Structuring Public–Private Research Partnerships for Success

Structuring Public–Private Research Partnerships for Success

Empowering University Partners

Gordon Rausser

University of California, Berkeley, USA

Holly Ameden

Independent Researcher, USA

Reid Stevens

Texas A&M University, USA

Edward Elgar
PUBLISHING

Cheltenham, UK • Northampton, MA, USA

Published by
Edward Elgar Publishing Limited
The Lypiatts
15 Lansdown Road
Cheltenham
Glos GL50 2JA
UK

Edward Elgar Publishing, Inc.
William Pratt House
9 Dewey Court
Northampton
Massachusetts 01060
USA

Paperback edition 2018

A catalogue record for this book
is available from the British Library

Library of Congress Control Number: 2016935805

This book is available electronically in the **Elgar**online
Economics subject collection
DOI 10.4337/9781849805759

ISBN 978 1 84980 574 2 (cased)
ISBN 978 1 84980 575 9 (eBook)
ISBN 978 1 78897 047 1 (paperback)

Typeset by Servis Filmsetting Ltd, Stockport, Cheshire
Printed and bound in the United States.
Printed on ECF recycled paper containing 30% Post Consumer Waste.

Contents

Abbreviations

ARS	Agricultural Research Service, US Department of Agriculture
AUTM	Association of University Technology Managers
BHEF	Business–Higher Education Forum
BP	British Petroleum
C2B2	Center for Biorefining and Biofuels
CEB	Center Executive Board of the Center for Biorefining and Biofuels
CEF	Cooperative efficiency frontier
CEO	Chief Executive Officer
CFS	Complete feasibility set
CHI	CHI Research Inc.
CNR	College of Natural Resources, University of California, Berkeley
CRADA	Cooperative Research and Development Agreement
CSHE	Center for Studies in Higher Education
CU	University of Colorado
DARPA	Defense Advanced Research Projects Agency
DOE	Department of Energy
EBI	Energy Biosciences Institute
EEF	Economic efficiency frontier
EFS	Economic feasibility set
EST	Expressed sequence tag
EU	European Union
GCEP	Global Climate and Energy Project
GDP	Gross Domestic Product
GE	General Electric
GEUSAP	General Electric's University Strategic Alliance Program
GMO	Genetically modified organism
GUIRR	Government–University–Industry Research Roundtable, National Academies
IFAS	Institute for Food and Agricultural Standards, Michigan State University
IP	Intellectual property
MIT	Massachusetts Institute of Technology

NADI	Novartis Agricultural Discovery Institute
NC	North Carolina
NDRC	National Defense Research Committee
NIH	National Institutes of Health
NSF	National Science Foundation
OECD	Organisation for Economic Co-operation and Development
ONR	Office of Naval Research
OSRD	Office of Scientific Research and Development
PEBB	Power Electronic Building Block
PFI	Private finance initiative
PMB	Plant and Molecular Biology Department, University of California, Berkeley
PPP	Public–private partnership
PPRP	Public–private research partnership
R&D	Research and development
RFP	Request for proposals
RPI	Ribozyme Pharmaceuticals, Inc.
TTO	Technology transfer office
UC	University of California
UCSF	University of California, San Francisco
UIDP	University Industry Demonstration Partnership
UIUC	University of Illinois at Urbana–Champaign
UIP	University–Industry Partnership
US	United States
UT	University of Tennessee
WU	Washington University
WUMS	Washington University Medical School

1. Public research enterprises: The changing landscape

1.1 PUBLIC FUNDING TRENDS AND RESEARCHER INCENTIVES

A major driver of US economic development since the Second World War has been productivity growth. The university research system has played an essential role in fostering productivity growth by consistently generating outputs with public good characteristics that have been easily reproducible and thus have not lent themselves to private market development and appropriation. Despite the success of this system, the scientific research establishment has come under increasing scrutiny and federal and state research funding (in real dollars) has been on a downward trend since the 1980s (Just & Rausser, 1993). More importantly, the scientific research establishment has received a declining share of the federal budget. Scientific research and development (R&D) received nearly 12 percent of the federal budget in the mid-1960s, but this share has fallen below 4 percent in recent years (Figure 1.1). This decline in federal public research funding has coincided with a slowdown in productivity growth, which has slowed since the 2008 Financial Crisis (Fernald & Wang, 2015). The composition of federal funding reflects similar patterns with the exception of National Institutes of Health (NIH) biomedical research which continues to receive support from federal legislative bodies (Figure 1.2).

State and local government research funding has declined along with federal funding. Historically, many states have provided a significant share of public research university revenue. From 2002 to 2010, state support for public research universities fell 10 percent, while enrollment increased by 8 percent (NSF, 2012). This meant that state support per student fell by an average of 20 percent over that period (NSF, 2012). Though some of these funding cuts were driven by the Great Recession and funding rebounded somewhat after 2010, no state has restored funding to its pre-recession levels as of 2014 (Center on Budget and Policy Priorities, 2014). Over the six years following the Great Recession, the average state cut funding per student by 23 percent, in line with pre-recession trends (Center on Budget and Policy Priorities, 2014).

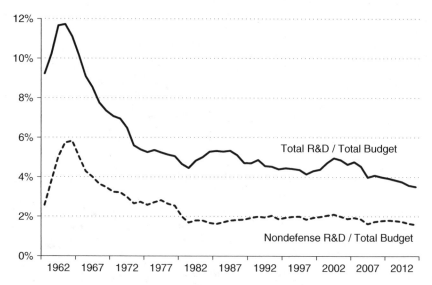

Source: American Association for the Advancement of Science.

Figure 1.1   Public sector R&D funding

As the public sector contributions to university research budgets have declined, the need to seek out alternative sources of funding has become increasingly imperative. R&D funding from the private sector has steadily grown over the last 50 years, and now accounts for over 70 percent of national[1] R&D budgets (Figure 1.3). In effect, the federal government and private enterprise have essentially switched roles in terms of the execution of R&D funding. Private industry frequently offers a viable alternative, not only because of its financial resources but because of the dramatic synergies of knowledge that arise from successful alliances. Unsurprisingly, many universities have responded to the changing budgetary environment by readily accepting funding from the private sector. Nevertheless, even though the proportion of privately funded research has increased significantly, it remains a small portion of total funding for university- and college-led research (Figure 1.4).

In most universities, researchers have been encouraged to replace federal funding with external research grants, many of which are sourced from private commercial interests. As a consequence, many researchers' marginal research time and the generation of ideas are focused increasingly on specific private interests. As a result, private firms are leveraging their R&D funds to redirect a larger share of

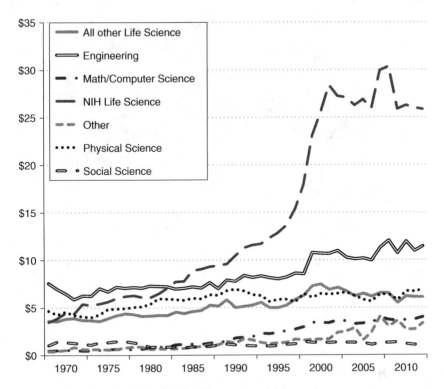

Source: American Association for the Advancement of Science.

Figure 1.2   Funding by discipline

universities' research efforts, gaining increasing influence over the public research agenda.

The changing landscape exists not only for universities but also for public sector research conducted at governmental agencies. For example, the President's Council of Advisors on Science and Technology (2012) recommended that the US Department of Agriculture research portfolio be rebalanced by the creation of innovation institutes funded through public–private partnerships (PPPs).[2] The justification, in part, for this recommendation was to overcome "congressional constraints" on research funding budgets sourced by the federal government.

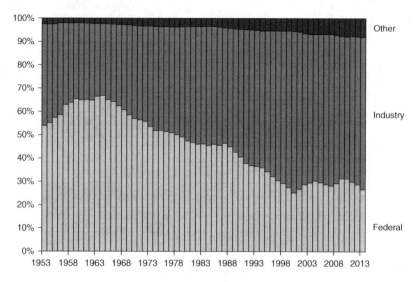

Source: American Association for the Advancement of Science.

Figure 1.3   Trends in research funding

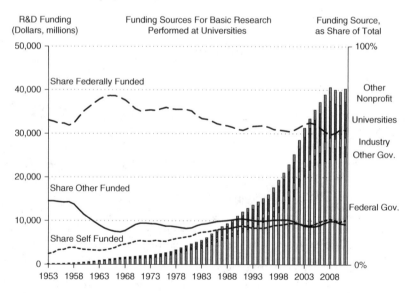

Source: National Science Foundation.

Figure 1.4   Basic research funding trends

1.2 INTELLECTUAL PROPERTY LAW AND RESEARCHER INCENTIVES

Along with changes to the research funding landscape, changes to IP (intellectual property) law have created new incentives for researchers to pursue innovations that have commercial value. Prior to 1980, the government was assigned property rights for major discoveries resulting from publicly funded research at universities. This structure had a chilling effect on university researchers' attempts to commercialize their research. Innovation was also hampered because the government did not typically allow exclusive rights to these discoveries, but would only grant non-exclusive licenses to firms interested in commercializing the research. Firms were reluctant to pursue non-exclusive licenses because successful commercialization would draw competitors that could simply incur a government licensing fee and gain access to the same IP. Given the incentive structure, it is not surprising that only 5 percent of patents owned by the federal government were licensed for development by the private sector (Schacht, 2009).

As the US economy stalled in the late 1970s, policymakers searched for ways to increase the use of academic research discoveries by the private sector. Efforts to increase the commercialization of government funded research focused on changing the assignment of property rights from the government to the research institution. Critics were concerned that this reform would allow private companies the lion's share of new discoveries, where the burden of financing the underlying research is borne by the US taxpayer (Stevens, 2004). Proponents countered that, without allowing research institutions to capture some of the benefit associated with their research, discoveries would continue to go undeveloped and a significant source of economic growth would go untapped. As a result of public discourse, legislation emerged from the US Senate in the form of the Bayh–Dole Act. This act gained support by only granting patent rights from federally funded research to universities and small businesses, not large private government contractors.

The passage of the Bayh–Dole Act in 1980 dramatically altered the incentives landscape by structurally changing IP rights and royalty distributions within a university (Washburn, 2005). Under the Act, IP rights are assigned to the universities where the research takes place, even if the research is federally funded, and it requires that universities share any license revenues with the inventors. This allocation of the royalty stream gives university researchers incentives to select areas of research that are likely to result in commercially valuable innovations. In essence, by directing their research toward private sector interests and commercially applicable innovations, university researchers can increase the likelihood of receiving remuneration. Researchers commonly receive one-third of licensing fees with the remainder split evenly between the university and other university units (in many instances, the academic department where the researcher resides), though some universities use a sliding scale to split net revenue with researchers (Jensen & Thursby, 2001). There is much variation by university; for example, researchers at Oxford retain 16 percent of net revenues above £720,000 (Isis Innovation, 2003). University of Washington researchers receive 27 percent of net revenue (University of Washington, 2015) while Johns Hopkins University researchers receive 35 percent of net revenues in addition to the 15 percent of net revenues their personal lab receives (Johns Hopkins University, 2011).

IP law also incentivized researchers by expanding property rights for researchers over discoveries in the field of biotechnology. In 1980, the US Supreme Court ruled in Diamond v. Chakrabarty (US Diamond v. Chakrabarty, 1980) that researchers could patent the genetically modified organisms (GMOs) they create. This ruling helped revolutionize the biotechnology field. In the decades following the ruling, thousands of biotechnology companies were founded, which employed hundreds of thousands of people, and spent tens of billions of dollars on R&D (Robinson & Medlock, 2005). Research conducted in unversities has been crucial to the success of the biotechnology companies; many have been started by professors and most employ research professors as consultants (Zucker et al., 1998). These companies provide significant compensation for professors willing to conduct commercially valuable research.

The Bayh–Dole Act has had a dramatic and sustained effect on licensing by universities. According to surveys by the Association of University Technology Managers (AUTM), over 4,000 firms have been spun off from universities (AUTM, 2012). Licensing contributes an increasing share to university revenues, as average yearly license executions have nearly tripled from 1997 to 2013. And this growth has continued despite federal research funding declines. For example, in 2014, new commercial product licenses jumped 34 percent despite a 5 percent decline in federal research funding (AUTM, 2015). To illustrate how quickly the university research landscape has expanded its organizational structure, largely as a result of the Bayh–Dole Act, there were only 27 technology transfer offices (TTOs) at universities prior to the passage of the Bayh–Dole bill. The trajectory of TTOs began with 7 that were founded before 1960, which increased to 113 in 1979, 200 in 1990 and then more than quadrupled by the turn of the century.

The growth of technology firms near universities is another indicator of the impact of the Bayh–Dole Act. Research at Stanford University was one of the major engines of growth in Silicon Valley, discoveries at the Massachusetts Institute of Technology (MIT) and Harvard developed businesses along Route 128, and similar research discoveries in Austin, Texas and in the Research Triangle in North Carolina drove economic growth in nearby cities. The potential positive linkage effects on local business, utilizing the expertise of faculty as entrepreneurs or consultants, have resulted in many attempts to establish university research parks. One study on the formation of university startups within university research parks has been conducted by Link and Scott (2005). Their results suggest that, for biotechnology private firms, startups have a more pronounced presence than established firms while more established firms are more pronounced in parks or locations associated with elite research universities. These successes have spawned countless university imitators who have been said to experience "MIT Envy" (David, 1997). Universities have been quick to develop technology transfer offices, but the licensing revenue remains highly skewed toward the most successful research universities (AUTM, 2014).

Independent of the Bayh–Dole Act, it has always been in the financial interest of research universities to actively pursue monetization of their patents. The classic example is the University of Wisconsin Alumni Research Foundation. It is not a technology transfer institution, but instead frequently monetizes the value of the University of Wisconsin patent portfolio through litigation. This foundation has represented that it has over the years generated more than $1.5 billion for the University of Wisconsin–Madison, an average contribution of $18 million per year (Washington Post, 2015). In the most recent academic year, it generated more than $72 million, amounting to 2.5 percent of the university's budget. Recently, this foundation filed a claim against Apple for infringement of a micro-processor patent that was developed through research at the University of Wisconsin–Madison and was awarded $862 million in potential penalties by a lower court. In 2015 Carnegie Mellon University won a $1.1 billion award from a jury against Marvell Technology Group, an amount that was later reduced on appeal from a lower court to $278 million. According to Reuter's (Chung, 2015), universities are the source for filing 45–50 patent lawsuits every year. Aside from litigation, the Wisconsin Alumni Research Foundation holds the property rights for a number of patents; in 2013 alone, this foundation obtained the rights to 160 new patents. In terms of licensing revenues, the University of Wisconsin ranks 10th among US universities. "The University of California system, Northwestern University, Columbia University, New York University and Princeton University all made more than $100 million in 2011 from patent licensing" (Washington Post, 2015).

1.3   THE CONFLICT BETWEEN PUBLIC AND PRIVATE RESEARCH INTERESTS

As government funding has declined, the need to seek out new sources of funding has become increasingly imperative. Private industry frequently offers a viable alternative, not only because of deep financial resources, but also because of the dramatic synergies of knowledge that arise from successful alliances. These public–private research partnerships (PPRPs) offer university faculty funding for research that could not be conducted using government funds and charitable contributions alone. In a survey of natural resource faculty conducted by the University of California (UC), Berkeley (UC Berkeley, Academic Senate, Committee on Educational Policy, 1998), survey responses include the following observations from individual faculty: "If the state won't support departments appropriately, it is proper for the faculty to seek outside support"; "Do you really believe the state is going to fund Plant & Microbial Biology's research? Please, get real"; "Arrangements like this may be the only way for Microbial Biology faculty to do cutting-edge research in a field currently dominated by industry"; "For those interested in research in the target area, this may be the only way to fund and perform pioneering research"; "Some sort of alliance of the type proposed is the only way academic research in genetic research has a chance in hell of staying at all up-to-date."

Opponents of these research partnerships suggest that private support for university research is a departure from the norm when, in fact, research universities have always been heavily dependent upon outside funding to sustain their research activities. A faculty member stated: "I believe that we have been subsidizing industry for too long and that [research partnerships] provide an opportunity to get something back . . . . In my view [the research partnership] merely makes explicit what we have long done, removing the illusion and increasing the financial responsibility of industry for the benefits it receives."

Rather than viewing research partnerships as an act of "privatization," a number of faculty noted their huge potential to place in public service what are currently private technologies. One respondent stated: "[Research partnerships are] an excellent new opportunity for a public institution to be involved in this area, with public values of what previously had been exclusively private, to be realized."

Within the university, not all professors view PPRPs as an essential component of the university's research system, and PPRPs have remained controversial across research university campuses. Such controversies extend well beyond the potential non-alignment of interests among universities and private companies in the formation and implementation of research agreements. At a fundamental level, these controversies will always be with us. Their origin has a long history, emerging initially with the establishment of the National Science Foundation (NSF), to provide subsidized research grants to university researchers (see Chapter 2).

PPRP agreements, by their very nature, are attempts to pursue and capture commercial value. Many intellectual leaders strongly believe that the pendulum at research universities, as well as non-research universities, has swung too far in the direction of neoliberalism (Deresiewicz, 2014). Deresiewicz (2015) asserts, "Neoliberalism is an ideology that reduces all values to money values. The worth of a thing is the price of the thing" (p. 26). It is the humanities and liberal arts educators who are generally opposed to the establishment of PPRPs on research university campuses. PPRPs are another source of commercial values that biases the educational experience toward commercial interests. This may come at the cost of pursuing ideas for their own sake, not directed at some commercial value. What is lost is the capacity "to make autonomous choices – to determine your own beliefs, independent of parents, peers, and society. To live confidently, courageously, and hopefully" (Deresiewicz, 2015, p. 26). This perspective of the humanities and many social sciences, however, fails to realize that PPRPs are engaging only faculty researchers and graduate PhD students in agreements between private firms and universities. The graduate students have already selected their professional or commercial interests. There is no attempt or interest in engaging undergraduate students to pursue any commercial value associated with PPRPs. Accordingly, the opposition of humanities and liberal arts faculty to PPRPs, regardless of their contractual structure and implementation, is largely misplaced on neoliberalism grounds.

Still, humanities and social science faculty often express concerns over PPRPs invading their campuses. They contend that the conflicting interests of the public and private partner are irreconcilable. They fear that the private partner will have complete control over the research process and will curb academic freedom. Though these professors have a different view on research funding, since they do not typically have the research budgets of the hard sciences nor have they historically relied on private research funding, their fears about capture are well founded. There have been many poorly structured research partnerships where the public interest was not served.

An immediately recognizable example of a poorly structured research partnership is the Boots–University of California, San Francisco (UCSF) partnership. In 1995, Boots Co., a British pharmaceutical company and drugstores chain, spent $250,000 to sponsor a study at UCSF investigating the bioequivalency of their drug, *Synthroid*, and three generics. In the contract, Boots Co. retained the contractual right to approve or disapprove publication of the study (a clause that was in fact against UCSF researcher policy). If they were found to be bioequivalent, Boots Co. would be expected to lose $600 million in business per year. If *Synthroid* was judged to be biochemically unique, Boots Co. would maintain monopoly power and a pharmaceutical division valued at $1.4 billion.

The study, led by Dr. Betty Dong of UCSF, found the four drugs to be bioequivalent. Since this was an unfavorable outcome for Boots Co., the company attempted to discredit the study. After review, Boots Co.'s criticisms were deemed to be unfounded and the study was ready to be published. However, Boots Co. threatened a costly and drawn out legal battle based upon the terms of the contract. Ultimately, the study was not published.

The experience of the UCSF researchers does not appear to be an isolated incident. Lexchin et al. (2003) reviewed 30 studies, which analyzed over one thousand clinical trials, on the effect of industry sponsorship of academic pharmaceutical research. The authors found that research funded by the pharmaceutical industry is more likely to produce results supportive of industry than research funded by non-industry sources. This statistically significant finding is robust across medical fields and over time. The authors also find that industry-supported research is less likely to be published in peer-reviewed journals, which appears to indicate a level of discipline-wide wariness of research that supports the claims of its funders. Surveys have also found that 20 percent of university research scientists admitted to delaying the publication of research to protect proprietary data (Blumenthal et al., 1997). This distrust and data withholding threatens to erode the foundations and core culture upon which many university research systems were founded.

The systemic bias in the pharmaceutical industry funded by the private sector validates the concerns of opponents of PPRPs. Academic integrity can be compromised and public resources can be captured when partnerships do not provide contractual protections for the public partner. Despite this danger, the question is not whether universities must deal with the outside world, but how effectively they will do so. Industry or private sector funding for academic research continues to replace government funds. This book provides a framework for optimizing the benefit to the public sector, especially research universities.

The task of forming research relationships is complex and delicate. Many lessons have been learned as public criticism and scrutiny of PPRPs has become increasingly intense (Press & Washburn, 2000). Issues, such as conflict of public and private interests, setting research priorities (Rausser et al., 2008), ownership of, and access to, IP (e.g., issues of hold-up and blocking patents), and publication delays, fuel the current debate and very often present insurmountable obstacles to forming research partnerships.

At the center of the PPRP controversy is the absence of a framework for structuring research agreements, whether formal or implicit, and for assessing the inherent merit of such contracts. No optimal contract structure has emerged for these partnerships. Most work examining research partnerships tends to focus on the source of research funding, basic provisions of these agreements, associated problems and consequences, policy recommendations for fostering these relationships, or specific aspects of a particular type of agreement (The University–Industry Research Collaborative Initiative, 2001; President's Council of Advisors on Science and Technology, 2008a). Although this literature is useful, it sheds little light on how these agreements should be structured, in particular, to protect public research interests.

Yet the call continues for creative collaboration across companies, universities, governments, and nations (Hamm, 2009). On November 26, 2008, European Commission President Jose Manuel Barroso announced the European Economic Plan, which proposes the formation of three PPPs for the R&D of energy-efficient buildings, new and sustainable manufacturing technologies for the "Factories of the Future," and the European Green Cars initiative (European Commission, 2008). The Lugar–Casey Global Food Security Act, introduced to the US Senate in February 2009, directs US assistance in developing agricultural technologies and specifically promotes public–private alliances. In September 2009, the Obama Administration released its "Strategy for American Innovation" calling for investing "more than three percent of GDP in public and private research and development" (National Economic Council, 2009).

This is a critical time to push beyond limited policies and develop a more comprehensive approach to structuring and evaluating PPRPs. We present a framework for analyzing the structure of contracts for PPRPs, recognizing that the essence of PPRPs is a set of "control rights" or embedded options. The four-stage framework, rooted in incomplete contracting and control rights theory, shows how control rights can be effectively identified, valued, and allotted between research partners.

1.4 UNCERTAINTY AND CONFLICTING RESEARCH OBJECTIVES

The Boots Co. case study illustrates two key obstacles that prevent successful research partnerships: conflicting objectives and uncertain outcomes. Private firms and public research institutions have divergent interests. Public research institutions allow researchers to establish their own research agenda and publicly disseminate the results of that research. Private firms typically give researchers less autonomy to create a research agenda, and do not release their findings publicly.

Opponents of PPRPs are convinced that corporations make inherently unsuitable partners because of their profit motivation. However, the history of innovation in the United States shows the obviously critical role that the potential for economic reward plays. Few important innovations could, or would, have occurred without the financial support of corporate backers. Such motivational incentives are embodied in the establishment of patent property rights in the United States. For example, as previously noted, the UC has been the beneficiary of this federally mandated IP system, adding to its coffers $118.2 million of gross licensing revenue system-wide in the 2014 fiscal year alone (UC, 2014).

Despite the inherent conflict, successful research partnerships can be created in areas of mutual interest to both public and private researchers. To overcome the obstacle of conflicting objectives, the partners should create contracts that recognize the existence of conflict and clearly lay out a framework for resolving that conflict. There will always be conflict in the design and implementation of a research plan, and contracts must directly address these conflicts. If both partners can commit to resolving conflict in a mutually agreeable fashion, the likelihood of success is increased.

We use the field of collective choice to evaluate conflict in PPRPs. The lens of collective choice will help us frame the conflicts between the public and private partners that naturally arise in research partnerships. At their core, PPRP contracts should be designed to promote collective decision making that maximizes both private gains and social welfare. We investigate how collective choice can link governance structures and the distribution of political power in the design and implementation of PPRPs.

Partnerships are further complicated by the uncontrollable, unforecastable nature of scientific research. Research is an uncertain process; there is no way to guarantee a blockbuster discovery. The partnership's contract must directly address unanticipated events. There is no such thing as a complete contract. The contract must contain a set of implementable actions to be taken when events occur in the research partnership in unanticipated ways. The power granted in these situations is called the "control rights." These control rights must be allocated with constraints that protect academic freedom. Clearly assigning decision-making authority in unanticipated situations is necessary to prevent capture of public resources by the private partner.

Scotchmer (2004) has argued that PPRPs are particularly well suited for large science projects. For certain large projects, the public sector may face the problem of choosing the right investments, in particular those with a high probability of success. On the other hand, the private sector would typically have the expertise needed to screen likely successful projects, but can on occasion reap unappropriable social benefits, and thus will be unable to recover the cost of the research that they finance (Sheridan, 2007). This, of course, implies that asymmetric information may exist between the public and private partner with the latter having superior information about the probability of success, which in turn might allow the private firm or industry to strategically engage the public sector in subsidizing its privately profitable projects.

Once again, the question is not whether universities must deal with the outside world, but how effectively they will do so. In this respect, we provide a unique model for maximizing the benefit to the university and, therefore, to the public. This book is an operational document that gives specific guidance regarding the creation and execution of research partnerships. This guidance is based on both the successful and unsuccessful PPRPs of the last 30 years.

1.4.1 Setting the Bargaining Space

Typically, the university and its faculty wait passively until they receive Requests for Proposals (RFPs) from governmental agencies or private companies and then generate a response on the other party's terms. As a result they must live with, and never dictate, the critical terms of the relationship. By contrast, we recommend staking out a strategic advantage and inverting the typical process; universities can generate the RFP, allowing private companies with appropriate R&D interests to respond, guided by the university's principles and on the university's specific terms.

This approach was engineered by Berkeley in the late 1990s, when the College of Natural Resources (CNR) issued an RFP and the industrial candidates were asked to compete with each other to meet its conditions. The principles established by the CNR included capturing consistency between the research objectives of the faculty and the private research goals and established intellectual capital of the partner; maintaining absolute faculty freedom and autonomy; obtaining otherwise cost-prohibitive technological resources for the faculty; and maximizing discretionary resources for infrastructure and graduate programs.

1.4.2 Preserving Academic Freedom

Universities should be wary of ceding control by placing private employees on university committees. However, it may be appropriate to involve the private partner in allocating funding among research projects. Naturally, the private partner will be interested in allocating portions of the research funding it contributes, but it would be inappropriate to cede control of the process entirely. In a major case study, research funds were allocated by a board which was comprised of three elected faculty members from the university faculty and two private firm officials. The inclusion of these private company officials was requested by the participating faculty; it was not a condition imposed (or for that matter, requested) by the private partner.

No faculty member should be required to sign a confidentiality agreement, or, for that matter, participate in any fashion in the research alliance; involvement must be strictly voluntary. Confidentiality agreements are absolutely standard for those who choose to conduct research with private industry but, in a preferred alliance, the participating faculty are free to choose whether to commit to such confidentiality.

1.4.3 Private Sector Presence on Campus

Another question regards company scientists being present on the campus as adjunct faculty. No special privileges should be extended to private sector employees. Contracts should include a provision that states clearly that (like everyone else) the private partner's employees are subject to standard university employment policies. This means that any particular adjunct appointment must satisfy the university's personnel and employment policies as a process separate from the PPRP.

1.4.4 Dealing With the Inevitable Controversy

Certainly, there are conflicting views regarding partnerships with the private sector, and the differing perspectives of all stakeholders should be thoughtfully considered. Every university should carefully monitor and study the results of research partnerships so that they may sharpen their best practices for collaborating with the outside world, rather than turning their back on them in fear. It should be the mission of university administrators and faculty to foster diverse (and often conflicting) avenues of investigation and search for points of possible integration. Along the way there will inevitably be disagreement, but contention cannot be allowed to block the innovation, risk taking, and academic independence which characterize the university's culture. If a minority of students and faculty are allowed to control the research agenda for the university, fewer outstanding professors will be hired, fewer of the best students will enroll, and ultimately, the university will attract less public support. The public interest is best served when divergent approaches are required to compete on the level playing field of science in lieu of the rough terrain of politics. Rather than yielding to fears about PPRPs, research partnerships should ultimately be measured by their results.

1.5 OUTLINE OF BOOK CHAPTERS

We begin our examination of PPRPs in Chapter 2 by reviewing two competing paradigms for modeling the scientific research process: the linear decomposition and the non-linear, chaotic, feedback research paradigms. The discussion of research paradigms is not simply an academic exercise, as each paradigm has important implications for universities contemplating PPRPs. We present empirical evidence on the distinction between public good and private good research in Chapter 3 while in Chapter 4 we explore whether private funding crowds-in or crowds-out public good research in a non-linear, chaotic, feedback paradigm. We pivot from these abstract models to knowledge creation and the R&D process in Chapter 5. Both the theoretical and empirical literatures on the knowledge generation process have important implications for PPRPs. In Chapter 6 we turn to real-world examples, assessing a few notable case studies. Over the last 30 years, the private sector has funneled hundreds of millions of dollars into university research through PPRPs, and we review the basic terms and conditions of such contractual commitments. We also present guidelines universities have developed to manage these partnerships and assess consistency across these guidelines.

In Chapter 7 we advance a collective choice framework to interpret the selection and implementation of PPRPs in the face of conflicts between private self-interest versus the public interest. We isolate the political, economic, and ideological forces that emerge in the strategic interactions among the partners. This allows us to formally demonstrate the crucial role that the assignment of authority, control, or decision rights plays in the collective choice arising from PPRPs. Based on this core result, in Chapter 8 we present the key insights from the finance literature on incomplete contracts and control premiums, or decision rights, in the generation of private and public goods. In Chapter 9 we extend this analysis to impure goods that are generated from a PPRP. In Chapter 10 we develop a four-stage process for forming and managing a PPRP. Central to this process is the concept of the control premium, or the right to make decisions when unanticipated events occur. The optimal assignment of control rights will vary by PPRP and is a function of the type of good produced by the partnership. Finally, in Chapter 11 we offer summary remarks and present practical suggestions to universities interested in forming a PPRP.

NOTES

1. These data include funding data from the "business sector, federal government, nonfederal government, universities and colleges, and other nonprofit organizations" (NSF, 2013).
2. For the purpose of clarity, in this book we use the term "public–private partnership (PPP)" to refer to any partnership between a public entity and a private firm. When a partnership specifically focuses on research and development, we use the designation "public–private research partnership (PPRP)."

2. The scientific research process

Prior to the twentieth century, university researchers focused on creating knowledge and training students, without particular concern with the application of their research. During the twentieth century, the role of university research evolved as scientific discoveries began to help drive economic growth. University researchers were viewed as significant contributors to the economy and the government funded them accordingly (David, 1997). Increased research funding brought with it an expectation that universities would generate the scientific capital, both in the form of relevant research and well-trained students, that would ultimately advance growth in the private sector.

Government funding of university research has led to dramatic breakthroughs across disciplines, including public health through the NIH; science, engineering, education, and technology through the National Science Foundation (NSF); and national defense through the Defense Advanced Research Projects Agency (DARPA). Despite the countless discoveries that were funded through these programs, the government has been under pressure to decrease their funding budget. The government has generally attempted to spare university support from cuts they have imposed on their own laboratories, though they have not always been successful (David, 1997). In contrast, R&D efforts in the private sector have grown dramatically, especially in biotechnology research. As previously noted in Chapter 1, universities are increasingly attempting to offset declining public funds with private resources. Universities recognize that private funds are not perfect substitutes for public funds, and research partnerships with the private sector present a unique set of challenges.

In advancing our framework for structuring research partnerships between universities and the private sector that benefit both parties, we must first visit the nature of the scientific research process and the two principal types of goods that can be generated. In this chapter, we identify two alternative paradigms that provide competing lenses on scientific research processes.

The university research funding system that developed in the United States following the Second World War was based on the linear decomposition paradigm of scientific research. This paradigm assumes that scientific research progresses linearly from basic research conducted by the public sector, including universities, to applied research conducted in the private sector (basic research → applied research). In this simple paradigm, applied researchers do not make discoveries that drive basic research; information only flows from, and not to, universities. This paradigm also presumes that the output of the university, basic research, is a public good. This public good is non-rival, meaning that basic scientific research discoveries are not diminished through use, and non-excludable, meaning the use of basic scientific research cannot be restricted and is available to be used by anyone. Since private firms lack incentives to produce public goods, a result of this paradigm is that government has sole responsibility to fund university research. This paradigm dominated university funding decision making in the United States for much of the second half of the twentieth century.

This linear decomposition paradigm of scientific research has been challenged by the non-linear, chaotic, feedback research paradigm promoted by Kealey (1996). In Kealey's framework, the interaction between basic and applied research drives scientific discovery. Rather than an orderly linear progression, this paradigm envisions chaotic feedback loops between basic and applied research (basic research ↔ applied research). Kealey's paradigm blurs the distinction between the public good and private good output distinctions of basic and applied research. This paradigm also shifts some portion of the burden of funding basic research to the private sector.

Universities, in forming research partnerships, must first choose which paradigm characterizes their research process. Universities that embrace the linear decomposition paradigm should restrict their search for funding sources to the government foundation think tanks since collaboration with the private sector will not generally be mutually beneficial. However, universities that choose the non-linear, chaotic, feedback paradigm advocated by Kealey can expand the set of possible funding sources to encompass both the private sector and the public sector.

2.1 PARADIGMS

The choice between the two alternative paradigms is informed by the work of Thomas Kuhn (1962), which originally focused on paradigms formulated for natural sciences but has become fashionable in social sciences over the past several decades. In the present context, it is useful to note that a paradigm typically defines a large set of possible hypotheses and makes no claims for the validity of any particular member of that set. A paradigm in social sciences, as in the natural sciences, "defines the type of relationships to be investigated and the methods and abstractions which are regarded as legitimate within a particular problem area" (Christ & Rausser, 1973, p. 274). For example, accepted economic paradigms include the assumption that agents on average act rationally and that the laws of supply and demand apply. Paradigms, unlike the hypotheses to which they give rise, cannot be validated by experimental or statistical methods.[1] For example, the maximum principle or rationality is not a hypothesis but a paradigm; and although a specific hypothesis embodying some version of the maximum principle can, in effect, be tested, the maximum principle paradigm itself cannot.[2] This does not suggest that the maximum principle ought to be abandoned. On the contrary, since abstractions from details are essential, any usable model must be a misspecification of the system to which it refers. We have no option but to construct frameworks which fall short of a complete specification of the system under examination. In this sense all frameworks or models are partially reduced forms (due to omission of variables, distortion of relationships, aggregation, etc.) even though we frequently refer to them as structural models. It is always possible to imagine a more fundamental explanation of the phenomenon under examination involving more equations and thus endogenous variables. Hence it appears reasonable to suggest that (a) paradigm frameworks cannot be judged solely by the resemblance between their specification and the systems which they are designed to represent, and (b) the choice of different paradigm frameworks of the same system by different analysts implies no presumption that one of them must be in error. For these reasons, it is safer to investigate the "sufficiency" of a particular paradigm rather than its "realism;" that is, is the constructed framework, for the purposes designed, adequately sufficient.

The requisite conditions for any particular theoretical formulation are never likely to be met and thus they should be no more than a subsidiary concern. The important issue is how extensively such conditions can be violated without seriously impugning the results obtained. The impossibility of falsifying any theory on the basis of observation is far more reasonable if couched specifically in terms of paradigms and not testable hypotheses (whether of the nested or non-nested type). Various paradigms of microeconomic theory (e.g., perfect competition, imperfect competition), of behavioral theory beginning with Cyert and March (1963), or of macroeconomic theory (e.g., neoclassical, neo-Keynesian) are not directly confronted with empirical evidence.

Although some would argue otherwise, a disregard for empirical evidence is generally appropriate for conflicting paradigms; in a conflict of paradigms the disagreement does not center on specific hypotheses but on the types of hypotheses and the types of data that might be presented for empirical investigation. Furthermore, it is difficult if not impossible to isolate criteria for judging among paradigms that are not products of the paradigms themselves.[3] For example, throughout much of economics there is a dominance of market paradigms which have conditioned most economists to view the firm as a basic element rather than as an economic system worthy of investigation. As Kuhn (1962) suggests, if criteria employed in an existing paradigm are used in judging between it and a new paradigm, the latter will typically perform rather badly.

To be sure, since social science must typically operate in an "open system" where non-controllable factors can always interfere with the operation of causal forces, social scientists can never be certain that the requisite conditions necessary to examine their hypotheses are actually obtained. Moreover, as a social science system may not be explicable as a simple, or even a weighted, sum of separate effects, it is the contrast, not the comparison, between social science and the natural sciences which is illuminated. Kuhn's analysis, which is directed chiefly to the physical sciences, requires some modification when applied to special cases that arise in social sciences. For the latter sciences it is not surprising that a paradigm, once established, is especially difficult to overthrow. This was, for many years, the case for the linear, decomposition paradigm. As its continued usefulness depends not only on the existence of unsolved problems but also on the prospects of their eventual solution by its application, there is no unequivocal standard by which it, the paradigm, can be refuted. Kuhn argues that the conflict among paradigms depends not only on their relative success, however measured, in explaining certain phenomena but also on judgements about which phenomena ought to be explained.

A paradigm helps to define a set of possible maintained hypotheses from which those most consistent with fundamental logic will be selected.[4] Given the limitations of real-world observational data, not all hypotheses are, in fact, testable. From any selected maintained hypotheses, it is necessary to isolate a still smaller set which represents the testable hypotheses.[5] In this setting the analyst in a sense becomes a prisoner not only of the maintained hypotheses but also of the paradigm within which he operates. Nevertheless, to deductively glean some information from a particular body of data, a paradigm is needed, as are maintained hypotheses involving in most cases arbitrary judgements with respect to forms of functional relationships, nature of lag distributions, and the like. An important part of the art of analytic work is knowing how much to include in the maintained hypotheses or model specification; the use of intuition, logic, and the "pragmatic test of validity" are often necessary to restrict the range of possible specifications.[6]

Some elements of the maintained hypothesis may, of course, be inconsistent with the parent population generating the observed sample observations regardless of whether the linear decomposition or the non-linear, chaotic, feedback paradigm is selected. To ascertain potential inconsistencies, we have no recourse but to relax and test certain presumed-crucial maintained hypotheses. This is perhaps the only objective ground for preferring one set of maintained hypotheses over some other set, assuming both are equally reasonable from a theoretical, intuitive, and/or technical standpoint.[7] All of this typically takes place within the context of a particular paradigm. Except perhaps for the case in which an alternative or new paradigm is "simply a higher level theory than those known before, one that linked together a whole group of lower level theories without substantially changing any" (Kuhn, 1962, p. 95), the possibility of relaxing maintained elements of one paradigm and moving into another is remote. Given this background on alternative paradigms, we turn to the two major paradigms of the scientific research process.

2.2 THE LINEAR DECOMPOSITION PARADIGM OF SCIENTIFIC RESEARCH

During the Second World War, the US government funded scientific research related to the war effort through the Office of Scientific Research and Development (OSRD) under the oversight of the National Defense Research Committee (NDRC). The NDRC was established "to coordinate, supervise, and conduct scientific research on the problems underlying the development, production, and use of mechanisms and devices of warfare" (NDRC, 1941). The program was intended to enhance communication between university researchers and the military, and ensure that no useful academic discoveries went unnoticed outside of the university. Academic researchers were given funding to conduct research that could be developed into wartime technologies. These scientists conducted research in many fields including weapons, communications, optics, physics, transportation, and medicine.

The OSRD was a resounding success. Researchers developed radar, vehicles, medical treatments, and, most famously, the atomic bomb. There were concerns at the time that the scientific discoveries from government sponsored R&D during the war would not be publicly disseminated and commercialized by the private sector. In response to these concerns, the head of the OSRD, Vannevar Bush, pushed the government to continue funding academic research. Bush articulated his view of the role of government in scientific research in a report to the President entitled "Science, the Endless

Frontier" (Bush, 1945). He argued that just as government support of scientific research was crucial to military success during the war, government support of university researchers was similarly critical to promoting economic growth in peacetime.

Bush's argument for government support of scientific research is grounded in a view of scientific progress as a linear process, advancing from basic research to applied research. In Bush's view, "Basic scientific research is scientific capital." In other words, the private sector production process requires basic scientific research as an input much like physical capital or labor. And this scientific capital is created by training scientists and funding their basic scientific research at universities. The private sector, or in the case of national defense, the government, applies this research to solve practical problems. Bush's view was not novel. This model of scientific research was also espoused by the top philosophers of science (see for example, Kuhn, 1962). The natural conclusion of Bush's paradigm was a call to action for the government to promote national defense and welfare by actively funding scientific research.

Bush's advocacy for government funding was met with some resistance. By embracing the Bush paradigm, policymakers endowed themselves with the ability to set the agenda for scientific researchers. And opponents were concerned that university researchers would cede their academic freedom to the funding agencies in the government or military. Echoing this sentiment, the Academic Senate at the University of California, Berkeley, adopted the following position: "The danger of undue political and military control of scientific research undertaken by universities under any plan of large scale grants from the government or from the Army and Navy, has been present in the minds of some who have questioned the wisdom of this policy" (UC Berkeley, Academic Senate, Committee on Educational Policy, 1947).

Despite concerns over capture of university researchers by the federal government and Defense Department, Bush's efforts led to the creation of the NSF in 1950. The NSF, along with other federal funding programs such as the NIH and the DARPA, dramatically increased university funding levels. Figure 2.1 illustrates the extent to which government funding for university research outweighed private funding until the late 1970s.

Since its peak in the mid-1960s, the share of R&D funded by the federal government steadily declined over the next 35 years. Though this trend was driven in part by the growth of R&D-intensive technology firms, the declining political will to fund research also contributed to the decline. Efforts to decrease the federal government budget deficit did not spare research funds. Though federal funding of R&D has stabilized relative to

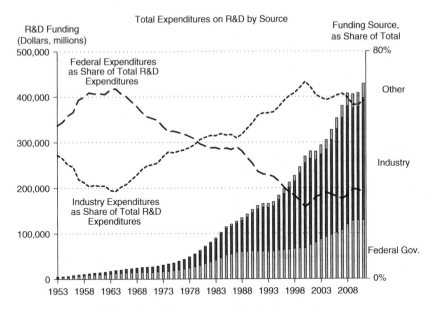

Source: National Science Foundation.

Figure 2.1 R&D expenditures by source

private funding, there are no credible forces to support increased public research funding over the near-term.

2.3 THE NON-LINEAR PARADIGM OF SCIENTIFIC RESEARCH

The Bush paradigm has been challenged by an alternative paradigm that admits nonlinearities and recognizes the chaotic nature of R&D processes. In this alternative paradigm there is feedback between both basic and applied research. The often meandering path of innovations into the wider economy is well known to scientific historians, who have repeatedly shown that innovations often emerge through a circuitous route (Ruttan, 2006). This route cannot be codified and, many would argue, is impossible to measure. An extreme variant of this view has been proposed by Kealey (1996), who goes so far as to argue that applied research drives basic science as much as, if not more than, basic science drives applied research. In Kealey's model of scientific research, reliance on government funding alone for research can hinder innovation by cutting off university researchers from a flow of information from the private sector. Echoing the concerns of the Berkeley Academic Senate 50 years earlier, for far different reasons, Kealey warns of the dangers of allowing policy-makers to set the university research agenda through funding decisions. Governments, Kealey claims, lack incentives to fund the most promising research agendas, and are less likely than the private sector to find and support the most innovative scientists.

Kealey's paradigm is not entirely novel, as scientists had long recognized that basic and applied science are closely tied. As early as 1850, Louis Pasteur noted that "There is no such thing as a special category of science called applied science; there is science and its applications, which are related to one another as the fruit is related to the tree that has borne it" (Debre, 1998). Though this view did not become widespread for more than a century, scientists warmed to the idea as technological progress fostered new questions for basic science researchers to explore.

Critics of Kealey were quick to point out that in many cases science progressed linearly and public sector R&D funding was successful (Nelson, 1997). Though biotechnology is often used as an example of a field with a non-linear, feedback relationship between basic and applied research, the field was formed by basic research, with no obvious practical application, that was conducted in universities and funded by the federal government. Critics also point out the danger of a world where funda-mental scientific research is not freely shared. Scientific progress could be stymied if fundamental research is proprietary and not publicly available. Critics also pointed out that in many countries, government R&D funding decreases were not followed by private sector R&D funding increases (Humphreys, 1997).

Kealey's paradigm is supported by the successes of private sector research labs. The private sector has long recognized the value of conduct-ing both basic and applied research. At the beginning of the twentieth century, several large private sector firms created in-house research labo-ratories to conduct basic and applied research in fields that lacked active university research. AT&T's Bell Laboratories and General Electric's Research Laboratory were among the largest laboratories that conducted basic and applied research to enhance innovations (Link, 2006). Research at these laboratories led to products that drove economic growth, includ-ing the transistor, photovoltaic cell, graphical user interfaces, and cellular phone technology. In many institutions, private as well as public, Kealey's non-linear paradigm began to replace the Bush paradigm toward the end of the twentieth century. New fields, like biotechnology, grew rapidly thanks to close relationships between universities and private firms.

Kealey's enthusiasm for private sector research misses an important feature of research in the twenty-first century: collaboration. Within universities, scientific research in complex fields increasingly requires collaboration across disciplines, and those research teams tend to produce more innovative research (Wuchty et al., 2007). Research teams tend to produce research that is more highly cited, and has a larger impact, than sole-authored papers. Collaboration has also led to highly productive, large-scale research projects like the ISIS project at Rutherford Appleton Laboratory, the Soleil Synchrotron operated by the French National Centre for Scientific Research, or the Advanced Photon Source at the Argonne National Laboratory. This trend toward collaboration has extended to the private sector. The president of Bell Labs recently discussed the shift in the type of research conducted at Bell Labs, particularly in the direction of collaborative research partnerships with universities and government. Bell Labs has been successful by working with research partners, rather than doing all their research in-house. As Bell Labs has shifted its focus toward collaboration, the size of the research staff directly employed by the Lab has fallen from a peak of 3,200 researchers to its current level of 700 researchers (Kim, 2009; Crozie, 2013).

2.4 UNIVERSITY RESEARCH: A PUBLIC OR PRIVATE GOOD?

Though the linear decomposition and non-linear, chaotic, feedback paradigms of scientific research each presume applied research is a private good, a key difference between the paradigms is the imposed hypothesis of type of good that is generated by basic scientific research. The maintained hypothesis of the linear decomposition paradigm is that the value associated with basic scientific research cannot be captured by the researcher because it is a public good. For the scientific research that results in a public good, the private sector has insufficient incentives to engage in such research with the linear decomposition paradigm, and, as a result, the government must provide funding for basic research, just as the government funds other organizations that provide public goods such as police protection or fire departments.

The non-linear paradigm blurs the distinction between basic and applied research by imposing the maintained hypothesis that both can generate private goods. In the non-linear paradigm, private firms can pursue the IP rights associated with their basic and applied research discoveries that will allow them to appropriate or capture all of the value associated with their research. Private firms are therefore incentivized to produce basic scientific research in-house. In Kealey's paradigm, the government funding of scientific research would only act to distort an efficient market. Whether the output of the basic scientific research process is a public or private good has implications beyond the paradigms from which we model the research process. We return to this discussion in Chapters 8 and 9, where we show that the type of good produced by a university research partnership will determine the optimal allocation of control rights in any PPRP.

NOTES

1. Some of the members may be mutually exclusive alternatives.
2. For example, the conditions under which the firm profit-maximization formulation of the maximum principle is unique, namely, the conditions of long-run static equilibrium and perfect knowledge, are never likely to be met.
3. The apparently objective notion of rationality is in fact very heavily paradigm-dependent.
4. Hayashi (2000, p. 33): "Sometimes the maintained hypothesis is somewhat loosely referred to as 'the model.' We say that the model is correctly specified if the maintained hypothesis is true" (emphasis added).
5. Christ and Rausser (1973, p. 275): "the selected maintained hypotheses . . . isolate a still smaller set which represents the testable hypotheses."
6. Clearly, if too much is assumed, there may be little or nothing left to test, while if too little is assumed, it may not be possible to reach any conclusion or else the analysis may become hopelessly complex.
7. The chief difficulty is that there are in principle an infinite number of hypotheses capable of explaining a given finite body of data.

3. Public good versus private good research: The empirical evidence

Available literature on the relationship between public and private forces in research has evolved from a focus primarily on relative inputs to R&D (i.e., research funding) to considering research outputs such as publications and patents. This chapter first examines research on the relationship between public and private R&D investments. We also assess prior joint efforts by university researchers and private firms to commercialize academic research. A discussion follows of more recent literature that considers research orientation, research productivity, and value creation.

3.1 PUBLIC VERSUS PRIVATE GOOD RESEARCH AT LAND-GRANT UNIVERSITIES

The land-grant university system, which is the centerpiece of the agricultural science establishment in the United States, has been one of the most successful innovations in the history of education (Kerr, 1987; Rasmussen, 1989). The future viability of the system, however, has become problematic. Bruce Gardner has shown that while the US agricultural sector was once fairly uniform, composed largely of family farms, and the benefits of new technologies were widely distributed, its benefits have become increasingly more concentrated while its costs have remained widely dispersed (Gardner, 2002). Since the Smith–Lever legislation augmenting the land-grant university system in 1914, the farm share of the population has declined from 33 percent to 2 percent and the farm size distribution has become highly skewed.[1] Correspondingly, the agricultural science establishment has received a declining share of the public research budget, roughly in line with the farm sector's declining share of overall economic activity: Agriculture received almost 40 percent of the federal R&D budget in 1940, but by 2007 this share had declined to 1.4 percent.

One study after another has demonstrated that, for example, publicly funded agricultural research experiences annual rates of return of at least 35 percent (Fuglie et al., 1996; Alston et al., 2000). Even so, federal government expenditures for R&D have not grown in real terms since the mid-1970s. In 1940, agriculture received almost 40 percent of the federal R&D budget, but by the 1990s its share had declined to less than 2 percent. In contrast, between 1960 and 1992, private spending for food and agricultural research tripled in real terms. Since 1992 it has expanded at an even more rapid rate. In 1999, commitments were made by private companies in the area of plant genomics that were approximately equivalent to the total private R&D expenditures in 1992. It is not surprising that private agricultural research has more than offset declining government funds (Huffman & Evenson, 1993). Many land-grant administrators, looking to supplement their shrinking public budgets, have found eager partners in the private sector to participate in research collaborations and partnerships. These administrators have become increasingly successful in forming industry research partnerships; in 2006 land-grant universities accounted for more than half of the top 20 schools in attracting industry R&D sponsorship (National Science Foundation, 2007).

Corporate sponsorship of land-grant university research has caused controversy in some states where deans and directors have tended to "direct" faculty to perform short-term profit-enhancing research (Beattie, 1991). Moreover, choice of research projects is often controlled by internal competitive grants, and/or the administration of extension has been separated from the administration of teaching and research, presumably to concentrate more directly on serving special interests. In other states, a rift has developed between extension and teaching/research faculty. As a consequence, extension activities have been slow to evolve beyond the farm sector in the same fashion as academic research activities. In both cases, the fundamental premise of the land-grant system is violated as research conducted for the private sector has tended to "crowd-out" public good research (Greenberg, 2007).

University administrators increasingly encourage researchers to replace declining governmental formula funding by research grants, many of which are motivated by private interests either directly through private grants or indirectly through public research grants sourced with private lobbying and pork-barrel politics. As a consequence, researchers' marginal research time and the generation of ideas are increasingly focused on specific private interests. The ultimate concern is that private interests will leverage their funds to crowd-out public good research at land-grant universities.

The motivations to acquire private funding have been amplified by changes in IP ownership and any royalty distribution within the university (Washburn, 2005). Following the passage of the Bayh–Dole Act, as previously noted, IP rights were assigned to the universities and research scientists have typically received some fraction of the royalty stream associated with the commercialization of their research. This allocation of royalty revenues provides university scientists with incentives to pursue lines of research that are likely to lead to commercially profitable discoveries. Moreover, since private industry funds are directed to commercially appropriable research, university researchers can increase the likelihood that their research will be licensed by pursuing private sponsorship. Again, this research funded by the private sector may well crowd-out public good research that is not generated elsewhere. Underemphasized research products include fundamental scientific knowledge and, in the field of social science, research on new institutions and policies, analysis of labor displacement effects of new technologies, and safety and environmental research on new biotechnologies and chemicals.

As land-grant universities work more collaboratively with private interests, questions are raised about the need for continued public funding and, more fundamentally, public justification for the land-grant research system. Some argue that privatization of university activities offers new potential for encouraging socially relevant research and facilitating transfer of technology. However, without proper policies and incentives, universities can become pawns of powerful private interests, and the unique and separable contribution that universities can make to the public good may be lost (Just & Rausser, 1993). PPPs cannot be allowed to leverage university resources and divert research from public good outputs not produced elsewhere.

The capture of land-grant universities can be expected to lead to increased public criticism and possibly more dramatic reductions in funding. However, capture by the private sector is not the inevitable outcome of public–private research collaboration. In fact, it is conceivable that with proper policies and incentives, universities can use PPPs to leverage industry resources to crowd-in public good research. Without such partnerships, there is little prospect that the private sector will replace the public good research that would otherwise take place at land-grant universities. Sufficient incentives simply do not exist for the private sector to effectively replace fundamental investments in public good research. Even though private investment in agricultural research is substantial, it is quite obviously aimed toward applied commercial research with transparent potential for profitability, viz. chemicals and hybrid or genetically engineered seed research.

3.2   SUBSTITUTES AND COMPLEMENTS IN RESEARCH ORIENTATION

David et al. (2000) produce an expansive survey of the econometric research examining the question of whether public R&D is a substitute or complement for private R&D. Under a complementary relationship, or "crowding-in," publicly funded research would not only directly generate public good research products in keeping with a public service mission, but would also stimulate private R&D expenditures through knowledge or training spillovers that enhance private R&D performance, spawning a flow of future research benefits.

In their analysis of the empirical research, David et al. note a few qualifications of their assessment. First, they do not include research on the relative productivity of public versus private R&D. Second, the empirical research considers one side of the public versus private relationship, specifically the impact of public R&D on private R&D. Thus, given that there is concern about the effect of private investment on public good research levels within the context of PPRPs, the findings of this survey have only partial relevance. Due to the absence from the empirical research surveyed of latent variables that may jointly effect both public and private investment decisions, the authors suggest that future analyses should include structural modeling of government and private R&D behavior and responses.

Even though David et al. (2000) assess a broad range of empirical research, their survey does not generate any specific finding concerning the magnitude of the relationship between public and private R&D. Instead, it presents an expansive review of the methodologies and results of various studies covering industry, aggregate, and firm-level data. The authors note important factors in interpreting results across studies – that about two-thirds of the studies rely solely on data from the United States and that observations for these US studies come primarily from the third quarter of the twentieth century and involve a high portion of defense contracts.

Despite the heterogeneity of the research conducted, David et al. identify several patterns. One-third of the studies indicate that public R&D acts as a substitute for private R&D; this result is more prevalent for analyses of firm-level data versus industry and higher aggregate levels. A positive effect on input prices due to public research spending, the authors note, may contribute to a complementary relationship observed at the industry and higher level. One of the more interesting empirical analyses included in the survey, Diamond (1999), evaluates annual aggregates of spending on basic research covering 1952 to 1995 from four funding sources: the federal government, industry, universities and colleges, and non-profit institutions. The Diamond assessment suggests that there may be a crowding-in or complementarity between federal and private spending on basic research. If these results are supported by further research, Diamond suggests they may indicate that private funding will not fill the gap left by decreasing federal funding of science. Diamond also raises the concern of missing latent variables, cautioning that the results should be interpreted with care and that the positive correlation between private and federal funding may be the spurious result of both funding sources responding independently to a factor not considered in his model.

Another potentially important observation from the David et al. (2000) survey relates to the regional differences detected in the results. Research in the United States is more likely to identify public and private R&D as substitutes than research from other countries, especially at the firm level or below. The authors note that this contrast may reflect underlying differences in the nature of US federal R&D contracts and more recent European government programs for funding private R&D.

In the decade since David et al. (2000), a new area of empirical research has developed that analyzes the effects of academic relationships with industry. For example, Larsen (2011) surveys the limited empirical research examining the relationship between "academic enterprise" and the nature of public research. Much of this literature is concerned with the question of whether universities may face pressure to move away from public good research toward more commercially relevant applied research. Assuming the first paradigm model of knowledge generation (see Chapter 2), this move toward applied research would eventually mean reduced basic research in the long term. In other words, fewer new basic science discoveries may be generated to serve as a foundation for new future research directions. In qualifying the findings from his survey of empirical analyses, Larsen points to the inherent difficulty in separating basic from applied or academic from commercial research.

Despite these difficulties, Larsen (2011) finds several studies using scientometric data (data on citations) that support the hypothesis that research with a commercial orientation may be complementary to more basic research, or that increased levels of applied research are not being substituted for fundamental research (Breschi et al., 2007; Ranga et al., 2003; Van Looy et al., 2004; Van Looy et al., 2006). These studies used data on research in Belgium (Breschi et al., 2007; Ranga et al., 2003; Van Looy et al., 2004) and Italy (Van Looy et al., 2006), and all use CHI Research Inc. (CHI) classification for scientific journals to measure basic versus applied research levels (implying a linear model of innovation). "This classification system of science is based on expert assessments of individual research journals, which are assigned to one of four categories ('levels' in CHI terminology) according to a journal's degree of 'appliedness' as reflected in its contents (Noma, 1986; Hamilton, 2003)" (Tijssen, 2010). Breschi et al. (2007) and Van Looy et al. (2006) use patent data while Van Looy et al. (2004) use contract research as indicators of applied research activity. On the other hand, Larsen also finds several studies (based on scientometric data or surveys) that indicate that industry funding or collaborating with industry makes researchers more likely to be influenced by commercial motivations (Blumenthal et al., 1996; Azoulay et al., 2006; Fabrizio & Di Minin, 2008) or more likely to shift research focus in a more applied direction (Gulbrandsen & Smeby, 2005; Godin & Gingras, 2000).

Shifting from research orientation to research productivity, Larsen (2011) finds significant support for a positive relationship between academic collaboration with industry and scientific performance. Of the studies examining research orientation, not only do Breschi et al. (2007) and Van Looy et al. (2004; 2006) find increased publications associated with industry involvement, but those researchers that find a negative impact on research orientation find positive relationships with productivity (Blumenthal et al., 1996; Azoulay et al., 2006; Fabrizio & Di Minin, 2008; Gulbrandsen & Smeby, 2005; Godin & Gingras, 2000). In fact, of the 20 studies reviewed by Larsen (ranging in publication date from 1996 to 2008) that analyze scientific productivity, only three do not find a positive relationship between indicators of industry involvement or commercial orientation. (These indicators were industry funding, research collaboration, co-publication, contract research, patenting, and spinoff creation.[2])

Thursby and Thursby (2011a; 2011b) address the question of whether rising commercial interests in the academic community have compromised basic research using faculty-level data on invention disclosures[3] as an indicator of commercial activity. The authors note this indicator is different from licensing or patenting data in that it shows faculty interest in licensing. In one study, Thursby and Thursby (2011b) test three hypotheses on the effect of Bayh–Dole; the first is no change or status quo, the second is a negative hypothesis (faculty have shifted away from basic research), and the third a positive hypothesis (both basic and applied research is greater when the faculty member can benefit from commercialization of his or her research). The authors track science and engineering faculty disclosures at eight universities across 12 or more years, use a citation-based measure for basic research, and include federal and industry funding for each faculty as one of several independent variables in the econometric models. All of their statistical analyses support the positive hypothesis indicating that prior disclosure activity is associated with an increase in basic research. These results support the earlier work of Thursby et al. (2007), who advance a utility maximizing model of faculty research. The equilibrium research choices from their model depend on the research production function, or what is the production possibility frontier for research.

Thursby and Thursby (2011a) use a similar dataset (for 11 universities, using disclosure data) to analyze research funding models (for government and industry funding). The results show that lagged invention disclosures have a positive effect on both government and industry funding, with a greater effect on industry funding. Moreover, government and industry funding have positive and significant effects, indicating that government and industry funding are complements (i.e., crowding-in). The disclosure relationship is complex, however. The results of the analysis show that if faculty disclose multiple times, the positive effect on government funding can decline and disappear, turning negative with substantial numbers of disclosures.

While the results from both of these studies offer strong support for the theoretical finding by Thursby et al. (2007) that licensing has a positive effect on basic research, several caveats must be recognized. Both studies (Thursby & Thursby, 2011a; 2011b) track faculty that have been at the universities since 1993, thus more recently hired faculty are not included. Also, the universities included in the studies are large with a major presence in scientific and engineering fields.

A number of other empirical studies have recently been published that investigate the heterogeneity of a private firm's scientific human capital. Subramanian et al. (2013) investigate the role of bridging scientists, distinguished in terms of their orientation toward basic versus applied research. They find that in PPRPs the basic science orientation of bridging scientists is a substitute in a firm's research alliances with the universities, while the more applied scientists are actually complements. In another study of collaborations, Stuart et al. (2007) find that early-stage biotechnology firms often form PPRPs with public research institutions and later commercial alliances with well-established firms. These early-stage firms are also more likely to acquire commercial rights to discoveries made by university scientists. A still more recent study has focused on alliances, which are funded in large part from NIH, between universities and biopharmaceutical companies (Blume-Kohout et al., 2015). They find that sustainable funding over an extended period of time increases the probability of a university forming at least one PPRP.

3.3   TACIT KNOWLEDGE AND RESEARCH COLLABORATIONS

Research by Zucker and Darby (1996) and Zucker et al. (1998) reveals the importance of involving university researchers with private sector firms to commercialize academic research. Though all private firms have access to the codified knowledge produced by professors in journal publications, usually only the professors themselves have access to the tacit knowledge gained through their research. In cutting-edge fields, like biotechnology, this tacit knowledge is essential for commercialization. Zucker and Darby (1996) use data from the biotechnology industry to show that private firms that collaborate with professors who have expertise in newly discovered research techniques are more likely to achieve commercial success than firms without input from university researchers. These results were confirmed in research by Jensen and Thursby (2001) using survey data from technology transfer managers.

Zucker et al. (1998) confirm that it is access to the tacit knowledge of professors, and not the generally available codified knowledge, that determines commercial success in biotechnology. The authors show that private firms with identifiable research partnerships with professors have more products in development than similar firms without such partnerships. The authors also find that these research collaborations help professors as well. University researchers that work on commercialization with private firms tend to be more productive, in terms of published papers and patents, than faculty that do not engage in such commercialization. This feedback process from applied to basic research is an important justification for PPRPs, and is explored in more detail in the model presented in Chapter 4.

In contrast to the work of Zucker, Darby, and their collaborators, Arora and Gambardella (1990; 1994) were the pioneers in evaluating formal types of collaborations. In their 1990 article, they analyze collaborations of well-established biotechnology firms in the form of research or joint development agreements with early-stage companies as well as research universities. They analyze data from the United States, Europe, and Japan and focus on strategic complements among the scientists in such R&D collaborations. A major conclusion from their analysis is the need for the private firm collaborating with the universities to have the necessary in-house capability to enhance the value of any research discoveries that are made by university scientists. They specify four forms of collaboration with a hypothesis about the critical firm characteristics, including absorption capacity and other distinguishing features related to the locational-specific effects.

In their subsequent work, Arora and Gambardella (1994) analyze collaborative agreements between universities (and other public research institutions) and 26 large US chemical and pharmaceutical biotechnology firms as well as smaller early-stage-research private companies, stretching over the course of the 1980s. Once again, the most important firm characteristic that they isolate from this empirical analysis is the in-house capability, or absorption capacity, of the private company. Two types of capability are emphasized: scientific and technological. Such capabilities directly correspond to a private company's ability to evaluate and implement any knowledge that might be generated. Not surprisingly, they conclude that in private company agreements with universities, greater company scientific capability has a positive impact on the ultimate commercial viability of any discoveries that might emerge. They also find that private firms often enter into agreements with universities seeking nothing more than an option for longer-term knowledge development and acquisition.

More recent empirical studies investigate informal relationships between private companies and university scientists. These studies do not evaluate the performance of existing PPRPs. Instead, they attempt to elaborate the informal relationships that may, in fact, provide the foundation for a structured PPRP. Gittelman (2005) investigates a number of objective sources of data, namely citations to private, company-authored articles that are recognized in the academic literature, as a measure of the quality of science that is conducted. This study finds that early-stage firms publish more highly cited articles, supporting the hypothesis that such firms exist to exploit the discovery of new knowledge. Still other empirical work has focused on different types of university scientists. Glenna et al. (2011) conduct a nationwide survey covering 60 research universities, distinguishing each university's orientation toward applied versus basic science. As expected, they find that applied science is associated positively with the percentage of industry funding and negatively with the percentage of research funding that is oriented toward basic science. Along similar lines, Beaudry and Kananian (2013) discover that university scientists are often listed as inventors of a patent innovation if they receive industry funding and have had successful collaborations with industry in the past. Guerzoni et al. (2014) evaluate data on patents from cancer research to reveal that university scientists have a high propensity to generate more original patents when they are also partially funded by their own university. In contrast, university scientists have a lower propensity to generate more original patents when they are funded by private industry.

For TTOs, Owen-Smith and Powell (2003) assess panel data from a number of research-intensive universities and find that when TTOs draw upon outside expertise to help assess invention disclosures, universities are more likely to develop higher-impact patent portfolios. In a subsequent study, Owen-Smith and Powell (2006) show that in the development of biotechnology firms, in both the Boston and San Francisco areas, linkages with venture capitalists dramatically improved the probability of success. In Boston, such linkages are positively affected by the existence of informal relationships with public research organizations. In the San Francisco Bay

Area, more pronounced linkages existed with venture capitalists and other private firms. In fact, Jong (2008) argues that private industry proved critical in establishing a scientific foundation for the rapid development of biotechnology by helping to motivate the restructuring of biology and life sciences at both the UC Berkeley and Stanford University.

3.4   AN ALTERNATIVE FORMULATION

Theoretical research examining the balance of public and private research efforts on the degree of substitutability or complementarity between basic science (public good) and applied science (private good) is limited. In one recent formulation, Just and Huffman (2009) present a theoretical model focusing on a university-level decision maker, imposing a two-period setting. In the model, the university gains utility from instruction, public good research, and private good research. Revenue is earned from tuition, royalties on each unit of private good research, and transfers from public and private sources. The mechanism for transfers aimed at public good research integrates general public support and lobbying efforts by individual universities pushing for federal and state congressional and legislative funds. The level of this public support depends on the reputation and past performance of the university. Transfers coming from private and public sources may support one of three areas: instruction, private good research, or public good research. In a subsequent period, transfers depend on how successful each component was in the first period. Transfers directed at private research in the second period also depend positively on royalty rates. Tuition revenue depends on public good research success (described as reflecting outreach activities, news accounts of research discoveries, and measures of prestige such as Nobel Prizes and university rankings) and student demand.

Solving the university's maximization problem, assuming no technological complementarities, it follows that as royalty rate increases, private good research is augmented while instruction falls (Just & Huffman, 2009). In other words, motivated by royalty revenue, a university will substitute production of private good research for either of the other two university outputs (public good research and instruction).

Given the structure of this model, Just and Huffman (2009) note that public good research and instruction can only increase if the indirect income effect of increased royalty income is great enough to offset the substitution effect, and that this can only occur if the university's utility function is highly skewed toward instruction. The underlying model assumptions drive this result. The authors model the utility of the university as being derived equally from instruction, public good research, and private good research. The weights that universities actually place on these three activities, however, are not likely to be equal. If a university's reputation is based on "success in public goods research," as stated by the authors, with examples reflecting this success given as "university outreach activities, popular news accounts of research discoveries, and measures of prestige such as Nobel prizes, the number of National Academy of Sciences members, and published university rankings" (Just and Huffman, 2009, p. 1107), then a university's utility function would be highly skewed toward public good research, reducing the rate of substitution between private and public good research.

Moreover, the processes underlying the budget constraint that Just and Huffman (2009) specify are limiting. Tuition revenue is driven by student demand for instruction, which is in turn positively dependent on public good research only. Given that successes such as "university outreach activities" and "popular news accounts of research discoveries" could be the result of applied, technological advances as much as basic research, it is likely that public attention and student interest could be associated with applied research products.

In the second period, the shift to private good research becomes more pronounced due to an endogenous funding effect through transfers. The introduction of royalties results in more private good research in the first period, leading to increased transfers directed at private good research in the second period. In addition, the substitution away from instruction and public good research in the first period means that transfers directed to these outputs are lower in the second period. The authors state that these indirect lagged effects of private good research, brought about by the Bayh–Dale Act, on future research funding is supported by the "growing university emphasis on public–private partnerships" (Just and Huffman, 2009, p. 1109).

When the analysis is expanded to allow for complementarities, the findings are more complex. If the complementarity of public good and private good research is strong (and the complementarity of private goods and instruction small), an increase in the royalty rate may well cause university public good research to increase. This result holds for complementarity in the cost function (due to decreased input prices) and is strengthened by complementarity in the utility function.

Another key assumption driving the results in the Just and Huffman (2009) model is that there is no feedback from applied to basic research, or using the author's terminology, no feedback from research discoveries that develop private goods to research discoveries that foster public goods. This specification is consistent with the Bush paradigm discussed in Chapter 2.

However, if research is a non-linear process, the lessons learned by applied researchers can drive basic research. In the next chapter, we introduce a model that allows for feedback from applied to basic research, as well as from basic to applied research (the second paradigm).

NOTES

1. The largest 7.1 percent of farms produce 75.1 percent of output value and the smallest 78.7 percent produce only 6.8 percent of output value (Department of Agriculture, 2002).
2. A spinoff creation is a firm that is created to develop university research discoveries into commercial products.
3. A formal document filed with university technology licensing offices by faculty members that believe they have an invention with commercial potential.

4. Crowding-in versus crowding-out of public good research

Based on the empirical evidence and conceptual formulations of Chapter 3, we present in this chapter the causal conditions that link public good and private good research. We focus on the bargaining that must necessarily take place in establishing public–private joint ventures and the incentives among the two agents: research administrators and private industry representatives. We assess the potential for crowding-in or crowding-out of public good research. In addition to private sector incentives, a governance structure is specified for university research administrators. Crowding-in and/or crowding-out is shown to depend critically on the bargaining structure between these two parties.

Two alternative frameworks will be used to model university research: static versus dynamic with feedback effects. The single-shot static research framework assumes research funding only affects the sponsored research, that is, there are no knowledge spillovers. This "worst-case scenario" in which there is no feedback between public good and private good research is overly simplistic. An alternative framework is then employed that admits the nonlinearities and feedback between public good research and applied research that characterizes the research process at universities. By accounting for knowledge spillovers, this alternative framework blurs the distinction between public good research and commercial research and, as a result, also blurs the boundary between public land-grant universities and the private sector research.

4.1 MODEL I: SINGLE-PERIOD WITH NO FEEDBACK STOCK ACCUMULATION

At the center of our model is a public research institution. To fix ideas, we'll label this research institution "the university." However, the model could apply with few, if any, modifications to a wide variety of public research institutions at any level of governmental organization.

The university produces two kinds of research: *theorems* and *mousetraps*. *Theorems*, denoted by k, are basic research that generates public good.

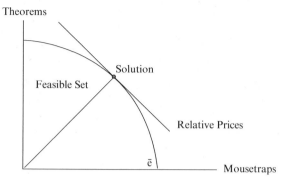

Figure 4.1   The production possibilities frontier and expansion path

As such, they can not be appropriated for direct commercial benefit. *Mousetraps*, denoted by *m*, are technologies and products resulting from applied research which are private goods that can be fully appropriated for direct commercial benefit.

In this model the technology available to the university to produce new theorems and mousetraps is simply a function of expenditure, denoted by *e*. These production technologies have the associated cost function $C(m, k) = m^{\beta_m} + k^{\beta_k}$, where β_m, $\beta_k > 1$. This cost function gives rise to a production possibilities frontier for the university which describes the set of feasible combinations of theorem and mousetrap research for a given level of expenditure, $\bar{e} \geq m^{\beta_m} + k^{\beta_k}$. This production possibilities frontier is shown in Figure 4.1.

The university's research allocation decisions are made by an administrator, who is given a *performance function* by the university's regents. This function is used to evaluate the quality of the administrator's decisions. Initially, we presume a simple linear performance function, namely,

$$P(m, k) = \mu m + (1 - \mu)k \quad \mu \in [0, 1] \tag{4.1}$$

This performance function gives the administrator μ *performance units* for each mousetrap she produces and $(1 - \mu)$ *performance units* for each theorem she produces. This function establishes a relative price between mousetraps and theorems equal to the ratio $p = \mu/(1 - \mu)$. For a fixed level of expenditure, the administrator will select the research mix along her production possibilities frontier defined by the usual condition that the rate of product transformation between mousetraps and theorems just equals their relative price, *p*. We consider later the effect of generalizing the performance measure to allow for imperfect substitution between mouse-traps and theorems.

To produce any research, the university must secure funding. The university has both public (government) and private commercial company funding sources.[1] Government funding, g, is presumed to be costlessly and exogenously obtained. Funding from the commercial company, denoted by f, is given in exchange for property rights over the produced mousetraps and is obtained through a bargaining process.[2] The outcome of this bargaining process is an (m, k) pair which is produced using funding from the commercial company and government, $C(m, k) \leq f + g$. If we normalize the price of mousetraps to unity,[3] the commercial company's profit function is given by

$$\pi(m, k) = m - f \qquad (4.2)$$

In the current static model, any investment in theorems is worthless to the commercial company; they only capture value from the mousetraps. However, depending on the bargaining outcome, they may also have to produce funding support for some theorems. We use the Nash cooperative bargaining solution concept to solve this problem (see Chapter 7). Based on the Nash formulation we will be able to neatly define a precise measure of what we mean by "crowding-out" or "crowding-in" and provide simple geometric interpretations.

The Nash solution is computed as the point in the bargaining set, B, that maximizes the product of the players' utility gains from cooperating:

$$(\hat{m}, \hat{k}) = \operatorname{argmax} \{ [\pi(m, k) - \pi_d][P(m, k) - P_d] : \forall (m, k) \in B \} \qquad (4.3)$$

π_d and P_d represent the disagreement outcomes (or threat points) for the commercial company and university, respectively. In the event of disagreement, the commercial company gets nothing – its threat point π_d is zero. In the event of disagreement, the university still has a funding level of g from governmental grants and can produce any allocation in the feasible set labeled g in Figure 4.2. The iso-performance line associated with this level of governmental funding is labeled P_d. The administrator would allocate this funding in accordance with the price, p, induced by its performance function. Let the chosen allocation be denoted by (m_g, k_g). The threat point for the university is $P_d = \mu m_g + (1 - \mu)k_g$.

For the problem in (4.3) to be well-defined, we must specify the bargaining set B. B is the set of efficient points that lie between the ideal research allocations for the university and company. This set is constructed as follows. First consider the commercial company's iso-profit curves labeled

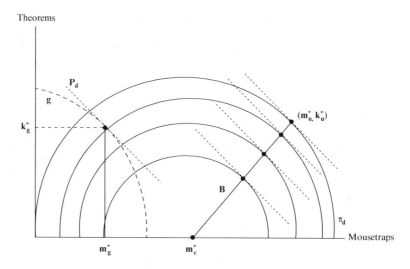

Figure 4.2   Construction of threat points and bargaining set, **B**

π in (4.2). The profit associated with these iso-profit lines is decreasing along the vertical axis. The commercial company's ideal point is on the iso-profit curve with the highest profit, which is the allocation (m_c^*, k_c^*), where $k_c^* = 0$ and the level of mousetraps is defined by the standard marginal condition $\frac{df}{dm} = 1$. The university has no global ideal point, as its preferences are monotonic, but does have a local ideal point for every iso-profit line. This local ideal point is determined by the tangency between the administrator's iso-performance line and the company's iso-profit line. For the commercial company to fund university research, the administrator must offer an allocation that gives the company at least its zero-profit disagreement outcome, π_d. Such allocations are found in Figure 4.2 along the iso-profit line labeled π_d that begins at the origin. The university's local ideal point along this iso-profit curve is the allocation (m_u^*, k_u^*) that lies at the tangency with its iso-performance line. The bargaining set **B** is the set of all such efficient points between this local ideal point for the university, (m_u^*, k_u^*), and the company's global ideal point, $(m_c^*, 0)$. This set of points is also the *core* of the bargaining problem, in which the solution must lie.

It is relatively straightforward to map this bargaining set from $m - k$ space to utility space to produce (a slight variant of) the well-known Nash bargaining picture, as depicted in Figure 4.3.[4]

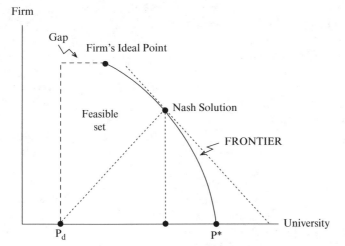

Figure 4.3   Nash bargaining set, disagreement point, and solution

4.2   MEASURING THE DEGREE OF CROWDING-OUT

As noted at the start of this chapter, a basic concern of this chapter is the allocation of research expenditures between public good research (theorems) and commercial applications (mousetraps). There is concern that as a result of reduced government funding, public good research will be neglected and research will be expanded that is more short-term in orientation, and more geared toward commercial applications. This chapter attempts to shed some light on the relationship between research priorities and the availability of public funding for university research. In particular, we use the model to investigate the claim that privately funded research can crowd-out or, in the alternative, crowd-in fundamental research, and that this can occur even when public funding becomes scarcer.

Two notions of crowding-out are easily captured, one a *research ratio* measure, the other a *negotiating leverage* measure. The research ratio measure focuses on the ratio of expenditure on mousetrap research to expenditure on theorem research. This ratio will be referred to as the $m - k$ *ratio*.

Definition: A fall in the level of government funding exacerbates the research ratio measure of crowding-out if it results in an increase in the $m - k$ ratio. That is, research ratio crowding-out exists if $\frac{d(m/k)}{dg} < 0$. Research ratio crowding-in exists if $\frac{d(m/k)}{dg} > 0$, i.e. a decrease in the level of government funding decreases the $m - k$ ratio.

This is a very natural notion that seems, at first blush, to capture the essence of the crowding-out metaphor. The first result from our model is that it exhibits research ratio crowding-out.

Proposition 1: In the context of the specified model, a decline in the level of government funding will increase the ratio of mousetraps to theorems produced by the university.

The intuition for this result is quite straightforward. Under extremely weak restrictions, publicly funded research in our model will generate a lower mousetrap to theorem ratio than privately funded research. The $m - k$ ratio compares *total* expenditure on mousetrap research to *total* expenditure on theorem research, aggregating across privately funded and publicly funded activities. As public research funds decline, so does the contribution of its relatively theorem-rich research mix to the aggregate mix, and so the $m - k$ ratio declines.

The above result is hardly surprising. Avoiding this research ratio form of crowding-out seems to be too much to expect. While administrators might wish that private agencies would share their enthusiasm for fundamental research, they can hardly expect this result. More realistically, administrators should expect that some dilution of the purity of their research activities is a necessary price that they must pay if they are to augment their public funds with private ones. For this reason, the research ratio measure of the crowding-out result is of little practical use as it tells us nothing about how policymakers could restructure incentives to ameliorate the deleterious effects of crowding-out.

For the remainder of this section we focus on a more subtle notion of crowding-out, which is intimately connected to the view that the research fundraising process should be viewed as a bargaining problem. The fundamental issue is: How will the decline in government funding affect the relative bargaining strength of the university administrator as she enters into negotiations with private funding sources for research contracts? A very natural concern is that as government funding declines, the administrator's need for funds will become more desperate, and hence she will be more willing to compromise in the bargaining process in order to secure funding. In this context, compromise will take the form of skewing research contracts in favor of mousetraps rather than theorems.

To operationalize this idea, we introduce the following negotiation leverage measure of crowding-out. The very best that the administrator can hope for in a negotiation with a private funding source is to drive the other bargainer to her reservation utility, that is, to extract *all* of the surplus from the bargaining relationship so that the other party is just indifferent as to whether or not an agreement is reached. We have already defined this as the administrator's local ideal point, (m_u^*, k_u^*). In general, of course, such a good bargain will never be struck, and the commercial company will secure some of the surplus. A natural way to measure the university's negotiation leverage, then, is to consider the gap between the realized bargaining outcome and the best possible outcome as a fraction of the total potential surplus that is available to the administrator from the bargaining relationship.

Definition: Formally, this measure of the university's leverage is:

$$\zeta = \left[\frac{P^* - \hat{P}}{P^* - P_d} \right] \tag{4.4}$$

where, as illustrated in Figure 4.3, P^* is the highest utility that the administrator can obtain from the bargaining relationship, $\hat{P}$ is the utility she obtains from the actual solution to the bargaining and P_d is the administrator's default utility.

This measure of leverage ranges between zero and one. When $\zeta = 0$, all the negotiation leverage resides with the administrator, while if $\zeta = 1$, the administrator is completely at the whim of the commercial company. Given this definition of leverage, a negotiation leverage measure of crowding-out may be defined that relates directly to the incentive structure of the underlying bargaining problem that can generate the crowding-out phenomenon:

Definition: The degree of crowding-out is measured by the change in the administrator's negotiation leverage as government funding falls. If $\frac{d\zeta}{dg} = 0$, we say the bargaining problem is neutral. The bargaining problem exhibits negotiation leverage crowding-out if $\frac{d\zeta}{dg} < 0$. Conversely, the bargaining problem exhibits negotiation leverage crowding-in if $\frac{d\zeta}{dg} > 0$.

4.3   NEUTRALITY

The key issue to be addressed is: Can a decline in the level of government research funding increase the university administrator's negotiation leverage? We begin by constructing a "neutrality" result. That is, we identify conditions under which the extent of negotiation leverage crowding-out is independent of the level of government funding. The theorem below is intended as a benchmark rather than as a positive result. Because the three assumptions upon which the result depends are all extremely restrictive, we can conclude that, in reality, the extent of crowding-out is indeed quite sensitive to the level of government funding.

Proposition 2: The following three separability conditions are necessary and sufficient for the bargaining problem to exhibit neutrality, that is, for the degree of negotiation leverage crowding-out to be independent of the level of government funding.

1. *Benefit Separability*: The commercial company only has property rights over the mousetraps that result from research that it funds. The university retains property rights over the mousetraps it produces with government funds.

2. *Cost Separability*: The cost *functions* for privately and publicly funded research are independent of each other.

3. *Performance Separability*: Theorems and mousetraps are separable in the administrator's performance function.

Under condition (1), the commercial company derives utility from any mousetraps resulting from the research program that it funds, but derives none from mousetraps resulting from publicly funded research. More generally, this condition reflects the idea that association with the university provides the commercial company with no externality whatsoever. In reality, of course, this is not the case. Private funding sources generally gain a great deal from these associations, over and above the utility that the research outputs generate. These benefits take many forms, ranging from the benefits of prestige to the benefits of public visibility, which increase access to research ideas and to potential employees at all levels.

An implication of condition (2) is that the marginal cost of producing an additional mousetrap or theorem depends *only* on the number of mousetraps and theorems already being produced *within the given research program* as opposed to depending on the outputs of other research projects. In particular, privately funded and publicly funded research programs cannot compete for the same scarce resources. Once again, this is an extremely restrictive assumption. In fact, it is typically the case that some fraction of the private research funds are earmarked for operating expenses rather than for infrastructure, so that at the very least, the university's opportunity cost of publicly funded research *does* increase with the level of privately funded research.

Condition (3) will be satisfied if and only if theorems and mousetraps

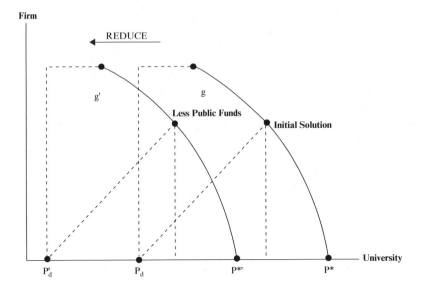

Figure 4.4   A geometric view of neutrality

are perfect substitutes in the administrator's performance function. To the extent that the performance function is intended as a realistic proxy for "social welfare," this condition is just as restrictive as any other assumption about perfect substitutability.

The proof of this neutrality result is illustrated by Figure 4.4. The figure depicts the two bargaining problems confronting the administrator and the commercial company, with different levels of public funding, as exact translates of each other. The neutrality result then follows immediately from the fact that the Nash bargaining solution is translation invariant.[5]

The key intuition for the proof lies in the demonstration that the problems are indeed translates of each other. To see this, note that under condition (1), the commercial company obtains no benefit whatsoever from the outputs of publicly funded research. Nor do its costs of doing business depend in any way on the level of public research. Hence, from the commercial company's point of view, all aspects of the bargaining problem are completely unchanged as the level of public funding decreases from *g* to *g'*. Similarly, the administrator benefits from publicly funded research by exactly the same amount, irrespective of whether or not it reaches an agreement with the commercial company, and irrespective of the nature of this agreement. In particular, note that by condition (3), the manner in which the administrator allocates public funds between theorem and mousetrap research is completely independent of whether or not, and how, she negotiates with the commercial company.

4.4   NONNEUTRALITY

In this section, we relax each of the assumptions of Proposition 2 in turn, and consider the effect of reduced government funding on the degree of crowding-out. We begin by omitting condition (1). For concreteness, imagine that the university administrator is authorized to offer to the commercial company property rights over all government funded mouse-traps as a "side-payment" that may induce more private participation. Specifically, consider a bargaining contract which assigns the commercial company property rights to *every* mousetrap produced, provided that *some* agreement is reached. If no agreement is reached, then the commercial company gets nothing.

As government funding declines, the size of the "pot" of bonus mouse-traps available for side-payments also declines. What is the implication of this for crowding-out?

Proposition 3: Nonseparable Benefits – If conditions (2) and (3) hold but not (1), then a decrease in the level of government funded research may either increase or decrease the degree of crowding-out.

This indeterminacy is at first sight unexpected. Intuitively, it would seem obvious that the larger is the pot of bonus mousetraps, the more the commercial company has to lose in the event that it fails to reach an agreement. It would seem that this device for enticing the commercial company into a bargaining relationship should strengthen the admin-istrator's hand in the bargaining process. After all, the more she brings to the table, the more leverage she has in bargaining with the commer-cial company. Hence, we would expect that a decrease in the level of government funding would *decrease* the degree of crowding-out. Clearly, this is not the case, however.

The intuition for Proposition 3 is provided by Figure 4.5 and Figure 4.6 for a non-linear university performance function. To highlight the problem, we consider two very extreme cases in which the university administrator's iso-performance lines are convex. Note, however, that the bargaining problems illustrated in these figures do not correspond to the problem at hand. In particular, their Pareto loci are not smooth. On the other hand, it will be apparent to the reader that we could construct smoothed ver-sions with the same properties that would be consistent with our model.

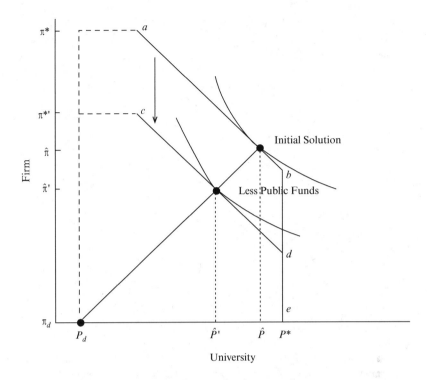

Figure 4.5   Nonseparable benefits can lead to crowding-out

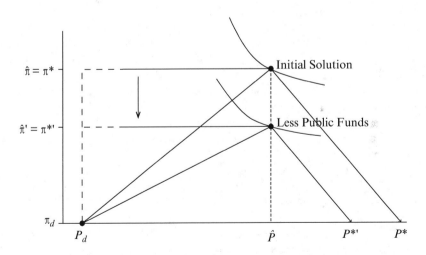

Figure 4.6   Nonseparable benefits can lead to crowding-in

In Figure 4.5, the original bargaining frontier is the line *abe*. After government funding has been reduced, the new frontier is *cde*. The explanation for this difference is that before government funding is cut, the university can offer a side-payment to the commercial company that the company values at $\pi^* - \pi^{*\prime}$ but the university values at zero. The commercial company receives this side-payment in full, provided *some* agreement is reached, but receives nothing in the event of disagreement. Note that the bargaining frontier is initially downward sloping but then vertical.[6] After the cut in government funding, government funded research dries up entirely, and the administrator cannot offer the commercial company a side-payment. Consequently, the entire bargaining frontier shifts down by precisely the amount $\pi^* - \pi^{*\prime}$. Note that because of the extreme specification of the frontier, the maximal utility level that the administrator can obtain from the bargaining relationship, P^*, is unaffected by the decline in funding. On the other hand, the *realized* outcome shifts back down along the ray through the default outcome, so that $\hat{P}$ exceeds $\hat{P}'$. Clearly, this example exhibits crowding-out.

Now consider Figure 4.6. The structure is exactly parallel except that the bargaining frontier starts out horizontal and becomes downward sloping. In this case, however, P^* exceeds $P^{*\prime}$ while $\hat{P}$ is unaffected by the decline in funding. This example exhibits crowding-in.

Since the "intuitive" result proved to be false, the reader will not be surprised to learn that the effects of relaxing the other two conditions are also indeterminate. First, consider what happens when costs are nonseparable. For concreteness, assume that research costs for mousetraps (similarly theorems) strictly increase with the *aggregate* number of mousetraps (theorems) produced. In this case, an issue of cost-sharing arises: Should private or public funding have access to the flatter part of the cost curve? To simplify the computations, we shall assume that public research has first access to the technology. That is, we will assume that public research costs are independent of private research activity, but the reverse relationship does not hold. In extensions to this work, we will consider the effect of including cost-sharing as an additional dimension along which bargaining can occur.

Proposition 4: Nonseparable Costs – If conditions (1) and (2) hold but not (3), then a decrease in the level of government funded research may either increase or decrease the degree of crowding-out.

Finally, consider the effect of introducing curvature into the administrator's performance measure. Specifically, assume that the administrator's performance measure is Cobb–Douglas in *aggregate* mousetraps and *aggregate* theorems. In this case, intuition strongly suggests a determinate result. We have already noted in Proposition 1 that as the level of public funding declines, the *aggregate* theorem to mousetrap ratio will decline also. Once we move to a Cobb–Douglas performance measure, a decline in public funding will have the effect of increasing the administrator's "hunger" for theorems. Being more "needy" in this regard, we would expect that the administrator's bargaining position would be weakened by the decline, and that crowding-out would increase. Once again, however, this intuition proves to be spurious. Specifically,

Proposition 5: Nonseparable Performance – If conditions (1) and (3) hold but not (2), then a decrease in the level of government funded research may either increase or decrease the degree of crowding-out.

4.5 MODEL II: MULTI-PERIOD WITH FEEDBACK EFFECTS

In our dynamic model, the production functions of mousetraps and theorems are dependent on the stocks of both basic and applied research. Since money spent on research in the current period increases the stock of theorems available for future research, this funding should be considered as an investment. The creation of theorems will also increase the stock of knowledge available to the creators of mousetraps; thus the stocks are public goods. However, there is also potential feedback from the accumulated mousetrap stocks to new discoveries in basic science.

Each period the university administrator chooses m_t and k_t and output is determined by:

$$M_t = \alpha M_{t-1} + m_t + h(K_{t-1}) \tag{4.5}$$

$$K_t = \gamma K_{t-1} + k_t + l(M_{t-1}) \tag{4.6}$$

Now the number of mousetraps (theorems) produced in period t is a function of the stock of mousetraps (theorems) available to researchers, M_{t-1}, mousetrap (theorem) research funding, m_t, and feedback from the stock of theorems (mousetraps), $h(K_{t-1})$. The feedback effects have the following properties for all $M, K > 0$:

$$h(K), l(M) > 0 \tag{4.7}$$

$$h', l' > 0 \tag{4.8}$$

$$h'', l'' < 0 \tag{4.9}$$

Properties (4.7), (4.8), and (4.9) capture the strictly positive, convex nature of feedback effects in university research.

Each period the administrator's performance is evaluated by a performance function, now stated in terms of the stocks of both applied (M_t) and basic (K_t) knowledge, that is

$$P_t(M_t, K_t) = \mu M_t + (1 - \mu)K_t \qquad \mu \in [0, 1] \tag{4.10}$$

Thus, over T periods, the administrator's objective is to maximize

$$P = \Sigma \beta^t P_t + \beta^T \psi(M_T, K_T) \tag{4.11}$$

where β is the administrator's discount factor and $\psi(M_T, K_T)$ is the value to the administrator of research conducted during the final year. This objective function establishing the relative price between mousetraps (applied research) and theorems (basic research) in every period is $p = \mu/(1 - \mu)$.

As in the single-period model, the university must obtain funding to sponsor research, but now the university has three potential funding sources: the government, a commercial company, and royalties from the university's mousetraps that have been commercialized by the company. As before, government funding, g_t, is presumed to be costlessly and exogenously obtained. Private funding, denoted by f_t, is obtained through a bargaining process that also determines royalties, $R(M_t)$. The outcome of this bargaining process is a pair of vectors ($m = m_1, \ldots, m_T; k = k_1, \ldots, k_T$) and a royalty rate, $R(M_t)$; the company agrees to provide a level of funding sufficient to produce a portion of this allocation, f_t, and to pay the university some fraction of the revenue from the commercialization of mousetrap research from the previous period as a royalty. We assume the administrator will only have $\theta \in [0, 1]$ of the royalties paid by the company at their disposal, while the remaining $(1 - \theta)$ is distributed to other groups in the university and has no impact on research. Note, the price of mousetraps is again normalized to unity.

The production of theorems and mousetraps in period t again has the following cost function: $C_t(m_t, k_t) = m_t^{\beta_m} + k_t^{\beta_k}$, where $\beta_k, \beta_m > 1$. This cost function gives rise to a production possibilities frontier for the university which describes the set of feasible combinations of theorem and mousetrap research for a given level of expenditure in period t,

$$C(m_t, k_t) \leq g_t + f_t + R(M_{t-1}) \tag{4.12}$$

where $R(M_{t-1})$ are the royalties paid by the company to the university in period t for the commercialization of mousetrap research in period $t-1$.

If a commercial company reaches a PPP agreement with the university, then each period that company sells mousetraps licensed from the university, funds university research, and pays royalties based on the commercialization of mousetrap research in the previous period. The company's profit in period t is therefore

$$\pi_t(m_t, k_t) = M_t - f_t - R(M_{t-1}) \tag{4.13}$$

where the private funding level in period t, f_t, is equal to the university's cost of producing the company's share of the total research output. The company's total profit is the sum of the profits from each period and the scrap value of an agreement, $W(M_T)$, discounted by the company's weighted average cost of capital, r:

$$\Pi = \sum_{t=0}^{T-1}\left(\frac{1}{1+r}\right)^t \pi(m_t, k_t) + \left(\frac{1}{1+r}\right)^T W(M_T) \tag{4.14}$$

Again, we use the Nash cooperative bargaining solution concept to solve this problem. Using the multi-period extension of the Nash bargaining framework from the first model, the solution is the pair of vectors $\hat{m} = \hat{m}_1, \ldots, \hat{m}_T$ and $\hat{k} = \hat{k}_1, \ldots, \hat{k}_T$ in the bargaining set, B, that maximizes the product of the players' utility gains from cooperating:

$$\begin{aligned}(\hat{m},\hat{k}) = \ &\text{argmax}\,[\,\Pi(m_1,\ldots,m_T,k_1,\ldots,k_T) - \Pi_d \\ &P(m_1,\ldots,m_T,k_1,\ldots,k_T) - P_d \\ &: \forall\,(m_1,\ldots,m_T,k_1,\ldots,k_T) \in B]\end{aligned} \tag{4.15}$$

Again, Π_d and P_d represent the disagreement outcomes for the commercial company and university, respectively. The company earns no revenue if it does not reach an agreement with the university, since no mousetraps are sold, and has no costs, since no research is funded, so its threat point, Π_d, is zero. The university still has a funding level of g from the government in the event of disagreement, which it will allocate in accordance with the price, $p = \mu/(1-\mu)$, induced by its performance function. Let the allocation chosen by the administrator for a funding level of g be denoted by $(m_{g_1},\ldots,m_{g_T}; k_{g_1},\ldots,k_{g_T})$. In the event no agreement is reached, the university administrator's performance function will be $P_d = \sum_{t=0}^{T-1}\beta^t[\mu M_{g_t} + (1-\mu)K_{g_t}] + \beta^T\psi(M_{g_T}, K_{g_T})$.

A new bargaining set, B, must be defined for this multi-period game for

(4.15) to be well defined. The company's ideal allocation is now the set of points $(m_{c_1}^*, \ldots, m_{c_T}^*, k_{c_1}^*, \ldots, k_{c_T}^*)$ which are determined by the first-order conditions given in Appendix 4A.1. Again, the university administrator has no global ideal point and must only offer the company an allocation that gives the company at least its disagreement outcome if there is to be an agreement. The set of efficient points between the company's global ideal allocation and disagreement outcome form the bargaining set, B, in which the solution must lie.

4.6   MEASURING CROWDING-OUT WITH FEEDBACK

As previously specified, we will use the two notions of crowding-out to determine the conditions under a research partnership with the private sector that can improve a university's public good research. Recall, the first notion, the research ratio measure of crowding-out, focuses on the ratio of applied research to basic research. We extend the single-period definition to this multi-period model by comparing the ratio of *total* expenditure on mousetrap research, $(m_1 + \ldots + m_T)$, to *total* expenditure on theorem research, $(k_1 + \ldots + k_T)$.

Definition: A fall in the level of government funding exacerbates the research ratio measure of crowding-out if it results in an increase in the $m - k$ ratio. That is, crowding-out exists if $\frac{d((m_1 + \ldots + m_T)/(k_1 + \ldots + k_T))}{dg} < 0$.

Though the first-order conditions (see Appendix 4A.1) indicate the profit-maximizing company will want to invest in some basic research because of the feedback loops, this model still exhibits research ratio crowding-out.

Proposition 6: For the specified model, there exists $\delta, r > 0$, such that for all $\beta > 1 - \delta$, a decline in the level of government funding will increase the ratio of total expenditure on mousetraps to theorems produced by the university.

The university administrator's linear performance function guarantees that for any $\mu \in [0, 1]$, the administrator values the production of theorems more than the commercial company, which leads the administrator to always prefer more basic research than the company (see Appendix 4A.1). Once again, public funding leads to a relatively theorem-rich research mix and, as private funding increases, relatively fewer theorems are produced. Even with large feedback effects, the private sector will not value basic research as much as the administrator.

As before, the negotiation leverage measure of crowding-out, in which private fundraising is viewed as a bargaining problem, focuses on change in the university administrator's leverage in her bargaining negotiations with the private sector as government funding falls. Note that we extend the negotiation leverage measure of crowding-out to this multi-period problem by simply using the weighted sum of the administrator's utility in the local ideal, actual, and default bargaining outcomes:

$$P^* = \sum_{t=0}^{T-1} \beta^t (\mu M_{u_t}^* + (1-\mu) K_{u_t}^*) + \beta^T \psi (M_{u_T}^*, K_{u_T}^*) \qquad (4.16)$$

$$\hat{P} = \sum_{t=0}^{T-1} \beta^t (\mu \hat{M}_{u_t} + (1-\mu) \hat{K}_{u_t}) + \beta^T \psi (\hat{M}_{u_T}, \hat{K}_{u_T}) \qquad (4.17)$$

$$P_d = \sum_{t=0}^{T-1} \beta^t (\mu M_{g_t} + (1-\mu) K_{g_t}) + \beta^T \psi (M_{g_T}, K_{g_T}) \qquad (4.18)$$

The university's leverage (4.4) is again measured as the distance between the realized bargaining outcome and the local ideal outcome as a fraction of the administrator's total potential surplus from the bargaining outcome.

Again, *negotiation leverage crowding-out* occurs if $\frac{d\zeta}{dg} < 0$ and *negotiation leverage crowding-in* occurs if $\frac{d\zeta}{dg} > 0$. If $\frac{d\zeta}{dg} = 0$, the bargaining problem is *neutral*.

4.7 NEUTRALITY WITH FEEDBACK

Two more neutrality conditions are needed to establish the "neutrality" result for the multi-period model with two feedback loops. These assumptions, like conditions (1), (2), and (3) from Proposition 2, are extremely restrictive, so the extent of crowding-out in this multi-period model is likely sensitive to the level of governmental funding.

Proposition 7: When conditions (4) and (5) are added to conditions (1), (2), and (3), the separability conditions are necessary and sufficient for the multi-period bargaining problem to exhibit neutrality, that is $\frac{d\zeta}{dg} = 0$.

4. Equal Weighting: *The university administrator's performance function assigns equal weight to basic and applied research. That is, $\mu = 1/2$.*

5. Equal Feedback: *The feedback functions are equal, $h(\cdot) = l(\cdot)$.*

Conditions (4) and (5) ensure the symmetry required for the neutrality result. Under condition (4) the administrator derives an equal amount of

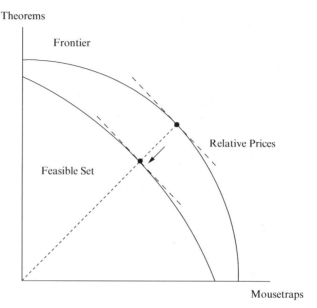

Figure 4.7   A geometric view of neutrality

utility from the production of basic and applied research. Because the administrator's performance function is a proxy for "social welfare," constraint (4) on µ is just as restrictive as the other substitutability assumptions. Condition (5) ensures the administrator's production possibilities frontier is symmetric about the 45° line. Though necessary to guarantee neutrality of governmental funding, this assumption is highly unlikely to be satisfied in practice.

Figure 4.7 illustrates why conditions (4) and (5) are needed to prove Proposition 7. The symmetry imposed by these neutrality conditions ensures that the administrator's leverage does not change as governmental funding changes. With feedback effects, a decrease in funding from the government has two effects: Conditions (1), (2), and (3) guarantee the end points of the production possibilities frontier shift down along their respective axis, and Condition (5) guarantees the frontier becomes less convex in a symmetric way so that the derivative of the frontier at the 45° line is −1. Condition (4) establishes that the allocation that lies at the intersection of the production possibilities frontier and the 45° line is optimal for the administrator. Figure 4.7 depicts a change in the university's $m - k$ space as funding decreases. Since the ray along which the administrator's preferred research allocations lie does not change with changes in the level of governmental funding, the bargaining problem is neutral.

4.8   NONNEUTRALITY WITH FEEDBACK

We now consider the effect of relaxing condition (4) of Proposition 7 on the degree of negotiation leverage crowding-out.

Proposition 8: If conditions (1), (2), (3), and (5) hold but not (4), a performance function that weights applied research more heavily than basic research, μ < 1/2, will increase the degree of negotiation leverage crowding-out, and a performance function that weights basic research more heavily than applied research, μ > 1/2, increases the degree of negotiation leverage crowding-in.

The effect of changing the relative weights of basic and applied research in the administrator's performance function is illustrated in Figure 4.8 and in Figure 4.9. The administrator's performance function gives more weight to theorems, μ > 1/2. A decline in funding leads to crowding-in as the university administrator's optimal allocation includes relatively more basic research. Figure 4.9 illustrates that for an administrator with μ < 1/2, a similar decline in government funding leads to crowding-out. The magnitude of crowding-in/out increases with the size of the drop in governmental funding.

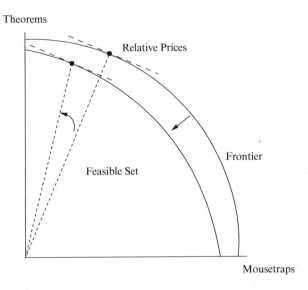

Figure 4.8   Decrease in governmental funding leads to crowding-in

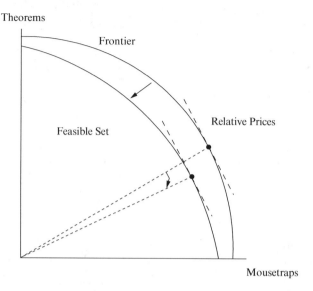

Figure 4.9   Decrease in governmental funding leads to crowding-out

Relaxing condition (5) of Proposition 7 can similarly lead to either negotiation leverage crowding-in or out.

*Proposition 9: If conditions (1), (2), (3), and (4) hold but not (5), then a
decrease in the level of government funded research will increase the degree
of negotiation leverage crowding-out if $h(\cdot) > l(\cdot)$, or increase the degree of
negotiation leverage crowding-in if $l(\cdot) > h(\cdot)$.*

First, assume the feedback from mousetraps to theorems is larger than
the feedback from theorems to mousetraps, $l(\cdot) > h(\cdot)$. Figure 4.10 illustrates the effect of a decrease in government funding. For a university
administrator who weights basic and applied research equally ($\mu = 1/2$),
it is optimal to fund relatively more basic research when government
funding declines. The intuition for this crowding-in of basic research is
simple: The university administrator gets relatively more bang for every
buck invested in applied research and, as funding declines and the asymmetric feedback effect becomes less pronounced, relatively more basic
research is funded.

Figure 4.11 illustrates that a decrease in governmental funding has the
opposite effect when the feedback from theorems to mousetraps is larger
than the feedback from mousetraps to theorems, $h(\cdot) > l(\cdot)$. Since basic

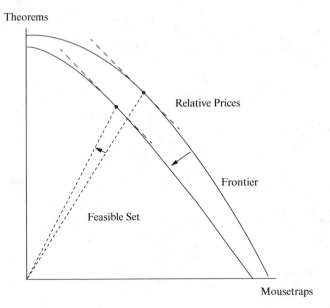

Figure 4.10   Asymmetric feedback leads to crowding-in

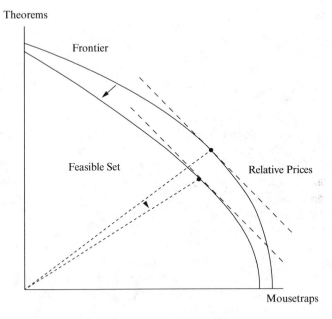

Figure 4.11   Asymmetric feedback leads to crowding-out

research gives relatively more bang for the buck, the administrator will fund relatively more applied research as governmental funding declines and the asymmetry becomes less pronounced.

4.9   CONCLUSION

Concerns that commercial sponsorship of university research will crowd-out basic research conducted for the public good, "theorems", are legitimate. Both models of the university research process used in this chapter show that commercial sponsorship agreements can lead to the crowding-out of public good research. The likelihood of crowding-out depends on the framework used to model university research. In the first model, there is an implicit linear evolution from public good or basic research to applied or private good research. For the case of no dynamic relationships, crowding-in only occurs under a set of highly restrictive assumptions. When there exists a linear decomposition of public good research and commercial or private good research, it is difficult for university administrators to form partnerships with profit-maximizing companies that, in accordance with the first paradigm presented in Chapter 2, do not crowd-out public good research.

In the second model we use a dynamic framework to model university research that admits nonlinearities and recognizes the chaotic nature of the R&D processes, consistent with the second paradigm presented in Chapter 2. Unsurprisingly, crowding-in becomes more likely as we allow for feedback loops from discoveries in applied science to expand the opportunity set for public good research. Astute university administrators can form partnerships that magnify these feedback loops and increase public good research while working with the private sector. University administrators should consider evaluating commercial sponsors based on the potential for significant feedback effects. For example, administrators can increase feedback effects by forming partnerships with companies that allow university researchers to access proprietary knowledge that is otherwise unavailable to the public. Identifying these complementarities will help university administrators create partnerships with the private sector that improve both public good and commercial, or private good, research.

We have structured the models presented in this chapter under the simplifying assumption that university researchers simply follow directions from the administrator and do not respond to other incentives. In practice, the potential for royalties from commercialized research entices university researchers away from conducting public good research. We expect these internal incentives to lead to more researchers working on applied science with commercial benefits than is socially optimal. Given these incentives underlying research pursuits, it is all the more important for administrators to acknowledge and exploit feedback loops by forming commercial research partnerships that enhance public good research. By establishing research partnerships with the private sector that maximize feedback from applied to basic research, administrators at universities can take advantage of this unique feature of scientific research and promote the public good while managing their needs for additional resources.

NOTES

1. We broaden our analysis to consider investment dynamics in the second model and consider a third funding source, namely, the royalties associated with any university mousetraps that have been commercialized.
2. In reality the university would not fully cede its property rights to the mousetraps, but would instead negotiate a royalties agreement. This complication is addressed in the second model.
3. We assume the commercial company can costlessly transform the university's mousetrap research into a marketable product. For simplicity, we assume every unit of the mousetrap research produced by the university can produce a single unit of marketable product for the commercial company. Relaxing this assumption by allowing for a costly, non-linear transformation of mousetrap research does not significantly alter our conclusions.
4. To maintain concavity of the Nash product requires some mild restrictions on the cost functions which essentially guarantee that the contract curve does not rise out of the commercial company's ideal point too quickly.
5. A monotonic decrease in government funding simply shifts the bargaining problem and the properties of the Nash bargaining solution do not change.
6. While this extreme specification is useful for heuristic purposes, the argument clearly holds for more general specifications.

APPENDIX 4A.1 MATHEMATICAL DERIVATIONS

The administrator's choices of m_t and k_t in the second model are determined by solving the following constrained optimization problem:

$$L = \sum_{t=0}^{T-1} [\beta^t P_t(M_t, K_t) + \beta^T \psi(M_T, K_T) + \lambda_{1t}(\frac{1}{1+r})^t (\theta R(M_{t-1}) + \bar{e}_t - m_t^{\beta_m} - k_t^{\beta_k})$$

$$+ \lambda_{2t}(K_t - \gamma K_{t-1} - k_t - l(M_{t-1})) + \lambda_{3t}(M_t - \alpha M_{t-1} - m_t - h(K_{t-1}))]$$

$$(4A.1.1)$$

The first-order conditions for the administrator's optimization problem in the second model are

$$\frac{dL}{dk_t} = \left[\sum_{j=0}^{(T-1)-t} \left(\beta^{t+j} \frac{dP_{t+j}(M_{t+j}, K_{t+j})}{dK_{t+j}} \frac{dK_{t+j}}{dk_t} \right) \right.$$

$$+ \sum_{j=0}^{(T-2)-t} \left(\beta^{t+j} \frac{dP_{t+j+1}(M_{t+j+1}, K_{t+j+1})}{dM_{t+j+1}} \frac{dM_{t+j+1}}{dh_{t+j+1}} \frac{dh_{t+j+1}}{dK_{t+j}} \frac{dK_{t+j}}{dk_t} \right) \Bigg]$$

$$+ \left[\beta^T \left(\frac{d\psi(M_T, K_T)}{dK_T} \frac{dK_T}{dk_t} + \frac{d\psi(M_T, K_T)}{dM_T} \frac{dM_T}{dh_T} \frac{dh_T}{dK_{T-1}} \frac{dK_{T-1}}{dk_t} \right) \right]$$

$$+ \left[\sum_{j=0}^{(T-2)-t} \left(\lambda_{1(t+j+2)} \left(\frac{1}{1+r} \right)^{t+j+2} \theta \frac{dR_{t+j+2}}{dM_{t+j+1}} \frac{dM_{t+j+1}}{dh_{t+j+1}} \frac{dh_{t+j+1}}{dK_{t+j}} \frac{dK_{t+j}}{dk_t} \right) \right.$$

$$- \lambda_{1t} \left(\frac{1}{1+r} \right)^t \beta_k k_t^{\beta_k - 1} \Bigg]$$

$$+ \left[\left[\sum_{j=0}^{T-1-t} \left(\lambda_{2(t+j)} \frac{dK_{t+j}}{dk_t} \right) \right] - \left[\sum_{j=0}^{(T-2)-t} \lambda_{2(t+j)} \gamma \frac{dK_{t+j}}{dk_t} \right] - \lambda_{2t} \right]$$

$$- \left[\left[\sum_{j=0}^{(T-3)-t} \lambda_{2(t+j+2)} \frac{dl_{t+j+2}}{dM_{t+j+1}} \frac{dM_{t+j+1}}{dh_{t+j+1}} \frac{dh_{t+j+1}}{dK_{t+j}} \frac{dK_{t+j}}{dk_t} \right] \right]$$

$$+ \left[\sum_{j=0}^{(T-2)-t} \left(\lambda_{3(t+j)} \frac{dM_{t+j+1}}{dh_{t+j+1}} \frac{dh_{t+j+1}}{dK_{t+j}} \frac{dK_{t+j}}{dk_t} \right) \right.$$

$$- \sum_{j=0}^{(T-3)-t} \left(\lambda_{3(t+j)} \alpha \frac{dM_{t+j+1}}{dh_{t+j+1}} \frac{dh_{t+j+1}}{dK_{t+j}} \frac{dK_{t+j}}{dk_t} \right)$$

$$- \sum_{j=0}^{(T-2)-t} \left(\lambda_{3(t+j)} \frac{dh_{t+j+1}}{dK_{t+j}} \frac{dK_{t+j}}{dk_t} \right) \Bigg] \Bigg] \leq 0 \tag{4A.1.2}$$

$$\frac{dL}{dm_t} = \left[\sum_{j=0}^{(T-1)-t} \left(\beta^{t+j} \frac{dP_{t+j}(M_{t+j}, K_{t+j})}{dM_{t+j}} \frac{dM_{t+j}}{dm_t} \right) \right.$$

$$+ \sum_{j=0}^{(T-2)-t} \left(\beta^{t+j} \frac{dP_{t+j+1}(M_{t+j+1}, K_{t+j+1})}{dK_{t+j+1}} \frac{dK_{t+j+1}}{dl_{t+j+1}} \frac{dl_{t+j+1}}{dM_{t+j}} \frac{dM_{t+j}}{dm_t} \right) \Bigg]$$

$$+ \left[\beta^T \left(\frac{d\psi(M_T, K_T)}{dM_T} \frac{dM_T}{dm_t} + \frac{d\psi(M_T, K_T)}{dK_T} \frac{dK_T}{dl_T} \frac{dl_T}{dM_{T-1}} \frac{dM_{T-1}}{dm_t} \right) \right]$$

$$+ \left[\sum_{j=0}^{(T-2)-t} \left(\lambda_{1(t+j+1)} \left(\frac{1}{1+r} \right)^{t+j+1} \theta \frac{dR_{t+j+1}}{dM_{t+j}} \frac{dM_{t+j}}{dm_t} \right) - \lambda_{1t} \left(\frac{1}{1+r} \right)^t \beta_m m_t^{\beta_m - 1} \right]$$

$$+ \left[\sum_{j=0}^{(T-1)-1} \left(\lambda_{2(t+j)} \frac{dM_{t+j}}{dm_t} \right) + \sum_{j=0}^{(T-2)-t} \left(\lambda_{2(t+j)} \alpha \frac{dM_{t+j}}{dm_t} \right) - \lambda_{2t} \right.$$

$$- \sum_{j=0}^{(T-3)-t} \left(\lambda_{2(t+j+2)} \frac{dh_{t+j+2}}{dK_{t+j+1}} \frac{dK_{t+j+1}}{dl_{t+j+1}} \frac{dl_{t+j+1}}{dM_{t+j}} \frac{dM_{t+j}}{dm_t} \right) \Bigg]$$

$$+ \left[\sum_{j=0}^{(T-2)-t} \left(\lambda_{3(t+j)} \frac{dK_{t+j+1}}{dl_{t+j+1}} \frac{dl_{t+j+1}}{dM_{t+j}} \frac{dM_{t+j}}{dm_t} \right) \right.$$

$$- \sum_{j=0}^{(T-3)-t} \left(\lambda_{3(t+j)} \gamma \frac{dK_{t+j+1}}{dl_{t+j+1}} \frac{dl_{t+j+1}}{dM_{t+j}} \frac{dM_{t+j}}{dm_t} \right)$$

$$- \sum_{j=0}^{(T-2)-t} \left(\lambda_{3(t+j)} \frac{dl_{j+t+1}}{dM_{t+j}} \frac{dM_{t+j}}{dm_t} \right) \Bigg] \leq 0 \tag{4A.1.3}$$

where

$$\frac{dK_{t+j}}{dk_t} = \alpha^j + I_{j \geq 2} \sum_{i=2}^{j} \alpha^{j-i} \frac{dl(M_{t+i-1})}{dM_{t+i-1}} \frac{dM_{t+i-1}}{dK_{t+i-2}} \frac{dK_{t+i-2}}{dk_t} \tag{4A.1.4}$$

$$\frac{dM_{t+j}}{dm_t} = \gamma^j + I_{j \geq 2} \sum_{i=2}^{j} \gamma^{j-i} \frac{dh(K_{t+i-1})}{dK_{t+i-1}} \frac{dK_{t+i-1}}{dM_{t+i-2}} \frac{dM_{t+i-2}}{dm_t} \tag{4A.1.5}$$

In the second model, the commercial company wants to maximize the sum of the profits from each period, $\pi_t(m_t, k_t) = M_t - f_t - R(M_{t-1})$, and the scrap value of an agreement, $W(M_T)$, discounted by the weighted average cost of capital, r:

$$\Pi = \sum_{t=0}^{T-1} \left(\frac{1}{1+r}\right)^t \pi(m_t, k_t) + \left(\frac{1}{1+r}\right)^T W(M_T) \qquad (4A.1.6)$$

where f_t is the funding the company provides to the university to produce the company's share, (m_c, k_c), of the university's research allocation each period, $f_t = C(m_c, k_c)$.

The company's first-order conditions are

$$\frac{d\Pi}{dm_t} = \sum_{j=0}^{(T-1)-t} \left(\frac{1}{1+r}\right)^{t+j} \frac{dM_{t+j}}{dm_t} - \left(\frac{1}{1+r}\right)^t \frac{dC_t(m_{c_t}, k_{c_t})}{dm_t}$$

$$- \sum_{j=0}^{(T-2)-t} \left(\frac{1}{1+r}\right)^{t+j+1} \left(\frac{dR(M_{t+j+1})}{dM_{t+j+1}} \frac{dM_{t+j+1}}{dm_t}\right) + \left(\frac{1}{1+r}\right)^T \frac{dW(T)}{dm_t} = 0$$

$$\frac{d\Pi}{dk_t} = \sum_{j=0}^{(T-2)-t} \left(\frac{1}{1+r}\right)^{t+j+1} \frac{dM_{t+j+1}}{dh_{j+t+1}} \frac{dh_{j+t+1}}{dK_{t+j}} \frac{dK_{t+j}}{dk_t} - \left(\frac{1}{1+r}\right)^t \frac{dC_t(m_{c_t}, k_{c_t})}{dk_t}$$

$$- \sum_{j=0}^{(T-2)-t} \left(\frac{1}{1+r}\right)^{t+j+1} \frac{dR_{t+j+1}}{dM_{t+j+1}} \frac{dM_{t+j+1}}{dh_{j+t+1}} \frac{dh_{j+t+1}}{dK_{t+j}} \frac{dK_{t+j}}{dk_t} + \frac{dW(T)}{dk_t} = 0$$

5. Knowledge creation and the research and development process

In this chapter we focus on the very nature of knowledge, within the context of public versus private funding for R&D processes and knowledge generation. Too often, we speak loosely of the frontiers of knowledge and how innovation may expand such frontiers without attempting to quantify the critical linkages. A simple roadmap for investigating the crucial linkages is presented in Figure 5.1.

5.1 KNOWLEDGE ASSETS

Knowledge is not homogeneous but a differentiated asset. As Polanyi (1958) recognized, it is useful to draw the distinction between two types of knowledge. Tacit knowledge cannot be easily articulated. It draws on skills and techniques that are acquired experimentally, and is transferred slowly by demonstration, apprenticeships, personal instruction, and the provision of expert services. Such knowledge is slow and expensive to

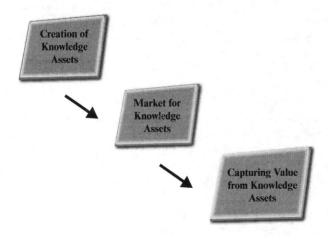

Figure 5.1   Road map

transmit (Tsoukas, 2003). In contrast, codified knowledge can be reduced and converted into messages that can be easily and quickly communicated. The more codified a particular set of knowledge is, the more economically and rapidly it can be transferred. Codification allows simple transmission, verification, storage, and reproduction of knowledge (Kabir, 2013).

In all sectors of research, codified knowledge has assumed an increasingly important role. Such knowledge assumes the form of a non-rivaled good in that sharing information will not reduce the amount of information held by the originator. Codified knowledge can be held and used jointly by multiple parties. This joint use is a key feature of public goods, yet this knowledge does not satisfy all the criteria for a public good because it is possible to exclude others. This excludability is certainly true of such knowledge assets as patents and trade secrets. It is this form of knowledge that has dramatically changed the landscape of jointly conducted public and private research.

Knowledge is a durable good with atypical characteristics. Its services tend to grow with use and decay with nonuse. It is frequently both a consumption good and a capital good. Its productivity can, in fact, have an intrinsic worth. It can be both observable and non-observable in use. Some knowledge is observable once a transaction has been recorded. This is often not the case, however, for process technologies. While reverse engineering may ascertain the fingerprint of a process embedded in a product, this is often not possible if the knowledge owners have been skilled in protecting their trade secrets. Finally, there is a significant body of literature that addresses embodied versus disembodied knowledge.

A useful distinction can be drawn between science and technology, especially when considering the generation and distribution of knowledge. The scientific research process can be viewed as a non-market allocation mechanism, with knowledge treated as a pure public good. The presumption is that discoveries must be completely and rapidly disclosed. In contrast, technology can be seen as a market allocation mechanism with knowledge treated as a private good. In this sense, patents, copyrights, and trade secrets preserve property rights. Findings may not be partially or fully revealed to the public in the short or long term. At the risk of oversimplification, science seeks to increase the public stock of knowledge by encouraging originality, while technology seeks rents from knowledge.

The creation of new knowledge occurs through multiple processes and takes many forms and shapes. Innovations that generate new knowledge are often the direct result of R&D processes in either the public or private sector. In the past century, the public sector played a major role in supporting R&D efforts. During this time, R&D efforts in the private sector have steadily increased and exploded in certain areas (e.g., computer and communication science, software, the Internet, pharmaceuticals, medicine, and agriculture). With the evolution to a "shared economy," it is vital to understand the exact nature of knowledge creation processes and the interaction of public and private good research.

Nowhere have these unfolding trends in public versus private sector R&D commitments been felt more dramatically than at research universities throughout the country. Developed-country governments have held steadfastly to the conviction that basic science is a public good and that much of it should be conducted at research universities. These trends in private versus public research support, when confronted with the significant increases in the cost of scientific research (especially modern molecular biology), have also been another force motivating public–private collaborations.

As noted in Chapter 2, for some years the general belief has been that there exists a linear evolution from public good, or basic science, to private good, applied research. The simplicity of this perspective allows analytically tractable representations. The presumption that innovation processes follow a linear process from basic research (conducted in governmental laboratories and mainly at research universities) through to applied R&D (conducted mainly by firms) is attractive to governmental policymakers and university administrators, and some would argue self-serving.

Again, as noted in Chapter 2, the alternative paradigm is one that admits nonlinearities and recognizes the chaotic nature of R&D processes. Many analysts have documented the meandering flow of innovations into the wider economy. Under this process, innovations emerge through a circuitous path that cannot be codified (Ruttan, 1982), and many would argue, cannot be measured. Kealey (1996) proposed an extreme variant of this view, going so far as to argue that innovation tends to drive basic science, not the other way around. Regardless, this alternative paradigm blurs the distinction often made between basic and applied science. As a result, it also blurs the boundary between the research university and the outside world.

If we accept that the path from innovation to the marketplace is not linear but circular, then productivity increases and economic growth are generated by innovation, which in turn fuels further public good and private good research and additional discoveries. Just as the economic course of innovation is often circular, the underlying process of generating knowledge is itself a series of feedback loops. In many cases, curiosity-driven investigation may be the product rather than the progenitor of a technological adaptation developed in the marketplace.

Moreover, if the widely accepted paradigm for the distinction between public good research and private good research is rejected, the alignment of the incentives between public interest and private self-interest is even more pronounced. Industries cluster around universities that produce usable research and supply the highly trained graduates needed for business success. Informed students know this, and elite universities integrate it into their curriculum as demonstrated by the invitation to corporate sponsors to provide input into the graduate education process and ensure that universities continue to produce the needed highly-skilled workforce. The cooperative exchange with industry not only allows universities to compete for the best faculty and students, but also to contribute to their own discretionary support by generating licensing revenues.

The research engine at major universities requires increasingly expensive fuel. Quality research required for innovation does not happen with top-flight faculty without adequate research funding. In almost all sciences, library research is simply inadequate to advance the frontiers of knowledge. Without modern laboratory facilities and access to commercially developed proprietary databases (such as the gene expression profiles and genome mappings), universities can neither provide first-rate graduate education nor perform the fundamental research that is part of the university's mission.

5.2   BAYH–DOLE ACT AND OTHER FORCES

As emphasized in Chapter 1, the incentives to obtain private funding increased with the passage of the Bayh–Dole Act and the accompanying changes in IP ownership and royalty distributions within a university (Washburn, 2005). Under the Act, IP rights are assigned to the universities where the research takes place, even if the research is federally funded, and research scientists are required to receive some portion of the license revenues earned from the commercialization of their research. This allocation of the royalty stream gives university researchers incentives to select areas of research that are likely to result in commercially profitable innovations. Moreover, by directing their research toward private sector interests and commercially applicable innovations, university researchers can increase the likelihood of receiving remuneration, typically one-third of licensing fees.

Another major structural change in the assignment of property rights has emerged in the form of utility patents. Until 1980, the only legislation in the United States that protected the innovative investments of plant breeders came through the Plant Patent Act of 1930 and the Plant Variety Protection Act of 1970. The first act protects asexually produced varieties, whereas the second act extends to sexually reproduced varieties.

Until the landmark Supreme Court ruling in the matter of Diamond v. Chakrabarty in 1980 (US Diamond v. Chakrabarty, 1980), plant-related inventions based on genes or cells from nature or applied to living organisms were viewed as natural phenomena and thus unpatentable. In this matter, however, the court held that "anything under the sun that is made by man" is patentable subject matter. Specifically, the court found that "the patentee has produced a new bacterium with markedly different characteristics from any found in nature and one having the potential for significant utility. His discovery is not nature's handiwork, but his own; accordingly it is patentable subject matter under the section 101." As a result, this decision broadened the reach of utility patent laws to encompass living organisms as patentable subject matter. Accordingly, utility patents are now granted in the United States for genetically engineered organisms, processes of transforming cells, and expressing proteins and the genes themselves. Note that protection provided by the Plant Variety Protection Act certificates has fallen significantly since the early 1990s, from a high of over 300 awarded certificates in 1992 to less than 70 awarded in 1998 to 78 in 2014. Over the same period, utility patents rose from 48 to almost 500 per year.

5.3 MARKETS FOR SCIENCE AND TECHNOLOGY

The augmented strength in IP regimes has provided the foundation for more active technology markets. To some degree, this has spilled over to markets for scientific knowledge. This should not be surprising. Since the 1990s, with the rapid liberalization of markets and the creation of many types of "intermediate" products, what is tradable has expanded significantly. This is especially true in security markets where derivatives, index futures, securitization, exotic options, barrier options, and an array of put and call options on both listed and non-listed assets are actively traded. The sudden burst of such markets has been aided by developments in computer and information technology.

Under the alternative nondecomposition paradigm, integrating forces exist between pure science and marketable technologies. In particular, successful executors of technological knowledge often need to be well versed in the development and acquisition of upstream knowledge. Such technological sophistication on the part of purchasers in knowledge markets often requires significant in-house fundamental research capabilities (Cohen & Levinthal, 1989; Rosenberg, 1990). As increasingly knowledgeable buyers internalize fundamental research, the position of specialized technology producers is naturally diminished. Nevertheless, the vertical integration between research and technology production has been supplanted to a large degree, beginning in the 1980s, with the growth of specialized technology suppliers.

For codified knowledge, knowledge and information are largely synonymous. For this form of knowledge, the traditional nexus between the economics of goods and services and the economics of information is decoupled. To be sure, sufficient information can be collected over the internet to enable customers to engage in comparative shopping at significantly lower transaction costs. As a result, traditional marketing and distribution channels are under siege. In many instances, more "virtual" structures are viable with new information technology facilitating specialization. In some channels, the erosion in knowledge or information control, combined with the decrease in customer switching costs, will result in the emergence of niche markets. With the decoupling of information from goods and service flows, information is commonly sold in bundles (e.g., magazines are bundles of articles and subscriptions are bundles of magazines). The advantage of customized bundles is that it reduces dispersion in users' willingness to pay. When a supplier's span of control covers sufficient information necessary for bundling, this can be attractive. This is especially the case where complementarities naturally arise. Information components can be guaranteed to be effectively integrated and there are some economies of scope from combining the various component parts. Accordingly, the price of the bundle is typically less than the sum of the component prices.

The significant interest in the markets for technology and the focus on IP is driven by the well-known phenomenon of increasing returns. To the extent that the phenomenon of increasing returns is operative, the Marshallian and Hicksian frameworks of how markets operate and how firms compete must be revisited. These well-designed traditional analytical frameworks, which presume diminishing returns and increasing marginal product costs, do not hold for knowledge-based industries (Arthur, 1988; Arthur, 1996; Milgrom & Roberts, 1990; Teece, 1986). In particular, as Arthur (1996) has argued, "John Hicks warned that admitting increasing returns would lead to 'the wreckage of the greater part of economic theory.' But Hicks had it wrong" (p. 102).

Products generated from knowledge-based industries incur large fixed costs and inconsequential, in many instances zero, marginal cost. This phenomenon exists in agricultural biotechnology, the pharmaceutical industry (whether chemical or biological based), and generally in the development and use of information technologies; the first copy can cost hundreds of millions of dollars with the cost of the second and subsequent copies zero or nearly zero. In this setting, the typical analytical frameworks and standard comparative static results are no longer relevant. Instead, non-convexities prevail and we are forced to turn to supermodularity frameworks (Milgrom & Roberts, 1990).

Increasing returns are driven by several factors: technology, standards, and network externalities; the existence of tacit knowledge; and customer lock-in. The form of the technology drives the relative fixed and marginal costs. Network externalities and standards focus on critical customer mass. Once critical mass is achieved, network externalities (Katz & Shapiro, 1985) establish the basis for positive feedback economics and bandwagon effects. Here, consumer expectations are critical; perceptions drive what ultimately becomes the competitive standard in the minds of customers. If such standards are proprietary, those entities establishing the dominant standard can reap significant rents. As we see again and again in information technology, customer lock-in arises from significant switching costs. These costs are sourced in customer investment in knowledge accumulation.

With the complexity of knowledge markets, new products are rarely stand-alone. Instead, they are components of integrated systems. Dependence on such integrated systems means that firms must focus not only on their competitors but also on their collaborators. In order to establish an active market for information, there already must be a significant stock of accumulated knowledge (Arrow, 1962). As Mowery (1983) has found, it is generally impossible to internalize all the R&D that is needed to integrate the technical know-how to arrive at marketable products. Accordingly, the demand for alliances, joint ventures, and institutional arrangements has never been greater.

In biotechnology, the relevant IP needed to bring specific products to the market is almost never owned, or controlled for that matter, by a single firm. As a result, serious problems arise with respect to the fragmentation of IP rights. This fragmentation challenges the effective functioning of markets for technology. These limitations arise from "hold-up" and other forms of opportunistic behavior, informational asymmetries, and antistacking licensing arrangements.

From the standpoint of markets for technology, many plant biotechnology discoveries have been cumulative and systemic. Prior to much of the consolidation that has taken place, for example in agricultural biotechnology (Marco & Rausser, 2008; Marco & Rausser, 2011), the pace of progress depended on the separable actions of many firms responsible for the production of needed components. Thus, in order for a particular firm to use the available technology, that firm had to collect all the rights for the use of its components. In a world with no transaction costs, this would not be a problem, as we could expect the parties to bargain to a Pareto superior solution given any initial distribution of property rights over the components. In the realistic world of opportunistic behavior, hold-up problems result in unrecoverable detours from such bargaining solutions. This has led to serious questions of "freedoms to operate" motivated by blocking patents or other forms of IP.

In the presence of "blocking patents," market failures are often induced. In the case of complex fragmentation, there is little incentive for a system integrator to arrange transactions in the technology components sequentially. This is quite obviously because once the integrator has obtained some control of only a portion of the necessary components, the associated costs are sunk, and as a result bargaining power is diminished. The transaction costs faced in simultaneous transactions or even contingent transactions make this option almost impossible to execute.

IP fragmentation in agricultural biotechnology has experienced a number of patent infringement and patent validity lawsuits. Particular concern has arisen regarding property rights for isolated gene fragments. In a different context, but equally applicable to plant biotechnology, Heller and Eisenberg (1998) have argued that the proliferation of such patents held by different owners (and only licensed through stringent "pass through" provisions) results in a serious obstacle to research and the development of commercial products. For example, in the case of Roundup Ready Corn, nine critical patents had to be bundled in order to deliver this product to the market. At one point, five major firms controlled one or more of these patents, but as a result of mergers and acquisitions, they are now controlled by only two firms. This fragmented control resulted in costly patent infringement litigation during the late 1990s and early 2000s (Rausser et al., 1999).

Counters to the fragmentation problem include cross-licensing agreements, especially where large transaction costs are faced in any attempts to bundle patent portfolios needed for marketable products. A more effective solution that is yet to emerge in the agricultural biotechnology industry is patent pools.[1] Other institutional arrangements that have been used for copyrights, especially for artists and entertainers, are a potential solution. Ultimately, public policy is also largely responsible for the unintended consequence of IP right fragmentation. Unfortunately, the US Patent Office has issued overly broad and imperfectly specified patents. To be sure, this in turn is the direct consequence of the lack of expertise as well as the lack of necessary funding to search for and evaluate prior art.

Transaction costs and opportunism are the major sources of inefficient knowledge markets. Because of the increasing decoupling of information or knowledge from tangible goods as well as the fragmentation or non-existence of well-articulated property rights, it is no surprise that knowledge markets are often inevitably "thin." There is an unfortunate paradox.

For an exchange to be conducted efficiently, both buyer and seller must know with some precision the characteristics and attributes of what is being traded. However, once the information is assimilated by a potential buyer, the buyer might have no incentive to conclude the transaction; the seller cannot prevent the prospective buyer from benefiting regardless of whether confidentiality agreements have been signed. The difficulty of quantifying the value of knowledge without understanding its inherent attributes and characteristics was noted long ago by Arrow (1962).

A number of separate obstacles arise in the case of tacit knowledge. Here, the context-dependent features of knowledge production as well as the significant cost of transferring technology across contexts can be a serious limitation. Consider, for example, producer learning and knowledge accumulation in the context of natural resource industries. As shown in Rausser (1974), Rausser et al. (1972), and Rausser and Lapan (1979), knowledge augmentations can counter the limitations of nature's endowments. In their frameworks, knowledge augmentations are endogenized as tacit "learning-by-doing" processes in joint production, investment, pollution abatement, and consumption models. In the current context, their results demonstrate:

Proposition 1: Producer learning is internalized and its value can be captured but only by organizations that control the tacit knowledge.

The tacit knowledge accumulation process structured by "learning by doing" generates intermediate goods. There is very little transparency, with only some implicit imputed values associated with the indirect impact on productivity or intangible assets/goodwill appearing on corporate balance sheets.

5.4   CAPTURING VALUE FROM KNOWLEDGE ASSETS[2]

Creating knowledge is one thing, but capturing the value of knowledge is quite another. The existence of incomplete markets for technology provides no assurance that the potential value of new discoveries or innovations will be captured. Moreover, as economists have long realized, the questions of value capture turn on "appropriability regimes." Appropriability enhances value capture both when knowledge is inherently difficult to replicate and/or when IP provides legal barriers to imitation. To the extent that replication and imitation cannot be accomplished, knowledge assets become the foundation for value capture through product differentiation.

The inherent nontradability of many knowledge assets is a source of competitive advantage. This is especially true for tacit knowledge when coordination costs discourage outsourcing or virtual organizations and increase incentives for the internalization of R&D activities. Specialized tacit knowledge assets create rents for their owners. As a result, imperfections in the market for know-how can be both a blessing and a curse.

In the case of codified knowledge, the strengthening of IP is the most effective counter-force to imitation. If such assets are marketable, they can be accessed by all agents. Accordingly, the domain over which competitive advantages can be structured narrows as markets expand. For well-articulated IP, however, it is indeed difficult to infringe without significant penalty even though it can be traded, in some cases reverse engineered, and in others invented around.

As markets for codified knowledge expand, new competitors emerge, and rents normally accruing to the innovator dissipate. Licensing of such knowledge or technology generates royalty revenues or, in the case of agriculture, technology fees that must be balanced against the rent dissipation effect. The rent dissipation impact depends critically on the structure of the industry (i.e., the degree of control the innovator has in the product market). Where the technology rights are not controlled by a monopolist, a "commons" problem emerges in which profits from an oligopolistic market constitute the "commons" (Arora et al., 1998).

Under this structure, the innovative firm that licenses its technology does not fully internalize the rent dissipation effect; the rent dissipation is shared with other users of the commons, whereas the innovative licenser is able to internalize the value of the license. Thus, it is quite possible for the revenue effect from licensing to outweigh any potential rent dissipation effect. This is especially true under well-articulated IP rights that lower the associated transaction cost of licensing. Such rights may also enable the licenser to capture not only the licensing revenues but also a larger share of the rents. However,

Proposition 2: To the extent that broad IP rights result in greater product differentiation, licensing will decline.

This is because if the licensing firm creates a rival who sits closer to the licenser in the product space than other product suppliers, the rent dissipation effect is internalized to a greater extent. Furthermore, as we have witnessed in biotechnology,

Proposition 3: Trait developers that lack downstream assets to operate final markets sell more licenses.

Simply, such technology suppliers have no rents to dissipate under more intense downstream competition. In markets in which there are many innovators and many potential licensers, including universities, the rent dissipation effects will necessarily arise. As a result, in this world:

Proposition 4: Licensing by rivals increases the propensity of other technology holders to also enter into licensing agreements.

Under these circumstances, the markets for technology, once they arise, can become quite robust.[3]

5.4.1 Knowledge Assets and Conservation

An important example of knowledge value capture to environmentalists and much of the developing world is bioprospecting. This activity has been touted as a source of finance for biodiversity and environmental conservation. In a world of no knowledge assets or informative priors, the value of the "marginal unit" of genetic resources is likely to be vanishingly small, creating essentially no conservation incentives. However, ecological and taxonomic knowledge can change the beliefs about potential locations of genetic materials that are candidate sources for the development of new products. In this search, leads of unusual promise are distinguished with the aid of scientific information gleaned from biological and ecological science. Such knowledge developed by researchers, when filtered through a model that provides differential success probabilities, can serve to tag those creatures most likely to display economically valuable characteristics.[4]

As demonstrated in Rausser and Small (2000), when search procedures are optimized to take advantage of knowledge assets through useful prior information, high probability leads command information rents associated with their contribution to the chance of success. Such knowledge allows search costs to be avoided. These rents augment any scarcity rents arising from any bound on the total number of leads available for testing. From this analysis, the following proposition emerges:

Proposition 5: The magnitude of information rents depends on the degree to which ecological and taxonomy knowledge turns leads into "differentiated products," creating a monopolistic competitive market in research opportunities. Rents for high-quality leads can be significant even when the aggregate supply of genetic materials is large.

When biological resources are abundant, an increase in the potential profitability of product discovery has virtually no effect on the value of any lead, whereas technology improvements at lower search costs induce (weakly) a decline in the value of every lead. Empirical analysis suggests that bioprospecting information rents can in some cases be sufficiently large to finance meaningful biodiversity conservation.

5.4.2 Complementary Assets

Any efforts to embed knowledge in differentiable and marketable products must confront the issue of access to complementary assets. Successful attempts (to succeed) in the value creation process will depend not only on the appropriability of innovation rents but also on access to complementary assets. If such assets are already controlled, no obstacle need arise. However, because the market for complementary assets is itself riddled with imperfections, such assets might become the "choke point" in the value chain. It is, in fact, the integration of complementary assets and the need to identify the incremental returns of their components that are the focus of supermodularity frameworks.

In the case of technological advances in plant biotechnology, the complementary assets include, inter alia, research capacity, scale-up experience, and access to seed research stations.[5] As noted by Graff et al. (2002), research or process technologies for plant transformation, access to traits and enhancements of elite germplasm, capacity to produce nonbiological chemical inputs (herbicides), distribution networks for seeds and other inputs, and legal and regulatory competencies are among the crucial complementary assets.

Any knowledge innovation rents will depend on a particular discovery's appropriability as well as the degree of specialization of complementary assets. If access to complementary assets is available through open-market transactions, the innovator will capture the rents. To the extent that this is not true, specialized complementary assets will capture a share of such rents. Obviously, there are varying degrees of innovation, appropriability, and the control of complementary assets (Teece, 1986).

The number and the complexity of contracts, joint ventures, and strategic alliances with other firms in the industry and with universities and other non-profit research institutions have increased the value of the complementary legal and regulatory competencies. New institutional arrangements, such as grower license agreements introduced by Monsanto to protect and capture IP value, resulted in an unprecedented number of legal claims (grower alleged violations through saved seed). The monitoring and enforcement of refuge requirements to manage potential insect resistance buildup is another element of legal and regulatory competencies. The net result of all these activities is to increase the entry barriers and thus often to keep imitators and other potential innovators at bay.

5.5 IP AND MARKET STRUCTURE

IP rights do not, by themselves, ensure the capture of value. This can be either because complementary assets are not combined efficiently (Teece, 1986) or because the joint profit available from an accumulative line of research is not divided such that the R&D costs of each innovator are covered (Green & Scotchmer, 1995). Both problems are especially critical in agricultural biotechnology from the standpoint of complementary assets. Even if a new and valuable trait is protected by a utility patent, it cannot generate value without being incorporated into the germplasm that is produced and sold to growers.

Much has been written on the rapid consolidation that has taken place in agricultural biotechnology since the late 1990s (Rausser et al., 1999; Marco & Rausser, 2008; 2011). In the popular press and industry publications, a number of hypotheses have been offered to explain this consolidation. One group of hypotheses focuses on contractual hazards associated with licensing, avoidance of appropriability hazards, and uncertain IP rights. Given the scope of some patents issued in plant biotechnology, there are justifiable concerns that hold-up strategies will be rampant. The second group of hypotheses is sourced with the exploitation of asset complementarities. The critical assets include "freedom to operate," enabling process technologies, bundled products (Roundup Ready seeds and the herbicide), and elite germplasm. To the extent that such complementarities lead to significant efficiencies, augmented R&D budgets and enhanced innovation are expected results. A third category of hypotheses focuses on anticompetitive behavior and the quest for market power. Here, the regulators (the Department of Justice and the Federal Trade Commission) face serious challenges. In the case of agricultural biotechnology, evaluating preconsolidation conduct and behavior in a world of commodities provides little, if any, insight into conduct and behavior in a differentiated product world.

A hypothesis has been advanced (Rausser et al., 1999) to formalize this explanation for selecting the "merger" option instead of different forms of licensing. This explanation focuses on heterogeneous beliefs and the causal connection between IP and the emerging increasing-returns perspective with differentiated products. In all knowledge-based industries, and agriculture is no exception, forces for increasing returns exist alongside those for diminishing returns. Moreover, there are critical segments of the industry that continue to perform not as a differentiated product business but instead as a commodity business. For the latter, products are fundamentally homogeneous, transactors can be anonymous, and markets are clearly delineated. For the former, the distinction between products and the boundaries between markets are blurred. Managers and entrepreneurs in the commodity world accept the notion of diminishing returns and the serious obstacles that are confronted as they attempt to expand. Because of the high degree of substitutability in this world, the value is more or less exogenously fixed with razor-thin margins.

Formally, consider a two-tier production process involving a trait developer and a seed producer. Vertical integration can be accomplished either by contracting (i.e., exclusive licensing) or by consolidation (i.e., mergers and acquisitions). To examine the possible causal connection with IP rights, two regimes are admitted in the proposed industry structure: one with clearly articulated property rights and another regime in which such rights do not exist.[6] To examine the fundamental question of whether there is anything that consolidation can achieve that contracting cannot, a primitive model can be developed in which markets are open for two periods. In the commodity world, all market parameters are identical in each period. In the first period a single agent develops an R&D product called a trait, incurring a substantial fixed cost and zero marginal cost. What happens in the second period depends on whether IP rights are clearly articulated. If they are, the trait developer obtains a patent and retains his monopolistic status in the second period; if they are not, other suppliers will imitate the trait developer's product in the second period, and price competition will drive the equilibrium price of licenses, and thus equilibrium profits for the trait developer, to zero.

For the differentiated product world, the distinctions of heterogeneity are introduced through subjective distributions on the demand for transgenic seed and the fixed cost of producing the trait. Both the trait developer and the seed provider hold beliefs about these variables, and their subjective beliefs might vary, depending on each agent's vision, management controls, and production and marketing operations. The results demonstrate that under homogeneous beliefs, consolidation and exclusive licensing contracts are equivalent routes to integration. Once heterogeneous beliefs about management are introduced, the equivalence between the two forms of integration breaks down. Under irreconcilable differences the distinction turns on the issue of control and control premiums. Provided that at least one party has sufficient faith in its own vision and strategy to warrant consolidation, the other will be willing to cede control in exchange for compensation that does not depend on a subsequent performance of the integrated enterprise. As a result, the following proposition holds:

Proposition 6: In a differentiated product world with a well-articulated IP regime, many parameter values exist for which integration via consolidation is feasible but for which integration via exclusive licensing is not.

In the pristine setting of the model sketched here, IP does affect incentives to vertically integrate either via consolidation or contracting in a world of differentiated products but not in a world of commodities. For the regime in which IP rights do not exist, the differentiated product world leads to the same conclusions with regard to the merger versus the licensing options as in the commodity world. Moreover, when such rights do exist and agents have heterogeneous beliefs about the causal determinants of industry profitability, there is a range of parameter values for which integration via consolidation will be profitable but for which integration via contracting will not.

Public policy, in its many dimensions, will continue to be a major force in the evolution of knowledge assets. The principal dimensions include competition, IP, food and health safety, and world trade policies. With regard to competition and IP policies, inherent conflicts show little sign of being resolved. The clash between these two sources of protections has been amplified by the recent Microsoft and Intel legal cases. The clash has only begun to emerge with the role of utility patents in plant biotechnology and the associated fears of knowledge monopolization. The Department of Justice and the Federal Trade Commission have grappled with the mergers and acquisitions over the last five years and can be expected to confront even more serious challenges over the future. Regardless, the pursuit of complementary efficiencies along with the accompanying increasing returns and, in some cases, even market power, will provide ample incentives for further consolidation and vertical integration.

Not only will US and international public policy continue to be a major force, but society could significantly benefit from private sector institutional arrangements for access to knowledge assets. The cost of litigation resulting from the award of overly-broad patents, patent fragmentation, freedoms to operate, and the lack of well-articulated property rights begs for the introduction for new institutional arrangements. The prisoner's dilemma problems that have emerged have been revealed in the exorbitant litigation cost associated with the patent infringement suits of one type or another. Institutional clearinghouses for IP and technology are a first step, with private sector patent pooling institutional structures representing a long-run potential solution (Graff et al., 2006).

5.6   CONCLUSION

We have witnessed an unparalleled information technology revolution and are on the verge of discovering the biological essence of life. Plant genomics, animal genomics, and nutritional genomics could, along with existing information technologies, provide the platform for not only pursuing but also achieving an enriched set of complementarities between economic well-being and environmental quality. To get from "here" to "there," tracking closely a virtuous cycle, requires an augmentation in the available "social capital." Life science advancements, especially biotechnology, have revealed that society's stock of shared values, principally manifested by trust, has not fared well in many communities throughout the world. It is in society's and the public's interest to enhance the incentives and institutional arrangements for the creation of knowledge; the incentives and institutional arrangements for well-functioning technology markets; the incentives and institutional arrangements for capturing the value of knowledge assets; and the public's understanding of the benefits and costs of innovative technology generation.

NOTES

1. In this regard, the agricultural biotechnology industry may have much to learn from the oil refining industry as well as the semiconductor industry.
2. This section relies heavily on collaborative research with Rachael Goodhue, Greg Graff, Susann Scotchmer, Art Small and Leo Simon (Goodhue & Rausser, 1999; Graff et al., 1999).
3. With respect to Proposition 4, the policies reflected in the Bayh–Dole Act, 1980, the Stevenson–Wydler Technology Act of 1980, and the Federal Technology Transfer Act of 1986 have strengthened the ability of universities and governmental research agencies to diffuse technologies. Because these institutions are generally technology suppliers with no downstream assets, a societal benefit emerges from inducing final producers to diffuse their technologies with related positive effects on investment, reduction of entry barriers, and thus more competition. The fear is that such societal gains come at the cost of some unintended consequences resulting from potential deleterious impacts on open access to the development of new knowledge.
4. Just as a catalog helps a library patron to focus quickly on those few volumes that are most likely to contain information he or she desires, so can an ecological model parse the living world into categories suggesting potential use.
5. For example "field research" refers to the extensive breeding programs of multiple stations that are operated by national companies. Specifically, Pioneer has 50 seed research stations in the United States and Canada, 25 of which conduct research on corn. It has 43 research locations outside the United States. DeKalb has 36 research locations in the United States and Canada. In addition to the national seed company breeding programs, approximately 25 to 30 regional seed companies have breeding programs.
6. Of course, this distinction is unnecessarily stark. More realistically, think of the weakly articulated property right regime as representing the period when agricultural IP was weakly protected under the Plant Variety Protection Act and of the well-articulated regime as representing more recent history where property rights are articulated through utility patents.

6. PPRPs: The benefits and risks of the bargain

The potential benefits from PPRPs are qualitative characteristics, easily articulated in terms of their potential. Complementarities between scientific and practical knowledge have the capacity to generate rapid and far-reaching innovation. Each partner is seeking attributes and assets in prospective partners that complement their own abilities and resources. Industry is interested in combining its knowledge of markets with information on new research and innovation in order to identify those developments that are likely to lead to commercial applications. This motivation may be obvious, but industry is also interested in other, less obvious assets such as access to academic expertise, networks, and first-hand information about up-and-coming scientists (current graduate students). And while universities are very clearly interested in financial capital,[1] they are also seeking intellectual capital, cutting-edge research technologies, and proprietary research tools (e.g., databases). Access to these research assets enhances a university's ability to provide a first-rate education to its graduate students and to serve the regional community's economic development goals.

Although the potential benefits of research partnerships are clear, the potential risks to both parties can be substantial. These risks can pose serious obstacles to the successful formation of PPRPs. In addition to the uncertainty inherent in any research process, the differences between university educational objectives and corporate goals are a primary source of risk in these relationships. With private financing comes the concern that the traditional orientation of the academic research agenda toward basic, public goods research will be directed toward more applied, appropriable research that serves the objectives of the private partner, and that this conflict of interest, in turn, may result in a loss of academic integrity. Certain partnership mechanisms, such as conflict of interest agreements and publication delays that often accompany collaborations with private partners, are seen to create barriers to the traditionally free and open research culture of public universities.

Planning horizons between university and industry partners tend to differ; university researchers focus on long-term research while companies often seek quick turnaround projects. The difference in university and industry turnaround time can make negotiating and managing research agreements a challenge. In addition, the cultures and values of research partners may simply clash, creating insurmountable blocks to a continuing relationship. University integrity may be questioned if the pressure to secure future research financing and to form future relationships negatively influences behavior under a current collaboration.

Issues concerning IP are especially contentious. Hold-up and background rights are of primary concern to an industry partner interested in commercializing the products of a research partnership (Business-Higher Education Forum, 2001). Researchers at universities and other public institutions often use proprietary research tools in their research without obtaining rights. They are blocked, however, from using these tools for commercial purposes. This is the basis for the collective research model: Generally, one researcher in an institution may freely access another researcher's patented research tool for academic study. Industry partners and researchers doing private research are often excluded from this type of arrangement. Thus a private institution looking to partner with a particular researcher, for example, may experience hold-up at the commercialization stage because the public research partner did not obtain formal rights to all research inputs (i.e., background rights).

Further, if numerous university researchers and graduate students are involved in a research project, industry risks loss of privacy and protection for proprietary information. In response to this risk, private partners may restrict researchers with confidentiality agreements. Private partners frequently indicate that long-term strategic partnerships provide a more successful mechanism than one-time specific research ventures for reconciling these issues (Hertzfeld et al., 2006).

The obvious risk to the industry partner is the loss of financial and other tangible assets committed at the outset of the research partnership if only *de minimis* discoveries are generated as the agreement unfolds. Embedded in the flow of financial assets from the industry partner are the indirect costs imposed by the university. Standard overhead rates, which vary from one university to another, represent a direct benefit to the university but increase risk for the private partner as these costs do not directly generate research products.

The interests of parties outside a research agreement (i.e., third parties) are also at risk under public–private research agreements. If an agreement is not effectively structured with regard to patenting and licensing rights, the public's interest (third-party interest) in having reasonable access to research products and innovations may not be adequately represented. In fact, blocking patents are a primary area of concern (Heller & Eisenberg, 1998).

6.1 CORE PRINCIPLES

The goal in forming comprehensive research partnerships is to balance the set of complex tradeoffs – to maximize research opportunities while controlling related risks. Research institutions must develop and use a set of "core principles" or values to guide their decisions in this process. For universities, which have diverse, complicated, and sometimes conflicting objectives, having well-conceived core principles before entering research partnerships is a prerequisite for forming successful relationships. If adhered to, these principles translate into a set of constraints on how much control may be relinquished (or must be retained) by the university in a research agreement in order to serve its mission.

Some core principles reflect the overall mission of a university and are widely recognized. Of these, certain values are shared by every university and are relevant for all activities, such as protecting academic integrity and freedom and serving the interest of students. These principles are the focus when research partnerships are scrutinized. Other principles such as serving the local community and pushing forward scientific knowledge matter to different universities to greater and lesser degrees.

More nuanced, and generally unrecognized, are the core principles that reflect the attributes of effective partnerships. For example, a high degree of asset complementarity, and incentive and cultural alignment, between partners means that a relationship has the opportunity for success. If the university adheres to the principle of active strategic positioning with respect to potential partners, as well as the principle of identifying and securing flexibility options, the university is likely to achieve the best arrangement for its researchers, students, and the community. Also vital is the degree of transparency, access, and oversight afforded to both those within and those outside of the agreement.

6.2 NEGOTIATING UNIVERSITY–INDUSTRY COLLABORATION

PPRPs can come in many forms ranging from large, multi-project, multi-year alliances to small-scale projects. Regardless of the form of any single university and private partner engagement, certain aspects of the negotiation and pre-negotiation process warrant special focus given the risks from these partnerships and the core principles of the public partner.

6.2.1 Partner Selection

At the initiation of a research partnership, the selection process for partners defines the range of possible outcomes. If a partner defaults on continuing an established relationship with an existing partner, the research outcomes are limited. If a new relationship is sought, then either the public or private partner can take the lead in initiating an agreement. Once the lead partner has defined its own primary research assets and goals as well as desired attributes in a research partner (in the case of a potential industry partner, a desired attribute may be a willingness to give access to proprietary information and non-codified or patented data and tools), it may then approach a single potential partner or several partners. Although deliberately seeking out partners, rather than waiting to be approached with a proposal, requires more effort up front, this will yield the greatest degree of control over the selection of research partners.

6.2.2 Governance and Research Agenda

The composition of the committee administering a research partnership and its general policies is a key factor in setting overall tone, defining process and conflict resolution procedures, and determining the focus of a research agreement. Previous relationship experience between the partners and the underlying level of trust are critically important considerations.

Although many aspects of a negotiated partnership, including the governance structure, help to shape the partnership research agenda, the two primary components in this process are the call for proposals and the proposal selection process. The call for research proposals can range from being open to any and all research proposals by faculty in broad or more defined research areas to directed calls by the private partner asking for proposals targeted at specific research areas. As the call for research proposals becomes more limited in scope and perhaps skewed to the interests of the private partner, the choice set for the public institution will become more restricted. The proposal selection process, or more specifically the composition of the committee selecting the proposals to receive funding, also has a significant role in defining the research agenda. Obviously, if the proposal selection committee is dominated by members representing the private partner, there is a risk that the resulting research agenda will primarily serve the private partner's interest.

6.2.3　Publication Delay and Confidentiality

While the university's academic mission is to share research findings rapidly and broadly, the private partner is interested in restricting access to research findings until IP rights are articulated and protected. Because of this direct conflict over publication dissemination, research agreements are guided by specific recommendations concerning publication delay (e.g., guidelines issued by the NIH (1999) recommend a delay of 30 to 60 days). Rather than the specified maximum publication delay period, a more important aspect of information dissemination is the control of the option for terminating the delay period through preparation of patent filings.

Confidentiality, always an issue when two partners work together, can be handled in various ways through contracting terms in research agreements. One approach is for the private partner to enter into confidentiality agreements with individual researchers when granting access to proprietary data or technology. Alternatively, the university can be held responsible for maintaining confidentiality.

6.2.4　Patents and Licensing

Both private and public partners have an interest in defining IP rights over research outcomes, including who is responsible for filing for patents, who holds the right not to file for a patent, who handles patent litigation, who oversees "know-how" transfer, and who owns the core technology. The partner that holds the right to file a patent application controls not only the publication delay period, but also the content of the application. In PPRPs, it is often the university partner who is responsible for filing the patent applications and the private partner who provides guidance and becomes involved in patent litigation to varying degrees.

Of vital importance for PPRPs is the nature of licensing options. Because of concerns about blocking patents, it is common for the industry partner to be given a first-to-negotiate licensing option for some subset of the innovations generated under the research partnership instead of right-of-first-refusal options. Generally, these options must be exercised within a specified time period, or else the option is extended to third parties. Another key aspect of licensing agreements is the percentage of total innovations for which the industry partner holds an option to negotiate an exclusive license. Third-party options are also a critical aspect of license agreements. These options are the rights that parties outside the partnership have to innovations generated by the partnership.

A more nuanced issue is whether a university is required to file for a patent if requested to do so by the private partner or whether the university maintains discretion. If the university retains control of the patent process and can elect not to file for a patent for those innovations the private partner does not intend to commercialize, it can make sure that innovations, or know-how, remain freely available to the public and that limited administrative resources are not diverted to pursue questionable patents.

6.3   UNIVERSITY–INDUSTRY INTERACTIONS

PPRPs come in many shapes and forms. Partnership agreements may be targeted, with private firms designating specific research agendas, or non-targeted. Collaborations may cover a single research project or, alternatively, may involve "mega-agreements" that cover a large range of collaborative interactions. Research projects may have short or long time horizons. Universities may enter agreements with a single private company or, instead, with groups of firms sharing a common interest (industry consortia).

The types of PPRPs include:

- *Single or multiple sponsored research projects*: The most common form of agreement, these are essentially service contracts involving direct funding of university research.
- *Spinoffs or startups*: Usually involve setting up new companies that have licensing rights to university IP and involve university researchers.
- *Strategic partnerships*: Longer-term, collaborative research agreements between one or more universities and one or more private companies that involve exchange of significant financial and other assets.
- *Open collaborative research*: A new model of PPRP that teams a private partner with several universities to pursue a common interest.
- *Consortia*: Groups of universities and private partners pursuing a shared research interest.
- *Research units/centers*: One or more private partners engage with one or more universities to establish research space that is separate from the campus to support research at various stages of development.
- *Informal agreements*: In most cases, more indirect, non-transparent arrangements such as corporate gifts that are not necessarily tied to any specific collaboration.
- *Technology licensing*: Licensing of university IP to companies that aim to develop a technology for market (Thursby et al., 2001).

- *IP sharing*: IP pooling or clearinghouses that consolidate a central portfolio of IP assets to facilitate exchange between partners (Graff & Zilberman, 2001).
- *Material transfer agreements*: The exchange of tangible research materials.
- *Clinical research and trials*: A specific type of sponsored project.

6.4   EXAMPLES OF PPRP AGREEMENTS

Certain types of partnerships such as sponsored research projects, technology licensing, and materials transfer agreements have become so commonplace that just about all research universities have specific offices set up to negotiate and govern these interactions. Other types such as strategic partnerships, research units and centers, and open collaborative research are more innovative. Informative insights and lessons about these more innovative partnerships are increasing.

In 2001, the Business–Higher Education Forum (BHEF) issued a report (2001), *Working Together, Creating Knowledge: The University-Industry Research Collaboration Initiative*, assessing the opportunities and challenges in forming university–industry collaborations. The report profiled several key, ongoing collaborations including one of the most long-running collaborations, that between Washington University (WU) and Monsanto. The relationship originated in 1981 when Monsanto approached nearby WU. Negotiators from both partners worked for several months to come to agreement. Once a contract was set, the partnership was revealed to the public and the faculty voted to approve the agreement.

One in a series of WU–Monsanto medical research agreements began in 2001 and involved a Monsanto financial contribution of $5 million per year. Under this agreement, the company issued "requests for applications" each year and interested faculty submitted applications. Both Monsanto and WU had senior scientists on the panel that reviewed the applications. Monsanto received the right of first refusal to license and develop the discovery it helped fund. Every three years a panel of outside scientists reviewed the research (Business-Higher Education Forum, 2001). The results of these reviews are apparently not available in the public domain.

The BHEF also profiled the partnership between UC Berkeley and the Novartis Agriculture Discovery Institute (Novartis). In 1998, Novartis entered into an agreement that provided $25 million in research support ($5 million per year for five years) to Berkeley's Department of Plant and Microbial Biology (PMB). The agreement with Novartis came after

UC Berkeley sent a request for proposals to fifteen companies and ultimately negotiated with four interested companies, one of which was Novartis. The governance of the agreement was controlled by a research committee, having a majority of university members. Under the agreement, research funds were available on a competitive basis to all PMB faculty that wished to participate in the research program, and each research project was to focus on that particular faculty member's respective areas of research interest. In return, Novartis was able to choose from all research generated from the participating faculty, up to the allowable percentage, and invoke a first right to negotiate. If Novartis chose not to pursue a license on an invention, or Novartis and the university could not agree on the terms, Berkeley could offer the discovery to other companies.

The BHEF provided another example of university–industry partnership in the form of a spinoff, Biolex, Inc. The company was established by a North Carolina State University (NC State) researcher and was based on processes for inserting foreign genes into duckweed, the smallest flowering plant. Duckweed's characteristics that allow it to reproduce swiftly and clonally make it commercially interesting. Although the NC State's technology transfer office (TTO) was able to offer advice, contacts for outside contracts, and encouragement and information through the contract negotiating process, there was a limit to the support that the TTO could offer for establishing an independent company. The researcher/founder had to navigate the relationships with venture capital and other private interests. In 2000, a few years after the spinoff was established, a patent was issued based on these processes. Biolex, Inc. grew for a time, acquiring other companies, but after the sale of certain company assets, Biolex, Inc. filed for bankruptcy in 2012.

Another innovative public–private relationship is the Power Electronic Building Block (PEBB) program that brings together the Office of Naval Research (ONR), Virginia Tech, Virginia Polytechnic Institute, and automotive companies. Under this program technological discoveries were spun out from government labs perfecting standardizations for transfer to the Navy, and then industry partners transferred the standardization to commercial markets. This partnership came together because both the Navy and industry partners needed technological discoveries, but the associated research was too risky for the industry partner and the Navy did not have sufficient or discretionary financial assets. As the partnership unfolded, the Navy pursued innovation of technologies with commercial promise (based on industry partner buy-in) and partnered with universities to drive research progress. The industry partner would then actively bring discoveries to commercial markets.

This partnership overcame several challenges with cultural differences, recruiting new partners and capitalizing on dual objectives (i.e., technologies that serve the interests of the Navy and industry). The Navy had to show trustworthiness, and industry had to have confidence that the research would result in discoveries and processes with civilian uses. In 2001, the ONR was making available $10 million per year to PEBB research through more than 100 grants and contracts involving more than 200 researchers.

The BHEF also profiled the experience of a small company partnering with a university. Ribozyme Pharmaceuticals, Inc. (RPI), a small biotechnology venture founded in 1992, proposed to the University of Colorado (CU) to provide a $500,000, five-year research grant with no restrictions on use in return for an exclusive option to license any ribozyme-related discovery made in CU laboratories, regardless of whether RPI funding was involved in the research. The agreement allowed the company to establish ties to CU scientists through collaborative projects, seminars at RPI's labs or at the university, and recruitment of CU scientists to RPI's Science Advisory Board. The financial commitment by RPI represented a significant percentage (5 to 10 percent) of CU's research budget. This presented more risk for RPI in comparison to the commitments that larger pharmaceutical companies can make to universities. However, smaller companies such as RPI have the advantage of being able to respond quickly. So with the issues of publication delay, a company like RPI can review material in a week and file for patents within a month.[2]

In 2008, the President's Council of Advisors on Science and Technology (2008b) issued a report, *University–Private Sector Research Partnerships in the Innovation Ecosystem*. The report, motivated by the concern over the growing demand for research funds at universities and the inability to meet that demand, profiled 14 partnerships representing a diverse set of successful partnerships.

One such partnership, General Electric's University Strategic Alliance Program (GEUSAP) is a joint research venture that matches a single industry partner, General Electric (GE), with eight universities in the United States, Europe, and China. The program focuses on specific research areas of technical importance to GE and guarantees three years of funding on a rolling basis with individual programs ranging from $25,000 to over $500,000. Specific IP policies govern the program:

> GE will not pay royalties, but will consider license fees. In the case of joint invention, patents will be jointly owned. In the case of gas turbines, GE retains exclusivity. GE encourages publication, provided that proprietary information is protected. Usually this entails waiting until a patent application is filed before submitting work for publication. GE has review rights; reviews are prompt and clear. GE has acknowledged that IP rights in other countries such as China

are more favorable for industry investments than they are in the United States. (President's Council of Advisors on Science and Technology, 2008b, p. 49)

Another partnership profiled in the report is the Energy Biosciences Institute (EBI), a R&D alliance focused on biology and the energy sector (see Chapter 9). The partners involved, UC Berkeley, Lawrence Berkeley National Lab, the University of Illinois at Urbana–Champaign (UIUC) and British Petroleum (BP), entered into a ten-year, $500 million contract. The EBI's research runs from basic research to applied proprietary projects for commercial applications in very specific areas of energy biosciences. The research takes place in an EBI building on the UC Berkeley campus and within the Institute for Genomic Biology on the UIUC campus. Co-location of researchers, with approximately 50 BP researchers placed on the university campuses, is one primary feature of the EBI, as is the co-location of open and proprietary research. The EBI utilizes a grant-making process with a rolling-basis approval and funds researchers who would not have been identified in a standard sponsored research process.

Examples of partnerships under a model of open collaborative research include Intel lablets and IBM's Open Collaborative Research program. Intel's program, launched in 2001, established a partnership with several universities that focuses on exploratory research with the aim of developing new technologies that may lead to new products or new business models for Intel (President's Council of Advisors on Science and Technology, 2008b). Initially, the partnership involved UC and the University of Washington in Seattle and then extended to Carnegie Mellon University and University of Pittsburgh Medical Center. Each lablet is co-directed by an Intel employee and a university professor. Budgets for the labs are determined annually and can fluctuate based on research agendas and priorities. The basis of the program is an Open Collaborative Research agreement that governs active collaboration by all partners and non-exclusive IP rights. Either an Intel or university researcher can propose and initiate joint research projects, and the results of the research are widely shared.

A different perspective on the university–industry lab is the Massachusetts Institute of Technology (MIT) Media Lab founded in 1985 (President's Council of Advisors on Science and Technology, 2008b). The research agenda of the lab has shifted over the years with the current focus on "Inventing a Better Future," facilitating human adaptability. The research is conducted on the MIT campus by Media Lab researchers. The Media Lab partners that are corporate sponsors join as consortium members for a minimum of three years. Corporate sponsors who join at the consortium level may place an employee in residence at the Lab and have access to full IP rights, license fee free and royalty free, for any discoveries emerging from any such lab during the period of sponsorship. Also, sponsors can recruit students to work as interns or hire them upon graduation.

Another organization evaluating PPRPs is the University–Industry Demonstration Partnership (UIDP), itself a PPRP that aims to facilitate other PPRPs. The UIDP was created by the University–Industry Partnership (UIP). In 2003, the UIP was constructed to represent a broad spectrum of university and industry partners with representation from many industry sectors (aerospace, agriculture, biotechnology, chemicals, consumer products, defense manufacturing, pharmaceuticals, and software), different company sizes, and both small and large public and private universities. The purpose of this partnership was to consider the causes of and potential solutions to the difficulties facing universities and companies as they attempt to partner. This group relied on key documents, including *Working Together, Creating Knowledge* produced by the BHEF (2001), and partnering guidelines. Representatives from the UIP convened five meetings and generated a set of Guiding Principles for University–Industry and Endeavors, and in 2006 established the new partnership alliance, the UIDP. From 2006 to mid-2015, the UIDP functioned as a project of the National Academies' Government–University–Industry Research Roundtable (GUIRR). The UIDP is now a free-standing membership, non-profit organization.

The UIDP presents several case studies of innovative partnerships including the Caltech Boeing Strategic Agreement. Built on a long-standing relationship, this specific agreement between Boeing Research and Technology and Caltech began in 2004 with a focus on systems integration technology and involving specific upfront terms on IP and other factors. As the research progresses, current projects are evaluated using set criteria and a subset are continued as sponsored research. Researchers and principal investigators from both partners work together with students to both expedite technology transfer and provide opportunities for students through scholarships and by extending their research to positions at Boeing. The partnership aims to leverage the relationship to attract government and other research center funding.

UIDP also reported on the partnership between the University of Tennessee (UT) and Scintillation Materials Research Center and Siemens Medical Solutions. This partnership has the fairly narrow research focus to develop new scintillators to enhance the performance of medical imaging devices manufactured by Siemens. A multidisciplinary team of faculty and students in the UT College of Engineering work with researchers at Siemens to discover and develop new materials technology with the goal to increase the competitive advantage for Siemens while providing research topics for students. Siemens provides $500k per year plus $1 million in equipment while UT supplies 2,000 square feet of lab and offices. As with most PPRPs, this partnership has resulted in journal articles, patents, and financial support of graduate students.

6.5   CASE STUDY OF THE BERKELEY–NOVARTIS AGREEMENT

An illustrative example of a strategic partnership is the so-called Berkeley–Novartis agreement. Formally, the agreement was between Novartis Agricultural Discovery Institute (NADI), a subsidiary of Novartis, and the PMB in the College of Natural Resources at UC Berkeley. This PPRP was presented to the Berkeley Academic Senate and to the university administration as an experiment from which much could be learned. Consistent with the shared governance structure between faculty and university administration on the UC Berkeley campus, the Dean of the College of Natural Resources sought and secured approval of the PPRP from both branches of governance, the Faculty Academic Senate and the Chancellor's Office. Given PPRPs' experimental nature, both the Academic Senate and the Chancellor's Office worked with the Dean to establish the funding for an ex post evaluation of the agreement to be conducted by the Center for Studies in Higher Education (CSHE), located on the Berkeley campus. As part of the PPRP, financial funding was obtained from Novartis ($300,000) to underwrite this formal extramural evaluation at the completion of the five-year PPRP. It is in large part for this reason that we present this case study to illustrate the possible benefits and risks. Ultimately, there was not only extramural ex post evaluation, but a number of internal reviews and an assessment by the UC Berkeley Associate Vice Chancellor for Research Office.[3]

The Berkeley–Novartis research agreement was a magnet for controversy from its inception. Much of this controversy was triggered not by the agreement, per se, but by the very nature of the research to be conducted, namely, plant biotechnology research potentially leading to the commercialization of transgenic seeds or GMOs. Debates in the Berkeley and wider academic community commenced as details of the agreement were shared in 1998. A cover story in the March 2000 issue of *The Atlantic Monthly*, which featured the Berkeley–Novartis agreement, conveyed the tone of the story through its title, "The Kept University" (Press & Washburn, 2000). An editorial in *Nature* (2001) gave the agreement as an example of the "down-side" of the PPRP, with the presence of Novartis employees on governance and research selection committees as cause for concern. Berkeley's Academic Senate raised several concerns about governance and resource allocation under the agreement, including the potential role of Novartis representatives in governance and resource allocations, the potential appointment of Novartis personnel as adjunct professors, the potential influence of an external funder on the allocation of space decisions, and the potential effect on faculty (recruitment, salaries, teaching loads, etc.). In response to the controversy, and true to Dean Gordon Rausser's statement in the report *Working Together, Creating Knowledge* (Business-Higher Education Forum, 2001) that "the university wants to learn from this experiment," Berkeley conducted a mid-agreement, internal evaluation, completed in 2002 (Price & Goldman, 2002). Berkeley then sponsored an external review orchestrated by a project officer at the CSHE (financed by the Berkeley–Novartis agreement) and completed in 2004 (Institute for Food and Agricultural Standards, 2004). As previously noted, this PPRP ex post evaluation and other analyses of the Berkeley–Novartis research partnership are unprecedented.

6.5.1 Internal Review

The 2002 internal review (Price & Goldman, 2002) noted that although the Berkeley–Novartis agreement "was initiated in a veritable storm of controversy . . . in practice the Novartis agreement has been quite different than what these critical commentaries expected." The report goes on to say that "virtually none of the anticipated adverse institutional consequences has been in evidence." The analysis used hard data on research agreement inputs and outcomes available from campus sources and also used the results of interviews with eighteen faculty members, five graduate students, two postdoctoral students, some PMB administrative staff, and the Chief Executive Officer (CEO) of Torrey Mesa Research Institute. The focus of the analysis was on areas of concern and controversy, including the magnitude of the Novartis funding for PMB relative to funding from other sources, governance of the agreement, research direction and academic freedom, resource allocations, IP, and the effect on students and teaching.

   The review found that during the first four years of the research collaboration, the $25 million in Novartis support constituted 27 percent of PMB's total extramural funding, and during this time period, extramural funding from all sources (federal, non-federal government, non-profit, UC grants, industry) increased by 170 percent, allaying fears that Novartis funding would crowd-out other extramural sources of funding. As far as governance and research direction, the review found that the agreement "did not grant to Novartis representatives any direct role whatsoever in the structures responsible for the general governance of PMB, nor have they played any such role during the period that the Agreement has been in effect." Under the agreement, Novartis's limited governance role did not extend to general governance of PMB, but came through minority representation on the Research Committee and Advisory Committee and their oversight of the $25 million grant to the PMB. The Research Committee, which met once a year, was directed to make awards based on three criteria:

- Quality of intellectual merit of the proposed research
- Potential advancement of discovery
- Past and present productivity of the principal investigator.

Price and Goldman (2002) note that the agreement stipulates that "the Research Committee will not make recommendations to PMB faculty as to the scope and long-term goals of the proposed research project." The review finds that interviews with PMB faculty indicate that the Research Committee operated as intended and, moreover, the Novartis Corporation and its successor, Syngenta, have assumed a "hands-off" posture with respect to the research conducted by PMB faculty, postdoctoral fellows and graduate students. "The industry representatives in the Novartis program's Advisory and Research Committees have not attempted to steer PMB research in any particular direction." The review found that the Novartis representatives on the governance committees did not seek to target funding toward particular research questions, did not block the publication of research results coming from the PMB department, and did not noticeably move "PMB's research agenda toward 'applied research,' as was widely anticipated." In fact, while the research agreement was viewed as a vehicle for collaborative research of a joint nature, the actual experience during the review period was somewhat different with less direct interaction between Novartis and PMB scientists than was envisioned, with no Novartis personnel having worked in campus laboratory facilities, nor with any industry scientists having received appointments as adjunct professors.

Another focus of concern with the agreement was in the area of IP and whether the relationship with Novartis would impose secrecy and publication delays. The review found that although the perception was that PMB researchers participating in the agreement were required to sign confidentiality agreements, this was not the case. There was no general confidentiality arrangement; rather, only those researchers accessing Novartis's genomic bioinformatics database and related microarray technology had to sign an agreement not to disclose the information associated with these technologies. This did not preclude publishing or reporting research results obtained through analysis with these technologies.

The review noted that yet another focus of concern was on the clause in the agreement that gave Novartis the first right to negotiate a license on a portion of patentable discoveries from PMB laboratories, whether or not the discovery came from research funded by Novartis. The portion was based on the percentage that Novartis funding represented of all outside funding, or approximately one-third of the research discoveries. While Novartis could negotiate a license, Berkeley retained ownership of all PMB research results and thus controlled the right to publish and disseminate research results (unless the results contained Novartis proprietary information). Under the agreement, participating PMB faculty were required to submit drafts of research to Novartis 30 days before submission for publication. This was to allow Novartis to determine if there were patentable discoveries or proprietary data in the research. This publication delay period could end once the invention was protected by the filing of a patent application. The review notes that delays and limits on the dissemination of information are not unique to the Novartis agreement and are a common part of the process of university researchers seeking to patent research discoveries.

The PMB faculty related that the availability of five years of funding "allowed them to pursue more novel and innovative lines of inquiry than would have been possible," and they have "continued to supplement their Novartis funds with extramural research support from other sources." As far as product from the research agreement, as of the report in 2002, the PMB faculty had "increased somewhat the pace of their publishing since the Agreement's initiation, but the large number of patent filings by Novartis, which some anticipated, has not materialized." With regard to graduate students, the review found a significant positive impact. The funds available under the agreement to support first- and second-year graduate fellowships enabled PMB to stay competitive in recruiting students and "has not significantly altered the nature of graduate or undergraduate education within PMB."

A review of the agreement published in the Chronicle of Higher Education (Blumenstyk, 2001) supports the findings of this internal review. Following extensive interviews, Blumenstyk was unable to find any occasion when the activities under the agreement involved overtly compromising research at Berkeley. Bob B. Buchanan, former PMB Chair, gives his appraisal of the agreement (Buchanan & Chapela, 2002) and why it differs from a standard university grant in terms of the significant academic development that resulted. In addition to significant funding, the research partnership agreement facilitated information exchange and access to expertise and facilities, resulting in an impressive increase in the quality and size of the research programs of the participating faculty. Graduate students and postdoctoral students were also given enhanced opportunity through financial support and access to technologies (10 advanced graduate students and 50 postdoctoral scholars). Contrary to the concern that the significant size of the funding from Novartis would crowd-out funding from other sources, Buchanan reports that faculty members continued to receive competitive federal and other grants and that programs both in plant biology and microbial biology were strengthened by the partnership. Financial benefits extended to the College of Natural Resources (funding was spent on such assets as new faculty and facilities) and to the greater campus for overhead support. And for its part, Novartis benefited from access to scientists and graduate students and increased access to potentially patentable discoveries.

6.5.2   External Review

In 2004, a group of academic sociologists from Michigan State University were selected from responses to a general RFP from CSHE. The external review team gathered various information resources (e.g., media reports, university press releases, committee notes), conducted semi-structured interviews of 84 people including members of the PMB (tenured and untenured faculty, graduate students, postdoctoral researchers, staff), as well as members of the broader Berkeley community, industry partners, and other interest groups, and utilized data from the PMB on graduate student activities and faculty funding.

The review found that "while the implementation of the agreement has been relatively uncontested and many of the critics' worst fears have not occurred, the fact that the agreement was widely challenged is important on a number of levels." The report detailed four broad reasons given by interviewees as to why the agreement was controversial: process, substantive concerns, local conditions, and broader issues. Only one of the four reasons, substantive concerns, focused on the content of the agreement.

Concerns about the agreement process included the perception that the formulation of the agreement was not transparent, oversight and governance did not follow normal channels, the broader university was not adequately involved, and the manner in which the agreement was presented added to misperceptions and angst. The review found there was a general lack of understanding and misinformation in the broader Berkeley community about how PPRPs work. The local liberal political climate, which welcomed public discourse and protests, provided an easily inflamed backdrop for this controversy. Given this climate, a broader examination of the changing university–industry relationship was sparked. The report also cited ideological conflicts between different branches of plant biology as well as conflicts between what some see as the true mission of the university, to serve the interests of the people of California, and generating public goods through university research.

The "substantive concerns" were sourced with perceptions of several aspects of the Berkeley–Novartis agreement. For example, the scale and scope of the agreement – $25 million, five years, the potential involvement of an entire academic department (each department faculty member was given the opportunity to participate if they wished), and being restricted to a single industry partner – all contributed to concerns about the agreement and its possible outcomes. The structure of the IP rights arrangement, with Novartis given first right to negotiate an exclusive license to all research conducted by researchers receiving Novartis funding, even research that did not necessarily involve Novartis funding, was the primary focus of concern about IP rights. Although the university would be expected to negotiate licensing terms that gave Berkeley fair compensation, the ability for Novartis to choose among the entire academic department's research was seen as giving Novartis an unfair advantage. Other issues with the agreement of concern to interviewees involved the possibility of developing a Novartis research facility near the campus and the possibility of giving adjunct status to Novartis researchers.

The report examined the role of the media in the Berkeley–Novartis controversy and found that the role of the media "in bringing the Agreement between UC Berkeley and Novartis to the public's attention cannot be overlooked, nor should it be overstated." The primary result of the media coverage of the agreement seemed to be increased friction between academic departments with differing views on PPRPs.

Turning away from potential concerns and perceptions of the agreement, the external review by the Institute for Food and Agricultural Standards (IFAS) (2004) reported on the implementation of the agreement over the entire period of engagement and found that all proposals submitted to the Research Committee were funded at the amounts requested, with an average award of $120,500. Twenty-five researchers received funding. During the five-year agreement, 20 of the 51 disclosures presented to Novartis were patented and 10 of those patented came from disclosures on Novartis funded research. Novartis optioned 3 of the 20 but never pursued commercialization of the discoveries. Although the provision that gave Novartis the right to negotiate on all disclosures had many concerned, as did the right of Novartis to wait until the end of three years to make decisions about patents, the evaluation found that this did not result in a great advantage for Novartis.

In addition to the "unstructured collaborations" that occurred between PMB and Novartis, annual retreats were the primary form of interaction between the research partners. The construction of a joint research facility and the appointment of Novartis personnel to adjunct positions that were allowed for in the agreement contract never occurred. Taken as a sign of the quality of the original agreement, few amendments were added to the original contract (IFAS, 2004, p. 85).

The external review considered the effects of the Berkeley–Novartis agreement on the PMB and found very few negative results:

- "All but two of the PMB faculty members agreed with the 'one company' strategy."
- "On the whole, the PMB faculty viewed the negotiation of the agreement as uncontroversial and not in need of adjustment."
- The Research Committee worked as most of the interviewees thought it should.
- Benefits of the agreement include funding for PMB and Berkeley, access to proprietary and confidential databases, benefits to the graduate program, and increased productivity (IFAS, 2004, p. 91).
- PMB faculty felt that funding from Novartis "enabled them to explore research questions they otherwise would have foregone or postponed until they had more initial results to support a government grant proposal" (IFAS, 2004, p. 95).
- As far as IP concerns and Novartis's first right to negotiate on an exclusive license, "PMB faculty generally reported that they did not see anything especially advantageous to Novartis from the 'peeking rights' to their disclosures."

Despite concluding that the direct impacts of the Berkeley–Novartis agreement "on the university as a whole have been minimal," and irrespective of the findings of the internal Price and Goldman review (2002), the primary recommendation from the IFAS review (2004) was that the Berkeley community should "avoid industry agreements that involve complete academic units or large groups of researchers" because of the potential controversy this may inflame. A response from UC Chancellor, Robert Berdahl (2004), questioned this recommendation given the review's overall positive conclusions. Berdahl notes that while the idea of industry funding university research makes some uncomfortable, as it should given that the credibility of university research is the "gold standard" and must be protected from self-serving interests, limiting connections with industry based on "impressions of a problem when none exists seems shortsighted." Chancellor Berdahl emphasized that the Novartis agreement and the associated controversy shows that "developing effective research partnerships with industry and ensuring confidence that core values of the university are preserved is a challenging task . . . for all universities."

Rather than shy away from future strategic alliances, Berdahl recommends that these agreements must:

- "Preserve the university's status as a truly independent source of public policy advice. This is especially vital in critical areas of technology policy related to areas of public health and the environment.
- Preserve the university's unique role as a completely open environment where the search for new knowledge is the highest ideal. And where all ideas are heard and the free flow of ideas and information is encouraged.
- Ensure that disclosure mechanisms are regularly reviewed and updated when needed to insure that faculty avoid conflicts of interest that may arise in various forms of industrial partnerships."

6.6 EMERGENCE OF UNIVERSITY AND PUBLIC AGENCY PPRP GUIDELINES

In addition to encouraging research, policies have also focused on guiding and imposing restrictions on PPRPs. For example, in the last decade the NIH has issued several sets of guidelines addressing such agreements (NIH, 1999). These policies provide models for "best practices" but they are not enforceable and therefore have limited reach. Other policies are binding. For example, in 1995 a federal regulation governing conflict of interest in federally funded research institutions was enacted (NIH, 1999). Although most universities have adopted conflict of interest policies that adhere to this regulation, there is variation in how they are administered (Business-Higher Education Forum, 2001).

Many universities provide standard contractual terms for non-federal institutions that sponsor research on the university campus. These documents provide guidance on publication delays, licensing options, IP ownership, confidentiality requirements, budgets, payment schedules, and other items typically included in PPRP contracts. Though these guidelines are modified and tailored to each individual PPRP, they do provide insight regarding the university's preferences and priorities. We review guidelines from Cornell,[4] MIT,[5] and Stanford,[6] and UC. Cornell provides two sets of guidelines, one for partnerships conducting basic research, the other for partnerships conducting applied research. MIT and Stanford each have one set of guidelines for all research partnerships.[7] These contract guidelines are quite similar and are representative of the typical provisions used by universities in PPRP contracts. The full text of these and other guidelines is available in the Appendix of this book.

Each university uses the following rules for allocating IP ownership for discoveries made by partnership researchers: IP for discoveries made solely by university employees is assigned to the university, and IP for discoveries made jointly by university employees and private partner employees is owned by both partners. Cornell, MIT, and Stanford also assign IP rights to the private partner when the discovery is made by employees of the private partner without use[8] of university funds or facilities.

Once a research discovery is made, the guidelines state that the university incurs the cost of filing and defending a patent, unless requested by the private partner, in which case the private partner funds the patent. Once the patent is filed, regardless of whether the research was performed by university researchers or jointly, each contract grants the private partner a time-limited first right to negotiate a license. The time limit varies somewhat by university: Cornell and Stanford allow the private partner 90 days and MIT allows the private partner 180 days. The guidelines allow for exclusive and non-exclusive licenses.

Cornell's guidelines also allow each partner unrestricted, non-exclusive, fee-free and royalty-free use of any IP created by the partnership for educational or research purposes. MIT and Stanford guidelines do not grant university researchers access to private partner research discoveries. MIT allows each partner to have an "independent, unrestricted right to license to third parties" any joint research inventions.

All contracts discuss publication delays and confidential information restrictions. Each contract allows the private partner to review manuscripts before submission to ensure confidential information is not published and to allow the private partner to review patentable research before it is disseminated. Before the results of partnership research can be published, Cornell, MIT, and Stanford allow the private partner 30 days to review manuscripts. Cornell and MIT allow an additional review period not to exceed 60 days.

The guidelines also place additional restrictions on the use of confidential information. All guidelines prohibit university researchers from publishing confidential data provided by the private partner, but only Cornell's guidelines put a time limit on that restriction. Cornell's guidelines require researchers to protect and not publish confidential information provided by the private party for two years from the date the information is disclosed. After that period, the researchers would not be restricted in their use of the confidential information.

Though the guidelines provide basic protections for university resources and give adequate mechanisms for private sector compensation, they contain little guidance on many important practical matters. For example, the current guidelines do not discuss the extent to which the private partner should influence research funding allocation decisions. Also, guidelines do not provide boundaries on negotiating the terms of IP licenses; neither do they address the extent to which the type of research should affect the partnership structure. More broadly, the guidelines do not provide guidance on how control rights should be allocated to resolve unexpected shocks or the inevitable conflicts between the partners.

UC provides only broad guidelines for constructing PPRPs rather than specific guidelines and standard contractual terms. The few guidelines that UC does address in detail are similar to the specific guidance produced by Cornell, MIT, and Stanford. For example, the UC guidelines allow for a publication delay by the sponsoring partner of no more than 60–90 days. Similarly, the UC guidelines also encourage faculty to avoid conflicts of interest when researching for a PPRP and include disclosure requirements when university researchers have a financial interest.

Unlike Cornell, MIT, and Stanford, the UC guidelines emphasize that university faculty are under no obligation to publish and that external funding should not determine whether research is or is not published. Universities typically focus on protecting the faculty's right to publish by minimizing publication delays in PPRP contracts while ignoring the right of professors to exercise their professional judgement when deciding whether the research generated by a PPRP should be submitted to an academic journal. To protect the academic freedom of university researchers, PPRP contracts should not guarantee the publication of research. The UC guidelines also require explicit protection of the academic freedom of student researchers in addition to the academic freedom of faculty members. This often overlooked provision is important given the reliance of graduate students on research funding.

A shortcoming of the UC guidelines relates to patent policy. The policy, which appears more restrictive than other universities' guidelines, is that any patentable invention discovered by university researchers or involving the use of university facilities or funds is the property of the university. Though the guidelines mention the importance of preventing the use of public funds for private gain, incentivizing private sponsors, and compensating the university, no guidance is given on accomplishing these laudable objectives. There are tradeoffs among these objectives and obvious conflicts; for example, incentivizing private sponsors with generous patenting terms runs the risk of inadequately compensating the university.

Overall, the collective university guidelines provide a useful starting point for negotiating and constructing PPRP contracts. These guidelines are based on the cumulative experience of university administrators and faculty over the 35 years since the passage of the Bayh–Dole Act. The guidelines could be improved by discussing in clear terms the assignment of control rights and how that assignment should change based on both the type of good the partnership is producing and the financial contributions of the partners.

In the United States, PPPs with federal government agencies and private firms are governed by a Cooperative Research and Development Agreement (CRADA). The CRADA is a federal-government-wide framework for PPP contracts that provides an outline of the legal terms, objectives, and expected outcomes of the partnership. Like the universities' guidelines, CRADA allows the private partner the first right to negotiate an exclusive license to any invention that is developed by researchers funded by the partnership, regardless of whether those researchers are employed by the government or the private partner. The CRADA allows much longer publication delays than academic partnerships: Partnership research can be kept confidential for up to five years, after which it is subject to Freedom of Information Act requests. Individual federal agencies sometimes provide additional guidelines for PPPs. For example, the Agricultural Research Service (ARS) at the US Department of Agriculture provides guidelines similar to those given by Cornell, MIT, Stanford, and UC.[9] The ARS requires a 60-day review period prior to research publication, during which time either party can request delays to file patents. The ARS also allows for joint ownership of research discoveries made jointly by researchers from each partner.

A unique requirement of the ARS partnerships is that scientific representatives of each partner are required to meet at least every six months to review the partnership. During these meetings mandatory progress reports are reviewed. In addition, each partner is required to maintain complete research records that must be available for inspection by either party upon request.

The Department of Energy (DOE) also supplements the CRADA with additional guidelines.[10] Given the sensitive nature of some DOE research fields (e.g., nuclear energy), DOE guidelines contain export control and confidentiality restrictions not typically found in PPRP contracts. The DOE guidelines also include provisions to ensure that research discoveries made in a PPRP directly benefit the US economy. The guidelines require products based on IP generated by the PPRP be substantially manufactured in the United States. In addition, the private partner is required to implement IP generated by the PPRP in US manufacturing facilities. Finally, the DOE guidelines require the establishment of a dispute resolution mechanism. PPRP contract guidelines rarely address the issue of dispute resolution in detail. The DOE guidelines require the use of outside mediators to resolve disputes that cannot be resolved through negotiations by the partners. The mediation can be tailored to each PPRP, and the guidelines allow flexibility in choosing binding or non-binding arbitration, confidentiality provisions, and mediation cost-sharing.

Overall, the CRADA, along with supplemental agency guidelines, provide much more detail than the typical university guidelines. Though some of the detail in the government PPRP guidelines is an unambiguous improvement over the university guidelines, there are limitations. For example, university guidelines could be improved by following the government's specification of explicitly detailing the conflict resolution mechanism in PPRP contracts. But universities are better off not including politically motivated restrictions on IP use that, though intended to benefit the US economy, will likely have a chilling effect on potentially beneficial PPRPs. In the final analysis, universities and federal agencies should provide sufficient practical detail in guidelines to ensure the interests of both parties are protected while avoiding excessive constraints that prevent forming an efficient PPRP.

6.7 CONCLUSION

PPRPs can be essential for advancing research, innovation, and technological progress. The benefits of bringing together research partners with complementary assets are clear. Universities are seeking financial and intellectual capital, cutting-edge technologies, access to proprietary databases, and competitive graduate education experiences. Industry partners are seeking access to new research and innovations, synergetic interactions with faculty and students, and leads on potential future employees. The clash of mission and cultures between research partners can lead to issues with academic freedom, conflict of interest policies, confidentiality, contract negotiations, indirect costs, IP, and background rights.

Research partners should look to their core principles to guide their negotiation process. University core principles include faculty freedom, knowledge advancement, protecting and enriching graduate student education, and maintaining academic culture. These core principles can be at risk when public and private partners negotiate issues such as agreement governance and research agenda selection, publication delay, and patent and licensing terms.

The types of PPRPs that involve active negotiations rather than template agreements or contracts are the strategic alliances or partnerships. The 1998 Berkeley–Novartis partnership provides a useful focus for a case study given the unprecedented extensive internal and external review of this one particular type of agreement. While the controversy and misperceptions around this agreement were multitude, the final evaluations found little fault with how the partnership actually unfolded. In response to concerns about academic capture by industry, the lessons learned from this strategic partnership provide the basis for a series of guiding principles for university–industry interactions to help ensure that the benefits of these partnerships are achieved and the risks are effectively managed.

NOTES

1. In addition to research funds, universities are interested in the accompanying overhead payment. While these indirect costs vary from one university to another, in some cases these costs to the industry partner are significant.
2. RPI became Sirna Therapeutics and was sold to Merck & Co. in 2006.
3. Unfortunately, no other case studies of a strategic PPRP are available that have been subjected to a third-party ex post evaluation.
4. https://www.osp.cornell.edu/Policies/Std_Agmt_Terms.html.
5. http://osp.mit.edu/grant-and-contract-administration/industrial-collaborations-and-agreements/sponsored-research-agree-7.
6. http://web.stanford.edu/group/ICO/industry/industrySRA.html#indTAgree.
7. MIT provides different templates for US and foreign sponsors, but the differences between the guidelines reflect tax issues associated with international funding.
8. MIT allows for non-significant use of university facilities.
9. Articles of Agreement (USDA) http://www.ars.usda.gov/Research/docs.htm?docid=9253.
10. DOE http://energy.gov/sites/prod/files/gcprod/documents/m4831-1.pdf.

7. Governance structures and collective decision making

Conflicts between the public and private partners naturally emerge in the design and implementation of research partnerships. Some research partnerships pursue the public interest by leveraging private resources to lower transaction costs, increase research resources, or enhance productivity. Still other research partnerships are the result of manipulation by powerful private firms actively exploiting public resources in the pursuit of their own self-interest. Regardless, conceptual formulations that attempt to explain or prescribe the formation of research partnerships emphasizing only one type of interest are doomed to fail.

In any PPRP, various self-interests naturally arise that play a critical role in resolving the strategic interactions among the partners. Ultimately, some alignment among the parties must be achieved if a cooperative solution is to be achieved. The partnership-making process endogenizes the contract as a function of university bureaucracy, the private firm, and the actions of stakeholders, as well as their strategic interactions. The strategic interactions in the partnership-making process involve interest groups competing by spending time, energy, and money on the production of pressure to influence both the design and the tactical implementation of PPRPs.

7.1 BARGAINING AND NEGOTIATION

Strategic interactions between a private company's interests and those of a potential partner, a university or governmental agency, will ultimately drive the formation of the PPRP as well as any policies, choices, or actions that are taken by the partnership once it has been formed. There is a rich literature on the modeling of such strategic interactions. Much of this literature has as its origin the so-called Nash solution to the bargaining problem. Originally, Nash presented a number of axioms that led to a cooperative solution to the two-person bargaining problem.[1] Initially, Nash focused on just the cooperative solution, which involved maximizing the joint payoffs that accrued to each of the partners in a PPRP.

The critical axioms in the original Nash formulation were (i) no party would agree to participate in a partnership that guarantees the party something worse than this partner would be able to achieve outside of the partnership (referred to as *individual rationality*); (ii) no partnership agreement represents an outcome that can be improved upon for one partner without making the other partner worse off (referred to as *Pareto optimality*); (iii) if the outcome for one partner is subjected to an order preserving linear transformation while the other partner's interest is unchanged, then the solution to the new bargaining game is simply subjected to an order preserving linear transformation (referred to as the *linear invariance axiom*); and finally, (iv) dropping from the set of possible outcomes a choice that is dominated by some other choice will have no effect on the bargaining process (referred to as the *independence of irrelevant alternatives*). These four basic axioms result in a collective choice problem that focuses on maximizing the joint payoff of the two partners, representing the gain improvement of the cooperative solution relative to some pre-specified disagreement outcome. The Nash axiomatic approach to bargaining and negotiation processes has been shown to lead to the same results even if such axioms are not imposed.[2]

Obviously, to reach a cooperative Nash solution, there must be a formal basis for conflict resolution. The mechanisms for formally addressing conflicts can be traced back to the work of both Nash and Harsanyi. In this work the cooperative Nash solution as well as the non-cooperative, or disagreement, outcome are jointly determined. As we demonstrate in Appendix 7A.1, the initial simple cooperative bargaining game first presented by Nash can be extended by turning a one-stage game to a more complex bargaining process. Conceptually, in the first stage of this more complex bargaining game, conflict strategies are specified that determine how a non-cooperative disagreement outcome will emerge. In this setting, both the cooperative solution and the non-cooperative solution are endogenously determined. As shown in Appendix 7A.1, there are five conditions that must be satisfied to completely characterize the two-stage cooperative solution to the bargaining and negotiation process.

The conditions for the solution to the two-stage bargaining process are also the basis for determining the governing criterion function for any PPRP. To establish this governing criterion function, there must be some assignment of authority among the two participating partners in the PPRP. If there is a single assignment of authority to one of the partner groups for making actual choices, for example, with regard to the allocation of research dollars across individual projects, a decision-making center can be established that actually selects particular choices. The basis for the derivation of this governing criterion function is developed in Appendix 7A.2. This appendix demonstrates that even though there may be an assignment of authority to one of the partners, the other partner will exercise whatever influence it may have through bargaining power and conflict resolution on the partner who is assigned authority. This influence is summarized by a bargaining or power coefficient of the non-assigned authority partner's interest over the partner with assigned authority. In terms of resolution of conflicts, this bargaining power is exercised through rewards and penalties imposed on the partner with the assigned authority. Ultimately, the degree of influence will turn on how responsive the partner who has been given assigned authority is to these threats and penalties generated by the non-assigned authority partner. The entire bargaining process leads to conflict resolution and equilibrium relationships that set out the inherent conditions for a cooperative solution. The cooperative solution can be viewed as including both the formation of the partnership and any actions or choices that are made once the partnership is formed. The conflict resolution that takes place within the bargaining or negotiation process is embedded in the bargaining power coefficient that appears in the governing criterion function.

Of course, it may turn out that not a single partner group will be assigned decision-making authority, but that authority may be held collectively by both partners (see Chapter 8). If both partners are assigned joint authority, then we have more than a single decision-making center. In particular, since we are talking about a two-person bargaining game between the public institution and the private company, there may be a bicentric configuration of actual policymaking. Under this circumstance, there are two decision-making centers that will reach a cooperative solution and a collective choice that is optimal for both partners. This joint assignment of authority or a sharing of the "control premium" is developed in Appendix 7A.3.

Regardless of whether a single or joint assignment of decision-making authority is made by the PPRP, the ideological position and self-interest of each of the two partners will be critical in the bargaining process. The ideological positioning and respective interests of each of the two partners must be reflected in the governance structure specified in Appendices 7A.2 and 7A.3.

7.2   IDEOLOGICAL CONFLICT

Each partner's ideological commitments are of crucial importance in shaping the research partnership contract. In this context, an important conceptual question arises: How should the role of ideology be integrated into the bargaining or negotiation process of research partnership formation? The ideology of each partner will determine its contractual arrangements to a material extent. The contract will set the rules for the organizational structure. As the ideological core of both public and private partners is critical in the bargaining process, it requires serious examination.

Undoubtedly, the conduct of interest groups in the contract negotiations depends significantly on the underlying organizational structure. Furthermore, the organizational structure of the university, the conduct of administrators and professors, and the behavior of academic departments are principal determinants of the policy formation process and should be examined in any systematic analysis of partnership formation. The organization of the private partner and the priorities of its Board of Directors, shareholders, and the private research scientists must be accounted for as well.

Attempts by economists to explain observed individual and group behavior as the pursuit of pure economic gain by individual agents (Williamson, 1993) have usually left a substantial part of observed behavior unexplained. Respect for property rights is a necessary condition for sustainable PPRP agreements. In addition to the respective property rights of the potential partners, cultural differences help explain the ideological origins of both the public institution and the private company. Faculty members and research scientists at a university, for example, cherish their academic freedom and research entrepreneurship while research scientists at private companies are more willing to accept direction, the authority of others, and specific task assignments. Such cultural differences often dictate the lack of interest alignment and the structure of strategic interactions in the bargaining and negotiation process.

It has been asserted that existing internal organizational forms are inconceivable unless the actions of participants in the organizations are to some extent constrained by participants' ethical attitudes (Zusman, 1993). North (1981) also contends that, in many cases, observed collective action would have been stalled by free riding had it not been for the ideological commitment of individuals. This view is further substantiated by empirical studies of the voting behavior of legislators in the US Congress. These studies find clear evidence of voting guided by ideological concerns (Kau & Rubin, 1979; Kalt & Zupan, 1984). The latter authors concluded that "economic interest variables play surprisingly weak roles in legislative outcomes, while the hypothesis of no ideological effect is quite easily rejected" (Kalt & Zupan, 1984, p. 280). Accordingly, the theory of contract formation of research partnerships must encompass the role of ideology and ethics – in the present context, the relationship between the bargaining power and ideology.

7.2.1   The Nature of Ideology

An ideology as a cultural system consists of (a) a set of beliefs concerning the way the world operates, social relationships included; (b) a set of ethical values by which social states are to be judged; and (c) a code of social behavior consisting of social norms dictating individual behavior in recurrent social situations. The various ideological components must, of course, be mutually consistent. Individuals acquire a particular ideology in the course of their primary socialization (e.g., family) and secondary socialization (e.g., church). In the process of socialization, individuals internalize a particular ideology that forms the foundation for both their personal preferences over economic and social outcomes and their cognitive apparatuses. Individual ideological attitudes also vary as a result of individual social experience. In fact, North (1981) views the theory of ideology as a theory of knowledge, and in this respect it is important to emphasize the social nature of ideology – individuals acquire an ideology in a process of interpersonal interactions in which the role of authority is far greater than in ordinary scientific evolutionary processes. Hence, symbols and imagery are especially important to the formulation of ideologies (Geertz, 1973).

To a large extent, ideology is an objective social fact and not merely a subjective individual commitment. Bearing in mind how rarely particular theories are rejected in the social sciences, especially because available data constrains the availability of conclusive evidence, one should not be surprised that ideologies are so likely to persist. Generally, ideologies serve as "cultural rather than genetic templates . . . [I]t is through the construction of ideologies, schematic images of social order, that man makes himself, for better or for worse, a political animal" (Geertz, 1973, p. 218).

Two distinct ingredients of ideology need to be distinguished. First, the set of ideological beliefs is clearly related to the person's cognitive processes. This ingredient consists of models of the environment, both physical and social, that define the set of possible events (states of the world) considered by the individual which determine the personal subjective probability distributions over these events at various points in time, contingent on actual prior realizations. The second component is composed of ideological values and social norms that are internalized by individual agents and that shape their preference structures. It should be obvious that while moral philosophy is largely concerned with the normative aspects of ethics (Hausman & McPherson, 1993), the paramount issues in a positive theory of PPRP formation are the ethical attitudes of university administrators and professors, as well as those of the private research scientists and executives.

A positive theory of individual ethical attitudes is presented in Sugden

(1986); individual ethical preferences and social norms are related to various conventions arising spontaneously in human communities. According to Sugden, natural law itself is related to conventions that evolve spontaneously. We contend that individual preferences, too, are shaped by ideologies as well as social conventions and norms. The domain of individual preferences considered by standard economic theory, namely, the space of consumption bundles, may be extended to also include the space of all social states and actions relevant to the person's ideological concerns. In particular, deviations from social standards of behavior defined by ideological norms are included in this space. In analyzing individual choices over the extended commodity-ideology space, it is possible to consider tradeoffs between consumption bundles (or incomes) and ideological commitments.

7.2.2   Ideological Commitment in Partnership Formation

As noted in Section 7.1 and in Appendices 7A.1 – 7A.3, under the Nash–Harsanyi axiomatic framework, the contractual equilibrium policy choice, $\bar{x}_0$, maximizes the PPRP governance function, W (see Appendix 7A.2). The equilibrium solution of the bargaining game, simulating the negotiation process that is obtained by maximizing the governance function, W, as shown in Appendix 7A.2, is

$$W(\bar{x}_0) \equiv \max_{x_0 \in X_0} [u_0(x_0) + b_1 u_1(x_0)] \qquad (7.1)$$

where $u_0(x_0)$ is the objective function of the partner with the assigned authority or the control premium, $u_1(x_0)$ is the bargaining objective function of the remaining partner, and b_1 denotes this partner's bargaining power coefficient relative to the assigned authority partner, whereas x_0 is the space of feasible policies or choices.

But underlying each partner without assigned authority is a number of secondary interest subgroups, say m. The term "interest subgroup" recognizes that each subgroup within, for example, the private firm's organizational structure has somewhat disparate interests. Hence, the objective function of the non-authority partner group, $u_1(x_0)$, is the governance function maximized in the Nash–Harsanyi bargaining game between its m organized secondary interest subgroups and the primary group's leadership. That is, the objective function of the non-authority partner group can be represented as:

$$u_1(x_0) = u_0^1(x_0) + \sum_{k=1}^{m} b_k^1 u_k^1(x_0) \,;\, x_0 \in X_0^i, \qquad (7.2)$$

The objective function of each potential disparate partner group can be determined if both the coalitional structure and the intra-group power structure of each partner are fully known. If some information concerning the actual coalitional structure and/or the power structure is unavailable, then Harsanyi's (1963) simplified theory of the multi-person cooperative game (bargaining model) and coalition formation can be employed instead.

As these specifications suggest, ideological commitments affect policy choices both through the bargaining power coefficients, b_1, and through the partners' policy objective functions, which in turn are themselves functions of certain power structures and interests of all organized secondary subgroups and all engaged policymaking centers. Obviously, all participants have certain ideological commitments, and such commitments should be reflected in the group's objective function in the same fashion as purely economic interests. Thus, if the public partner attaches ideological value to academic freedom, say, x_0 will likely include policy instruments protecting academic researchers from external influence. Similarly, if one or both partners are ideologically committed to fund graduate student research, x_0 should also include policy measures designed to financially support such students. It is likely that all members of a partner group are exclusively characterized by their unyielding commitment to a particular ideological objective, so that policy instruments, $x_{0e}(x_{0e} \subseteq x_0)$, contributing to the ideological commitment may lexicographically dominate all other policy instruments from a particular partner's perspective. As a result, all individual preferences may be defined on the extended space of consumption bundles and ideological commitments, and thus a partner's objective function also depends on policies affecting the group members' ideological interests.

The relationship between ideological commitments and bargaining power coefficients are multi-faceted. Legitimate power is an important base of power, and crucial changes in bargaining power often reflect variations in the legitimate base of power. This assertion may be interpreted as the bargaining power of a partner over the partner with the assigned authority increasing as the latter becomes more sensitive to the rewards and/or penalties by the former partner. By construction, the stronger the ideological commitment of the assigned authority partner to ethical public values requiring the sacrifice of personal interests in favor of public interests, the smaller $\frac{\partial s_i}{\partial c_i}$ from Appendix 7A.1 is, and the smaller the bargaining power of the partner without decision-making authority. Also, as the legitimate power of the assigned authority partners increases, the reciprocal power of the other partner naturally declines. If the partner without the assigned authority has a strong ideological commitment to respect the assigned authority partner's policy choices, the subjective cost to the non-assigned authority partner group of their attempt to influence the center's choice is high, and hence b_1 small.

Bargaining power over the policy center, b_1, depends on the extent to which the group leadership succeeds in overcoming free rider proclivities among its own members. In many cases, the individual calculus of personal costs and benefits induces the narrowly rational members to free ride. In such cases, the additional consideration of ideological commitment to group action as such may tip the scale in favor of collective action, thereby facilitating the mobilization of support of group action, which in turn reinforces the group's power over the policymaking center or partner with assigned authority (i.e., b_1 increases). In view of such relationships between ideological commitment and policy formation, it is not surprising that political entrepreneurs (group leaderships) seek to convince people to adopt an ideological position favorable to the leadership's interest.

7.2.3   The Organization of Interest Groups and Research Partnership Formation

The bargaining power theoretic approach to PPRP formation and actual policy choices clearly distinguishes between organized and unorganized partner groups. Organized partner groups are characterized by the existence of a group leadership capable of entering mutually binding agreements. Since such agreements commit the group to specific actions, some leadership control over group actions is presumed.

An unorganized partner group, though still consisting of individuals sharing a common interest, does not have a recognized leadership capable of committing the group. Consequently, organized partner groups engage the assigned authority centers in meaningful negotiations leading to a cooperative solution. Unorganized partner groups, on the other hand, are unable to reach such agreements; the most an unorganized partner group can do, provided it is not inert, is to respond to certain actions or policies in an uncoordinated fashion. That is, individuals belonging to the partner group act without central coordination by recognized leaders. The nature of a partner group organization determines the mode of group participation in the formation process and actual choices or policy implementation. Although this distinction of the group mode of action by the degree of group organization is crucial, organizational structure and functioning also determine other important performance characteristics of particular partner groups. To be sure, groups' objective functions and bargaining power bases are largely shaped by their organization.

7.2.4 Interest Groups and the Organization for Collective Action

In order to effectively influence PPRP formation and actual choices, group members must act in unison. Moreover, for their collective action to yield meaningful results, they must form a PPRP that would mobilize resources and direct individual action. Yet not all members of a particular partner group need partake actively in the organization, although it is reasonable to expect that the greater the number of active members in the organization and the more resources at its disposal, the greater its power base.

An individual guided by personal material well-being will choose to join the collective action only if the material benefits derived from this decision exceed the corresponding individual's or group's costs. The problem of the "decision to join" is thus introduced. As no one can be excluded from the material benefits of the selected action, individuals who are solely concerned with their personal costs and benefits may prefer to free ride. As stressed by Olson (1965), under such circumstances collective action by relatively large groups can come about only if free riding is controlled by means of "selective incentives" – that is, private goods desired by group members are provided by the group under favorable terms to those deciding to join and actively participate in the PPRP. Insurance and information important to partnership group members are examples of the selective incentives often provided by partner organizations to their members. In relatively small groups, collective action may be induced by intra-group direct interactions, even without the use of selective incentives.

7.3 CONCLUSION

In this chapter we explored how conflicts can be resolved as well as how the ideology of the public and private partners affects the contract formation process of a PPRP. Ideological commitments of each partner play an important role in the determination of bargaining power and help shape the objective functions of the PPRP participants during contract negotiations. Ideological commitments also assist group leaders in controlling the proclivity of partnership participants to free ride.

Ideological commitments can be incorporated in an empirical analysis of the contractual negotiations or the actual implementation of policy choices on the allocation of research and development resources. This can be done by including the policy instruments relevant to these commitments in the objective function. The political power captured by each of the partners may be one of the motives for individuals or firms to join a PPRP. Quite simply, they will join the PPRP if the benefit from doing so exceeds the cost involved in the process. Other reasons to join the organization may be symbolic social incentives and a commitment to collaborations among different types of intellectual capital.

NOTES

1. This, of course, was generalized to a n-person bargaining situation. See Harsanyi (1956; 1962a; 1962b; 1963; 1986) and see Rausser et al. (2011).
2. This equivalence has been established in a number of studies which are reviewed and evaluated in Chapter 2 of Rausser et al. (2011).

APPENDIX 7A.1   BARGAINING POWER: AN AXIOMATIC SPECIFICATION FOR COOPERATIVE VERSUS NON-COOPERATIVE OUTCOMES

In this formulation, the disagreement outcome or the non-cooperative solution, t, is made endogenous and the bargaining problem becomes: Given the bargaining set and a set of possible conflict strategies Σ_i ($i = 1$, 2), what will be the solution for $u = (u_1, u_2)$? To reach the solution, it is assumed that once the disagreement payoffs have been determined in the first, non-cooperative stage of the bargaining game, the solution to the second stage is the cooperative Nash bargaining solution, that is, the point $\bar{u} = (\bar{u}_1, \bar{u}_2) \in H^*$ satisfying

$$(\bar{u}_1 - t_1)(\bar{u}_2 - t_2) = \max_{u \in P}[(u_1 - t_1)(u_2 - t_2)] \qquad (7A.1.1.a)$$

such that

$$u_i \geq t_i \qquad (i = 1, 2) \qquad (7A.1.1.b)$$

To formalize the two-stage bargaining solution, let $H_1(u_1, u_2) = 0$ be the equation of Pareto frontier and assume that the partial derivatives, $H_1(\bar{u}_1, \bar{u}_2) = a_1$ and $H_2(\bar{u}_1, \bar{u}_2) = a_2$, are nonzero. Along the upper-right boundary of the (convex) payoff or bargaining set P, an increase in partner i's payoff must decrease partner j's payoff or that $\frac{du_j}{du_i}\big|_{H=0} \leq 0$. Note that since $\frac{du_j}{du_i} = -\frac{\partial H/\partial u_i}{\partial H/\partial u_j}$, it follows that H_1 and H_2 have the same sign. Without loss of generality, we can consider the case where $H_1, H_2 > 0$. Accordingly, the Kuhn–Tucker conditions for maximizing $(u_1 - t_1)(u_2 - t_2)$ with respect to u_1 and u_2 subject to $H(u_1, u_2) = 0$ are

$$a_1(\bar{u}_1 - t_1) = a_2(\bar{u}_2 - t_2) \qquad (7A.1.2.a)$$

where

$$a_i = H_i(\bar{u}_1, \bar{u}_2) \equiv \frac{\partial H}{\partial u_i}(\bar{u}_1, \bar{u}_2) \ (i = 1, 2) \qquad (7A.1.2b)$$

These conditions imply that for a given payoff space P^*, any pair of disagreement payoffs (t_1, t_2) that satisfy (7A.1.2a) yield the solution $\bar{u}$. This result is demonstrated in Figure 7A.1.1 where both t and t' satisfy (7A.1.2a) and both yield the solution $\bar{u}$.

Note that in Figure 7A.1.1 $C(\bar{u})$ represents the line in P satisfying the equation $a_1 t_1 - a_2 t_2 = a_1 \bar{u}_1 - a_2 \bar{u}_2$. This equation, $C(\bar{u})$, captures the set of

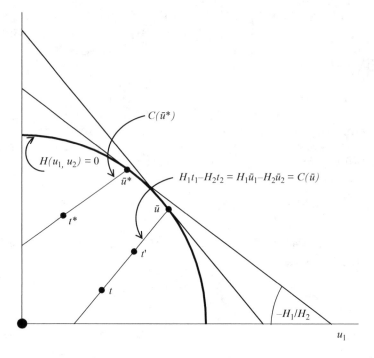

Figure 7A.1.1   Nash solution to the two-person bargaining game in the
(u_1,u_2) space

disagreement payoffs that satisfy (7A.1.2a) and yields the cooperative solution $\bar{u}$. As we move up and to the left along H, the outcome becomes more
favorable for partner 2. Because of this movement, $C(\bar{u}^*)$ hits the u_2 axis at
a higher point than $C(\bar{u})$ and this movement simultaneously decreases the
slope of the line $C(\bar{u}^*)$ compared to $C(\bar{u})$.

Because a given point (t_1, t_2) has a unique solution, no two lines $C(\bar{u})$
and $C(\bar{u}^*)$ can intersect. As a result, if $C(\bar{u}^*)$ lies above and to the left of
$C(\bar{u})$, $\bar{u}^*$ is more favorable to partner 2 than the solution $\bar{u}$. It can also be
shown, given (7A.1.2a), that if $\bar{u}$ is more favorable to partner 1 than $\bar{u}^*$
(i.e., $\bar{u}_1 > \bar{u}_1^*$), then

$$a_1\bar{u}_1 - a_2\bar{u}_2 > a_1\bar{u}_1^* - a_2\bar{u}_2^* \tag{7A.1.3}$$

Similarly, if $(\bar{u}^*)$ is more favorable to partner 2 than $\bar{u}$ (i.e., $\bar{u}_2^* > \bar{u}_2$), then

$$a_1\bar{u}_1 - a_2\bar{u}_2 > a_1\bar{u}_1^* - a_2\bar{u}_2^* \tag{7A.1.4}$$

Combining expressions (7A.1.2a) to (7A.1.4), it follows that it is in the interest of partner 1 to maximize $a_1 t_1 - a_2 t_2$, while partner 2's interest is to minimize the same expression. Consequently, the selected conflict strategies are given by

$$a_1 t_1 - a_2 t_2 = a_1 U_1(\theta_1^0, \theta_2^0) - a_2 U_2(\theta_1^0, \theta_2^0)$$

$$= \max_{\theta_1 \in \Sigma_1} \min_{\theta_2 \in \Sigma_2} [a_1 U_1(\theta_1^0, \theta_2^0) - a_2 U_2(\theta_1^0, \theta_2^0)] \qquad (7A.1.5)$$

where θ_1^0 and θ_2^0 are referred to as the *mutually optimal conflict strategies*. Note that the selected conflict strategies affect the ultimate bargaining outcome through their mutual effects on the disagreement payoffs, t_i.

Armed with the result (7A.1.5), the complete two-stage solution to the two-person bargaining model is determined by the following conditions:

$$H_1(\bar{u}_1, \bar{u}_2) = 0 \qquad (7A.1.6a)$$

$$a_1 = H_i(\bar{u}_1, \bar{u}_2) \qquad (7A.1.6b)$$

$$a_1(\bar{u}_1 - t_1) = a_2(\bar{u}_2 - t_2) \qquad (7A.1.6c)$$

$$t_i = U_i(\theta_1^0, \theta_2^0) \qquad (7A.1.6d)$$

$$a_1 t_1 - a_2 t_2 = \max_{\theta_1 \in \Sigma_1} \min_{\theta_2 \in \Sigma_2} [a_1 U_1(\theta_1^0, \theta_2^0) - a_2 U_2(\theta_1^0, \theta_2^0)] \qquad (7A.1.6e)$$

APPENDIX 7A.2   DERIVATION OF THE GOVERNING CRITERION FUNCTION

In order to simplify the analysis, we shall assume additive objective functions. The ith group's "extended objective function" is measured by $U_i(x)$. The index $i = 0$ is reserved for the partner with the assigned authority. The U_is are scalar functions expressed in terms of a common numeraire, say, dollars or pounds.[1] For the partner with the assigned authority,

$$U_0 = U_0(x)$$

$$= u_0(x_0) + \sum_{i=1}^{n} s_i(x_i, \delta_i) \tag{7A.2.1a}$$

where $u_0(x_0) = u_0(y(x_0), x_0)$, with $u_0 \colon \mathbb{R}^G \times X_0 \to \mathbb{R}$, and $y(x_0)$ the G-vector of endogenous variables whose values are determined by x_0; δ_i is a strategy indicator variable indicating whether a "reward" or "penalty" strategy has been adopted by the corresponding organized group in the strategic interaction; $s_i(\cdot)$ represents the "strength of power" function of the non-assigned authority partner, which is positive when this partner pursues a "reward" policy, and negative when a "penalty" policy is selected. The extended objective function for the non-assigned authority partner is

$$U_1 = U_1(x)$$

$$= u_1(x_1) - w_1(x_1, \delta_1) = u_1(x_0) - c_1 \tag{7A.2.1b}$$

where $u_1(x_0) = u_1(y(x_0), x_0)$ with $u_1 \colon \mathbb{R}^G \times X_0 \to \mathbb{R}$; $w_i(\cdot)$ represents the partner group's expenditures of pursuing actions (x_1) and a penalty or reward strategy(δ_1) in attempting to influence the assigned authority. Note that $w_1(\cdot)$ is positive whenever an active influence attempt is made by the partner without assigned authority, with c_1 representing the cost of exercising influence. The focus of such strategic influence is on the partner given authority.

The extended objective function, U_1, may consist of some or all of the following three components: (a) *the partner's policy objective function*, $u_1(x_0)$; (b) *the pressure function* (x_1, δ_1); and (c) *the cost of power*, c_1 *to the partner*. Note that in the structural specification, the pressure function and the cost of power function never appear jointly in any single extended objective function. Hence, $u_1(x_0)$ is group 1 evaluation of the consequences given the policy choice, x_0.

Each potential partner will seek to minimize the "cost of power," c_1, for given levels of pressure (strength, $s_1(\cdot)$, and the strategy, δ_1) it exerts on the assigned authority. This is achieved by a proper selection of actions, x_1. Let x_1^0 be the cost of the power minimizing combination of actions by interest group i. Recalling that x_1^0 may represent either a reward strategy or a penalizing strategy, the strength of power function, s_1, depends on the embedded cost of power, c_1, and the nature of the strategy, x_1^0, signified by δ_1. The foundation for these observations is

$$c_1 = c_1(\delta_1, s_1) = \min_{x_1 \in X} w_1(x_1, \delta_1) \qquad (7A.2.3)$$

Accordingly, c_1 refers to the partner group's least-cost combination of the means of power necessary for the partner group to achieve the "strength," s_1, over the assigned authority while δ_1 indicates the nature of the policy adopted by the partner group. Hence, the strength of power function, $s_1(\cdot)$, may be represented as follows:

$$s_1 \begin{cases} \alpha_1(c_1) \text{ when } \delta_1 \text{ is reward } (\delta_1 = \alpha_1) \\ -\beta_1(c_1) \text{ when } \delta_1 \text{ is reward } (\delta_1 = \beta_1) \end{cases} \qquad (7A.2.4)$$

Two concepts of the efficiency frontier may be distinguished for a cooperative solution: (a) an *economic efficiency frontier*[2] (EEF) – the set of efficient points $\{u(x_0) \in \mathbb{R}^2 : x_0 \in X_0$ and $u(x_0)$ is not dominated by any $(x_0^*), x_0^* \in X_0\}$ – and (b) the *cooperative efficiency frontier* (CEF) – the set of efficient points $\{U(x_0, \delta_1) \in \mathbb{R}^2 : x_0 \in X_0, \delta_1 = \alpha_1, c_1 \geq 0$ and $U(x_0, \delta_1, c_1)$ is not dominated by any $U(x_0^*) \in \mathbb{R}^2 : x_0 \in X_0, \delta_1^* \alpha_1^*, c_1^* \geq 0\}$.

The first set consists of efficient combinations of the policy objective functions attainable under the constraints imposed by the economic structure and technical and political feasibility, that is, with political rewards or penalties not considered in the determination of these efficient combinations. As we shall see later, the second efficiency concept is obtained from the first by allowing a partner to offer the assigned authority partner rewards for the cooperative solution as opposed to the non-cooperative solution where penalties are imposed.

Figure 7A.2.1 represents the economically feasible combinations of the assigned authority's (e.g., policymakers') and one partner's policy objective function, before taking into account the ability of this partner group to reward or penalize the assigned authority according to the functions $\alpha_1(c_1)$ or $-\beta_1(c_1)$ respectively. The policymaking or assigned authority center objective function, u_0, is plotted on the horizontal axis while the policy objective function of the other partner group, u_1, is represented on the vertical axis. The economic feasibility set (EFS) $\{u(x_0^*) \in \mathbb{R}^2 : x_0^* \in X_0\}$ is depicted by the shaded area *EFS*. The northeastern outer border of the EFS is the economic efficiency frontier, *EEF*, under the reasonable assumption that $u_i \geq 0$. It consists of the feasible combinations of policy objective functions (u_0, u_1) that cannot be dominated by any other feasible vector $[(u_0(x_0^*), u_1(x_0^*))]$ such that $x_0^* \in X_0$. That is, $(u_0, u_1) \in EEF$ cannot be dominated by any feasible vector $(u_0^*, u_1^*) \in EFS$.

If there is only one partner interest group and its extended objective function, U_1, is plotted on the vertical axis while the policymakers' extended objective function, U_0, is plotted on the horizontal axis, then the *reward function* appears as in Figure 7A.2.2 and the *penalty function* as in Figure 7A.2.3. Note that in both figures c_1 is measured downward along the vertical axis, and that both $s_1 = \alpha_1(c_1)$ and $s_1 = -\beta_1(c_1)$ are concave in c_1.

At this juncture, we explore the crucial properties of the equilibrium solutions and their implications for the analysis of power relations. The case of two players – the policy center partner and the remaining partner – is investigated. In accordance with Appendix 7A.1, the cooperative stage is preceded by a Nash–Harsanyi non-cooperative stage,[3] where the disagreement payoffs $[t_0(\tilde{x}), t_1(\tilde{x})]$ are determined by the players' threat strategies with $x \in X$. Given the disagreement payoffs, the Nash solution to the cooperative stage is the joint strategy $\bar{x} \in X$ which maximizes the product $[U_0(x) - t_0][U_1(x) - t_1]$ such that $U_i(x) - t_i \geq 0$, $(i = 0, 1)$, where $t_i \geq 0$, for all i. As shown in Appendix 7A.1, the non-cooperative equilibrium strategies $\tilde{x} = (\tilde{x}_0, \tilde{x}_1)$ are such that

$$t_0(\tilde{x}) - H_1 t_1(\tilde{x}) = \max_{x_0 \in X_0} \min_{x_1 \in X_1} [U_0(x) - H_1 U_1(x)], \quad (7A.2.5)$$

where $x = (x_0, x_1)$ and H_1 is a constant such that

$$H_1 \geq 0, \quad (7A.2.6)$$

and

$$U_0(\bar{x}) + H_1 U_1() = \max_{x \in X} [U_0(x) + H_1 U_1(x)], \quad (7A.2.7)$$

where $\bar{x}$ is the vector of cooperative solution strategies of both parties. At the optimal solution point, H_1 is the slope of the PEF, that is,

$$H_1 = -\left.\frac{\partial U_0}{\partial U_1}\right|_{x=\bar{x}}$$

Expressing the objective functions in terms of (7A.2.1a) and (7A.2.2b), condition (7A.2.5) becomes

$$t_0(x_0, c_1, \beta_1) - H_1 t_1(x_0, c_1) = \max_{x_0 \in X_0} \min_{c_1 \geq 0}$$

$$\{u_0(x_0) + s_1(c_1, \delta_1) - H_1[u_1(x_0) - c_1]\}$$

$$\delta_1 \in \{\alpha_1, \beta_1\} \qquad (7A.2.5)$$

The Kuhn–Tucker conditions imply that a necessary condition for (7A.2.5′) is

$$-\frac{\partial \beta_1(\tilde{c}_1)}{\partial c_1} + H_1 \geq 0, \qquad (7A.2.8a)$$

and the complementarity condition is

$$-\left(\frac{\partial \beta_1(\tilde{c}_1)}{\partial c_1} + H_1\right)\tilde{c}_1 = 0, \qquad (7A.2.8b)$$

where the strict equality of (7A.2.8a) holds whenever $\tilde{c}_1 > 0$. Notice that, due to the additivity of the objective functions, the interest group will always adopt a penalizing threat strategy under disagreement, namely, $\tilde{\delta}_1 = \beta_1$.

Stating (7A.2.7) in terms of (7A.2.2a) and (7A.2.2b), it turns out that due to additivity, the maximization of $U_0 + H_1 U_1$ in the cooperative game consists of:

(a) the interest group adopts a reward policy, that is, $\bar{\delta}_1 = \alpha_1$;
(b) $\bar{c}_i$ is selected so as to maximize $\alpha_1(c_1) - H_1 c_1$;
(c) $\bar{x}_0$ is selected so as to maximize $u_0(x_0) + H_1 u_1(x_0)$.

Consequently, the following condition holds:

$$\frac{\partial \alpha_1(\bar{c}_1)}{\partial c_1} - H_1 \leq 0, \qquad (7A.2.9)$$

and the complementarity condition is

$$\left(\frac{\partial \alpha_1(\bar{c}_1)}{\partial c_1} - H_1\right)\bar{c}_1 = 0, \qquad (7A.2.10)$$

where the strict equality of (7A.2.9) holds whenever $\bar{c}_1 > 0$.

In constructing the *complete* feasibility set (CFS) from the *economic* feasibility set (EFS), it must be kept in mind that the interest group can dole out rewards or penalties given *any* vector, x_0, which is chosen by the partner with assigned authority. A CFS can be determined by finding all the extended objective function combinations that can be attained through rewards or penalties starting from any utility combination in the EFS. That is $U_0 = u_0(x_0) + \alpha_1 \bar{c}_1 - \beta_1 \tilde{c}_1$ is feasible if x_0 is feasible, and U_1 is feasible if

$u_1(x_0) - c_1$ is feasible. Graphically, the CFS is constructed by sliding the origin of Figures 7A.2.2 and 7A.2.3 along the outer boundary of the EFS and marking the outer envelope of the points reached.

If only a reward strategy is implemented, the outer boundary of the CFS is constructed by sliding the origin $\alpha_1(c_1)$ from Figure 7A.2.2 along the boundary of the EFS represented in Figure 7A.2.1. The assumption of reward function concavity leads to a concave CEF. Intuitively, both the assigned authority center and the partner interest group win through cooperation; the policymaking center is granted a reward and the cost incurred by the interest group is compensated by a more favorable setting of x_0. The result is a CEF everywhere to the right of the EEF.

The partners could also reach a non-cooperative solution, that is, their respective disagreement payoffs. For this outcome, they independently choose a vector of threat strategies, $\tilde{x} \in X$, which determines the vector of disagreement payoffs, $t_0(\tilde{x}), t_1(\tilde{x})$. When only a threat or penalty strategy is implemented, the relevant CFS is obtained through shifting the punishment function, $-\beta_1 c_1$, along the boundary of the EFS in Figure 7A.2.1. As represented in Figure 7A.2.4, the resulting CFS from combining Figures 7A.2.1, 7A.2.2, and 7A.2.3, when both rewards and penalties are possible, contains a non-convexity. The non-convexity can be eliminated with free disposal of utility or intuitively if $U_1 \geq \min\{u_1\} = 0$. This latter assumption implies that a partner can never incur a cost that is larger than an interest group's utility in the EFS. Graphically, this presumption eliminates the bottom of the "rocket" in Figure 7A.2.4. (See the two areas designated by A.) When combined with the graphically implicit assumption that $\min\{u_1\} = 0$, we have a relevant CFS and CEF that appears only in the northeast quadrant of Figure 7A.2.4 as represented by the bold frontier.

The disagreement or non-cooperative payoffs are treated by the Nash–Harsanyi bargaining formulation as the first stage of a two-stage game. In the second stage, the "disagreement point" is taken as given, and Nash's cooperative solution consists of the joint strategy, $\overline{x} \in X$, that maximizes the product $[U_0(x) - t_0][U_1(x) - t_1]$, such that $U_i(\overline{x}) - t_i \tilde{x}_i \geq 0, i = 0,1$. Algebraically, the solution to the second-stage cooperative game can be obtained through the following steps. First, let the CEF be written as

$$H(U_0, U_1) = 0 \qquad (7A.2.11)$$

The Lagrangian for the second-stage problem can then be written as

$$L = [U_0 - t_0][U_1 - t_1] + \lambda H(U_0, U_1) \qquad (7A.2.12)$$

where we have assumed that the constraints, $U_i - t_i \geq 0$, $i = 0, 1$, are not binding. The associated first-order conditions for U_0 and U_1 can be combined to yield the equation,

$$\frac{\overline{U}_1 - t_1}{\overline{U}_0 - t_0} = \frac{H_0}{H_1} \qquad (7A.2.13)$$

where $H_i \equiv \frac{\partial H(U_0, U_1)}{\partial U_i}$ $(i = 0, 1)$.

Normalizing the ratio, $\frac{H_0}{H_1}$ in equation (7A.2.13) by setting $H_0 = 1$ and recalling that

$$-\left.\frac{dU_1}{dU_0}\right|_{U-\overline{U}} = \frac{H_0}{H_1} = \frac{1}{H_1}$$

we have for equation (7A.2.13)

$$\frac{\overline{U}_1 - t_1}{\overline{U}_0 - t_0} = -\left.\frac{dU_1}{dU_0}\right|_{U-\overline{U}} = \frac{1}{H_1} \qquad (7A.2.14)$$

There is a useful graphical interpretation of this equality. It states that the line segment joining the Nash bargaining solution to the second-stage game $\overline{U}(\overline{U}_1, \overline{U}_2)$ with the disagreement point (t_0, t_1) must have a positive slope equal to the absolute slope of the CEF at the solution point, $\overline{U}$. By implication, the second-stage solution would have been the *same* had the disagreement point been *any other point* on that same line segment or its extension into the interior of the CFS. This in turn suggests the entire strategy game can be solved graphically by working backward from the second stage. First, construct in Figure 7A.2.5, for any arbitrary point z on the outer CEF, the line tangent to the frontier at z. Next, find the line through z that has the same positive slope equal to the absolute slope of the tangent line at z (that is, the normal through z). The resulting line is then the set $C(z)$. This line has also been called the "isolation fiber." Repeating this process for many points, z_i, yields a set of line segments on the CFS that "fan out" if the CFS is strictly convex, as in Figure 7A.2.6.

The crucial point to note is that in the first stage of the game, given the property of the second-stage solution expressed in equation (7A.2.14), the two partners will only care which of their threat strategies, or equivalently, which of these "disagreement lines" $C(z_i)$ will take them to their best bargain. Given that the disagreement point lies *anywhere* on a particular one of these lines, $C(z_i)$, the solution to the game as a whole will then be given by the point at which that particular line crosses the CEF.

It is obvious from Figure 7A.2.7 that the assigned authority partner will prefer the disagreement point to lie on a line $C(z_i)$, that is, as far as possible to the southeast, whereas the organized interest group prefers a disagreement line as far as possible to the northwest. This is, of course, the content of equations (7A.2.5) and (7A.2.5').

In order to minimize the expression in braces on the right-hand side of condition (7A.2.5′), the interest group will always adopt a penalizing conflict strategy, that is, $\tilde{\delta}_1 = \beta_1$, and it will also choose $\tilde{c}_1$ as in equations (7A.2.8a) and (7A.2.8b). In order to maximize the same expression, the governmental center will choose $\tilde{x}_0$ such that $u(\tilde{x}_0)$ lies as far as possible in the east of the EFS. More precisely, $u(\tilde{x}_0)$ will be the point where the EFS touches the southeastern disagreement line $C(z_5)$ in Figure 7A.2.6.

In Figure 7A.2.7, the origin of the interest group's penalty function coincides with the most eastern point of the EEF. Starting from that point, the interest group will choose the penalty $-\beta_1(\tilde{c}_1)$ that reaches the most northwestern disagreement line, thereby satisfying condition (7A.2.8a). The disagreement point then is point (t_0, t_1) in the diagram, where the interest group's penalty function is tangent to the highest disagreement line (see Figure 7A.2.7).

The conflict strategies $(\tilde{x}_0)$ and $(\tilde{c}_1)$ are virtual strategies that never actually need to be carried out.[4] Instead, the two partners cooperate in stage two of the game to attain the point, $(\bar{x}_0)$, where the disagreement line on which (t_0, t_1) lies crosses the CEF. In order to attain this point, the assigned authority partner will implement the vector of policy instruments, $\bar{x}_0$, thereby inducing the vector of utilities, $u(\bar{x}_0)$, on the EEF. The remaining partner, in turn, rewards the assigned authority partner with additional utility, $\alpha_1(\bar{c}_1)$, at a subjective cost, $\bar{c}_1$, to themselves.

Figure 7A.2.7 also illustrates our core result that can be summarized as follows: To find the solution to the bargaining game, find the line tangent to the CEF at $U(\bar{x}_0)$ with the same slope as the line tangent to the EEF at $(\bar{x}_0)$. These lines are obtained by finding the solution $\tilde{c}_1, \bar{c}_1$ and $\bar{x}_0$ to the following problem:

$$\max_{x_0 \in X_0,\, \bar{c}_1 > 0,\, \tilde{c}_1 > 0} W(x_0) = u_0(x_0) - \frac{\partial \beta_1(\tilde{c}_1)}{\partial c_1} u_1(x_0) \tag{7A.2.15}$$

$$= u_0(x_0) + \frac{\partial \alpha(\bar{c}_1)}{\partial c_1} u_1(x_0)$$

where W is the *policy governance function*.

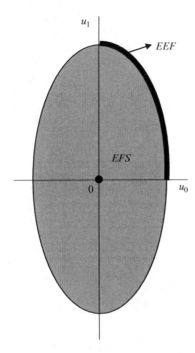

*Figure 7A.2.1   The economic feasibility set EFS and the economic
efficiency frontier EEF in the (u_0, u_1) space*

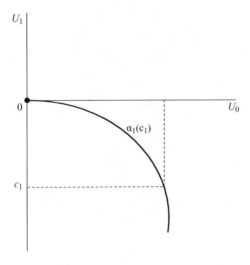

*Figure 7A.2.2   The reward function $\alpha_1 (c_1)$ when n =1, plotted in the
(U_0, U_1) space*

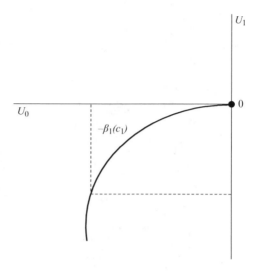

Figure 7A.2.3 The "penalty" function space $-\beta_1(c_1)$ when $n = 1$, plotted in the (U_0, U_1) space

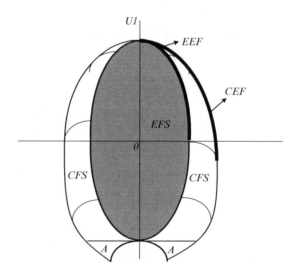

Figure 7A.2.4 The complete feasibility set CFS if both "rewards" and "penalties" are possible

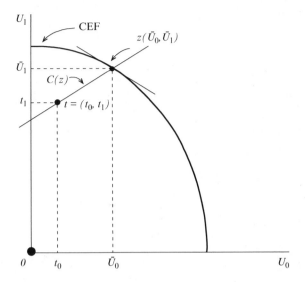

Figure 7A.2.5   Method of constructing the disagreement line set, $C(z)$
("isolation fiber"), through the disagreement point (t_0, t_1)
and the cooperative bargaining solution point $z(\overline{U}_0, \overline{U}_1)$

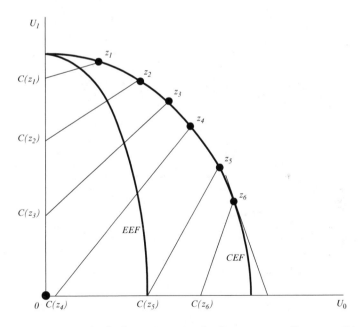

Figure 7A.2.6   Method of constructing the disagreement line sets, $C(z_i)$

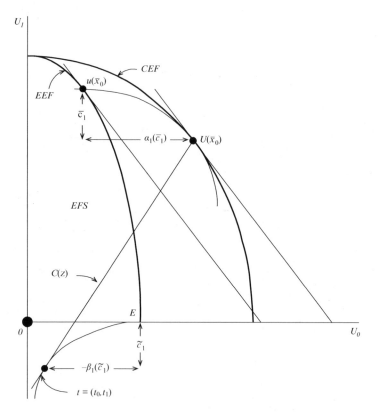

Figure 7A.2.7   Graphically derived solution when n = 1

Notes

1. No inter-group utility comparability is implied by our specification of the objective functions. The definition of U_i s in terms of a common numeraire implicitly assumes that members of each group are able to evaluate changes in the state of the political-economic system in terms of dollars and cents. This is a subjective value reflecting the group's own preferences; that is, $u_i(x_0)$ is a "money metric" utility function (Varian, 1992, p. 109).
2. The term "economic efficiency" used here is not necessarily synonymous with overall social Pareto optimality in the traditional economic sense. Rather, it applies only to the organized groups participating in a particular political economy bargaining process.
3. Throughout this section, the noncooperative stage's equilibrium is represented with the '~' sign, whereas the equilibrium of the cooperative stage is denoted with the '−' sign.
4. In fact, they need not be at all explicit. What is required is the perception of a potential threat by the participants (Nagel, 1968).

APPENDIX 7A.3   JOINT ASSIGNMENT OF AUTHORITY (OR CONTROL PREMIUMS)

If not a single assigned authority to one of the partners is established, but instead both partners jointly share such authority, we have in effect two policymaking centers. Under this circumstance, the policy governance function of Appendix 7A.2 must now be extended to:

$$W(x_0) = B_0 u_0(x_0) + B_1 u_1(x_0) \qquad (7A.3.1)$$

This governance structure follows from $\Gamma(U; t^0) = [U_0 - t_0^0][U_1 - t_1^0]$; and a bicentric bargaining game is obtained by maximizing $\Gamma(U; t^0)$ with respect to $x_0 \in X_0$. Considering only the cooperative solution, $\ln\Gamma$ is monotone increasing in Γ, and maximizing $\ln\Gamma$, $\ln\Gamma(U; t^0) = \ln(U_0 - t_0^0) + \ln(U_1 - t_1^0)$, also maximizes Γ. Let the outer boundary be given by $H(x_0) = 0$ and set the Lagrangian expression $L = \ln\Gamma(U; t^0) + \lambda H(x_0)$, where λ is a Lagrange multiplier. Assuming an interior solution, the first order conditions for maximing are $\ln\Gamma$

$$\frac{\partial L}{\partial x_0} = \frac{1}{(\overline{U}_0 - t_0^0)} \frac{\partial u_0}{\partial x_0} + \frac{1}{(\overline{U}_1 - t_1^0)} \frac{\partial u_1}{\partial x_0} + \lambda \frac{\partial H(\overline{x}_0)}{\partial x_0} = 0; \quad (7A.3.2a)$$

$$\frac{\partial L}{\partial c_0^1} = \frac{-1}{(\overline{U}_0 - t_0^0)} + \frac{1}{(\overline{U}_1 - t_1^0)} \frac{\partial s_{01}(\overline{c}_0^1, \alpha_0^1)}{\partial c_1^1} = 0; \qquad (7A.3.2b)$$

$$\frac{\partial L}{\partial c_0^1} = \frac{-1}{(\overline{U}_0 - t_0^0)} + \frac{1}{(\overline{U}_1 - t_1^0)} \frac{\partial s_{10}(\overline{c}_1^0, \alpha_1^0)}{\partial c_1^0} = 0; \qquad (7A.3.2c)$$

where $\overline{U}_0$ and $\overline{U}_1$ are the values of the corresponding, extended objective functions at the bargaining solution. Treating the values of $\overline{U}_0$ and $\overline{U}_1$ as given constants, it is easily shown that maximizing $\Gamma(U; t^0)$, that is, finding the solution to the two-person bargaining game, is equivalent to maximizing the policy governance function (7A.3.1) with respect to $x_0 \in X_0$ (i.e., $H(x_0) \geq 0$), where

$$B_0 = \frac{1}{(\overline{U}_0 - t_0^0)} > 0 \text{ and } B_1 = \frac{1}{(\overline{U}_1 - t_1^0)} > 0 \qquad (7A.3.3)$$

From (7A.3.2b) and (7A.3.2c), we also have

$$\frac{B_0}{B_1} = \frac{\partial s_{01}(\overline{c}_0^1, \alpha_0^1)}{\partial c_0^1} \text{ and } \frac{B_1}{B_0} = \frac{\partial s_{10}(\overline{c}_1^0, \alpha_1^0)}{\partial c_1^0} \qquad (7A.3.2c)$$

Equation (7A.3.4) suggests a power theoretic interpretation of the weights in the policy governance function; namely, the ratio, B_0/B_1, is the *marginal strength of power* of partner 0 over political center 1 relative to a marginal increment in interest group 0's *cost of power* over policy center 1. The ratio B_1/B_0 is likewise interpreted in terms of the reciprocal power relationship between the two policy centers.

8. Incomplete contracts and control premiums

A contract is incomplete if there is a set of events that can influence the partnership that has not been anticipated and addressed in the initial contract. Incomplete contracting theory provides the foundation for any framework evaluating PPPs. Control rights, the authority to make decisions in the case of both anticipated and unanticipated events, are a key consideration in incomplete contracting and, in particular, for PPP contracts. The allocation of control rights through a PPP contract can determine whether a partnership achieves efficiency as well as an equitable distribution of partnership benefits.

8.1 INCOMPLETE CONTRACTING THEORY AND PPPs

Any framework for evaluating PPPs must be rooted in the incomplete contracting theory literature and analyses of decision or control rights (Hart & Moore, 1988; Aghion & Bolton, 1992; Aghion et al., 1994; Dewatripont & Maskin, 1995; Hart, 1995; Aghion & Tirole, 1997; Hart et al., 1997; Hart & Moore, 1999; Tirole, 1999; Hart, 2003; Rausser & Stevens, 2009). At the heart of the concept of control rights and PPPs is the designation of the nature of the partnership output. PPP output can be designated as a private, a public, or an impure good. PPRPs that produce public or private goods are discussed in this chapter and PPRPs that produce impure goods are assessed in the next chapter.

8.1.1 Private Good PPPs

Grossman and Hart (1986), who provide a foundation for much of the incomplete contracting research, focus on the ownership of residual rights in a two-period model of integration of two private firms where the product of the relationship is a private good. In period 1, the firms form a contract that allocates control rights and allows each firm to make relationship-specific investments. In period 2, each firm makes production decisions based on the control rights designated under the contract. The production decisions and market outcomes determine the partnership value for each partner.

In the first period, the investments and the production decisions are uncontractable (Grossman & Hart, 1986). The firms make the relationship-specific investments non-cooperatively. The investments are observed, the second period begins, and the control rights allocated by the first-period contract are exercised. The production decisions can be non-cooperative or cooperative through costless renegotiation (the production decision becomes contractible in period 2). Because the partnership's value is unlikely to be maximized with non-cooperative decisions, the firms benefit from renegotiation in period 2 after observing investments. Assuming symmetric information, renegotiation will lead to an efficient ex post allocation. The distribution of ex post surplus, however, depends on the initial allocation of ownership rights, and thus distorts ex ante investment decisions. If the firms are assumed to divide the partnership surplus sym-metrically, both firms underinvest and fail to achieve efficiency. This result is further supported in a subsequent study by Hart and Moore (1990).

Grossman and Hart (1986) find that if the first-period investment of one firm has a larger effect on the partnership's value than that of the other firm, the contract should assign the firm with the more valuable invest-ment full control rights over decision making in the second period, giving this firm an incentive to invest optimally, and thus maximizing the part-nership's value. In essence, in the case of a jointly produced private good, the assignment of control rights to agents based on the value generated by investments can mitigate against underinvestment.

8.1.2   Public Good PPPs

Besley and Ghatak (2001) use incomplete contracting theory to evalu-ate a partnership that produces a public good, namely, a product that is presumed to be non-rival and non-excludable. In their model, two agents make relationship-specific investments. The benefits of the relationship are public and are dependent on the investment decisions. The two agents are assumed to have different valuations of the project. With no contracting problems, the agents choose investments that maximize joint surplus. If the contract is incomplete since investments cannot be specified ex ante, each party holds bargaining power after investments have been made and the first-best levels of investment are generally not reached. Besley and Ghatak (2001) show, however, that by allocating full ownership, and thus all control rights, to the partner with the highest valuation of the project, joint surplus will be maximized. Given this assignment of authority, the high-valuation

Table 8.1   Optimal allocation of authority or control rights in a PPP

Type of good	To partner(s) with the most valuable investment	To partner(s) with the highest valuation of output	Shared with greater share to low-valuation partner (output)	All rights to low-valuation partner (output)
Private good (Grossman & Hart 1986, Hart & Moore 1990)	X			
Public good (Besley & Ghatak 2001)		X		

partner has the incentive and ability to invest optimally. Accordingly, when a public good is generated by a partnership, the allocation of control rights should be based on the agents' valuation of the partnership output, not the relative value of their investment as found by Grossman and Hart (1986) and Hart and Moore (1990) for private goods. The major results for private good versus public good are presented in Table 8.1.

8.2   PROVISION OF PUBLIC SERVICES

Infrastructure development projects involve significant risks given the large capital investments and long project time periods needed to negotiate contracts and construct, operate, and maintain assets. Traditionally, these projects (e.g., bridges, roads, telecommunications, railroads, energy) were funded, constructed, and managed by the public sector because these projects produced impure goods. Increasingly, public agencies have looked to improve efficiency by using private sector expertise and financing through PPP mechanisms. When an infrastructure PPP is formed, the private partner usually manages the finance, planning, and construction of the asset base for the services to be generated. Once constructed, ownership or operating rights for public utilities can revert back to the public partner or may be assigned to private firms. Infrastructure development partnerships are quite similar to PPRPs and can offer valuable insights into the optimal partnership structure. In both types of partnerships, the private partner brings financing and subject-area expertise and the public partner grants the private partner rights to the revenue generated by the project either through a licensing agreement in the case of R&D or through operating fees in the case of infrastructure development. Another key similarity is that both partnerships deal with uncertainty and the potential reallocation of control rights. The outcome of infrastructure development, like the university research process, is uncertain, in terms of time to completion and revenue generation. The contracts that govern both partnership types must address many of the same issues.

Using PPPs for the development and maintenance of infrastructure allows the government to avoid levying distortionary taxes by using private sector funding repaid through project user fees. More important, these PPPs can transfer many of the risks associated with long-term capital projects (e.g., construction risk, operating risk, revenue risk due to demand shortfall, financial risk, regulatory risk, and environmental risk) to the private sector. Infrastructure financed by PPPs holds particular promise for developing countries as it allows governments that do not have sufficient financial resources, risk-bearing capability or intellectual capital to build their country's infrastructure (World Bank Latin American and Caribbean Studies, 1997; Alonso-Conde et al., 2007).

Economic theory predicts that given a full set of control rights, the private partner will exercise market power by setting prices above the competitive level and producing quantity below the competitive level. By forming PPPs, the government can retain some control over production and pricing decisions and can limit the private firm's use of market power. Of particular importance is the structuring of the renegotiation process so as not to distort each partner's incentives (Gausch, 2004). In practice, designing contracts for construction and operations of infrastructure that result in appropriate risk sharing and balance control rights is a challenge.

8.3   THEORETICAL RESEARCH

Hart et al. (1997) evaluate a government's decision whether to provide a service in-house, thereby retaining residual control rights over nonhuman assets generated by the partnership (e.g., a prison), or whether to contract out to a private firm, giving the private provider residual control rights. These residual control rights assign authority to make changes given unforeseen contingencies. The service provider chooses investments in quality improvement and cost reduction. The Hart et al. (1997) model shows that while the private provider has stronger incentives than a government employee for both quality improvement and cost reductions, the cost reducing incentives are too strong, sacrificing quality. Thus private provision may be preferred when cost reductions do not have a strongly negative effect on quality or when these cost reductions can be controlled through contracts and quality innovations are a priority. Hart et al. (1997) present the example of prisons as a case of private contractors reducing costs to an extent that can deteriorate quality. The authors cite data that indicate that the level of violence is higher in private prisons. The authors conclude that although some of this concern about quality can be addressed by adopting standards or "best practices," contractual incompleteness remains and, as such, their theoretical model makes a case against privatization of prisons.

Building on this research, Hart (2003) evaluates a PPP that creates infrastructure to be constructed and operated privately. The government can "bundle" the construction and operation by forming a partnership with a single private firm or "unbundle" the project using different firms, one to construct and another to operate the infrastructure. The advantage of bundling is that the private firm internalizes the benefits of investments made during construction. A firm that manages a bundled project (i.e., the firm holds control rights) will be more willing to make quality investments in construction that lead to more efficient operation than a firm that is responsible for construction alone. Hart concludes that if the quality of the building can be specified, but the quality of service cannot be specified (e.g., prisons or schools), "unbundling" or separate provision may be preferred. Alternatively, if the quality of the infrastructure cannot be specified in the contract, but the quality of the service can be (as may be the case with a hospital), a PPP could provide the best incentives for the private firm to invest optimally in construction.

Bennett and Iossa (2006a) also evaluate bundling of the construction and management of a facility and whether private or public ownership is optimal. Under their model, the project may affect social benefit, management costs, and the residual value of the facility. Under private ownership, the owner has the power to implement an innovation unilaterally. Under public ownership, renegotiation between the firm/consortia and the public authority must take place before an innovation is implemented. An innovation that increases social benefit may either decrease cost at the management stage (bundling results in a positive externality so bundling is optimal) or increase management costs (bundling results in a negative externality so unbundling may be optimal). Bennett and Iossa (2006a) find that with a positive externality, assumed ownership by the consortia (i.e., private partner) is not necessarily optimal. Under certain conditions, government ownership is optimal (i.e., the government partner should hold all control rights). It is not optimal, however, for these rights to automatically revert back to the public partner at the conclusion of the project because ex ante investment incentives are reduced. Instead, residual ownership should be allotted to the private partner, and the public partner has the option to negotiate a mutually beneficial transfer of ownership.

The theoretical research on the provision of public services provides several lessons. The private partner's incentives and the interplay of decision variables (e.g., the effect of cost reduction on quality improvement or the effect of increasing social benefit on management cost) are important to identify and consider. As can be expected, the private partner will not invest in an end product that does not generate private benefits unless it is accounted for in the contract. That said, assigning full, automatic ownership control rights ex ante to either the private or public partner is not always most beneficial. Residual ownership schemes that include the ability to bargain ex post over the transfer of ownership may be optimal.

8.4   EMPIRICAL ANALYSES

Formal empirical analyses generating testable hypotheses in the context of R&D relating to PPPs and incomplete contracting theory are minimal. More often, researchers turn to survey-based methods and case-study approaches as in Chapter 6 to assess current and past PPP relationships and to extract lessons for future partnerships. In this section, we discuss the recent empirical, survey-based and case-study research addressing contracting issues for PPPs generating impure public goods in the form of infrastructure and provision of public services, ultimately drawing the implications of these PPPs for PPRPs.

A primary finding from the theoretical research, that bundling of construction and operating processes through PPPs may increase efficiency (Hart, 2003; Bennett & Iossa, 2006a; Hart et al., 1997), has been the focus of some empirical research. Bundling transfers control rights over assets to the private partner, providing incentives for relation-specific investments. If the quality of the service can be specified, theory predicts that a PPP could provide optimal investment incentives for the private partner (Hart, 2003). Bennett and Iossa (2006a; 2006b) apply their model to the special case of Private Finance Initiative (PFI) PPPs in the United Kingdom. They consider how the transfer of ownership at the conclusion of a project affects PFI projects and find that asset specificity and service-demand risk are key considerations.

Chong et al. (2006) evaluate organizational choice and the performance of PPPs using regression analysis and a database of information relating to 5,000 French local public water authorities. The analysis finds that consumer prices are higher for water supplied under any of the four forms of PPPs accounted for in the analysis rather than water supplied under direct public management. Moreover, the form of PPP that represents the greatest allocation of control rights to the private partner, build-to-operate-and-own concessions, results in the highest consumer prices. The authors point to several factors that may contribute to these results, including inadequate ex ante competition between private partners and non-transparent partnership selection procedures. Although these PPP relationships in France are considered to be "administrative contracts," and as such give the public sector authority the right to unilaterally change the contract after signing, addressing concerns about ex post opportunistic behavior by the private partner, it is not clear how often this provision is invoked and, thus, how credible this threat might be.

Blanc-Brude et al. (2009) also evaluate PPP efficiency in contrast to traditional procurement for road construction projects. Using a database of 227 road projects, of which 65 are PPPs, financed by the European Investment Bank between 1990 and 2005 in all EU-15 countries and Norway, the authors evaluate ex ante costs in the form of bidders' construction prices. They find that a PPP road project which can be viewed as allocating greater control rights to the private partner is 24 percent more expensive, ex ante, than roads built through traditional procurement with more limited private control rights. The authors note that ex post cost overruns for traditionally procured roads are reported to be close to this estimate. While the authors argue that this finding may undercut the increased efficiency argument for bundling projects (i.e., transferring control rights over assets to the private partner), this finding seems to point to the need to compare ex ante contract costs to the full range of ex post costs, including construction cost overruns, renegotiation costs, and operating costs, in order for a determination of efficiency to be made.

Cabral and Saussier (2007) evaluate both quality and cost in PPPs and differences in control right allocations across countries. They use a case-study approach to evaluate PPP provision of prisons in three countries: Brazil, France, and the United States.[1] From previous research, they find that in Brazil, PPP prisons resulted in certain cost reductions and an increase in the quality of services provided; in France, PPPs led to an increase in both cost and quality; and in the United States, researchers observed reductions in both cost and quality. Cabral and Saussier attribute these differences across countries to differences in the assignment of decision rights (control rights). The authors assert that in the United States, all decision rights are assigned to the private partner, while in France and Brazil, decision rights are split between the private and public partners. The private ownership of control rights in the United States means that the private partner controls not only the building of the facility but also the operation, and it is difficult for the government to monitor the behavior of the private operator.

A second focus of quantitative and case-study research is the evaluation of PPP governance mechanisms, contract flexibility, and partner attributes. Zheng et al. (2008) use a case-study approach to evaluate how contractual and relational governance mechanisms are used in the management of two long-term, complex PPP supply arrangements. While contractual governance implies well-defined control rights, relational governance, which relies on informal arrangements based on trust and experience, rather than formal contracts, for managing relationships, implies more fluid control rights. Some researchers argue that relational governance promotes flexibility, solidarity, and information exchange while others argue that developing these arrangements consumes resources and may restrict new opportunities (Zheng et al., 2008). Zheng et al. (2008) find that relational and contractual mechanisms are complementary and, moreover, that relational assumptions frame the contracting process as either one of distrust or commitment. Contractual governance mechanisms, once set up, offer less flexibility but are stabilizing to the partnership whereas relational governance mechanisms are more fragile and can erode quickly.

Desrieux et al. (2013) also analyze the role of relational contracts in the form of repeated or multiple relationships between a local government and a private partner. After developing a theoretical model showing how multiple or bundled relationships can improve performance and reduce costs (due to the government's option to continue a relationship or end it, i.e., threat strategy), the authors formally test the model using a database of the contractual choices made by 5,000 French local public water authorities.[2] The regression analysis shows that the use of the same private partner for both the distribution and the sanitation of water is associated with a significant price reduction for consumers. While the authors point to the importance of relational contracts in generating their findings, the model results could also be interpreted as stemming from the retention of important control rights by the local government that gives them flexibility to respond to any consequences of the PPP implementation.

Athias and Saussier (2007) evaluate the tradeoff between rigid and flexible contracts using a database of 71 concession contracts for toll roads across eight countries. They find that several factors are related to increased flexibility in contracts, as defined by price renegotiation terms, including higher traffic uncertainty (i.e., revenue uncertainty), increased reputation as measured by the number of previous contracts between the partners, and stronger country-specific institutional frameworks for contract enforcement. This increased flexibility essentially gives the private partner more control rights over future contingencies. The analysis indicates that the characteristics of the partners affect contract design and thus control right designations.

Araujo and Sutherland (2010) provide a broad evaluation of PPPs in Organisation for Economic Co-operation and Development (OECD) countries based on an ad hoc OECD questionnaire on infrastructure investment and on data on nearly 2,000 PPPs. This study presents quantitative characterizations of PPPs in OECD countries, generating an indicator to assess how well-suited, country-specific policy frameworks are to benefit from PPPs, and provides guidelines for contract structure. The authors conclude that the heterogeneity of this indicator across countries suggests there would be gains from improved policy frameworks for some countries.

Contractual commitments on sharing the value of a project require an assessment of tradeoffs between cash flows and private benefits and how such tradeoffs are affected by the allocation of control rights. Aghion and Bolton (1992) consider a project that yields a cash flow as well as private benefits. Each partner in the project cares about different benefits; the investor in the project only cares about cash flow while the entrepreneur receiving the investor's funding is interested in maximizing both cash flow and private benefits, creating a conflict between the partners. In this context, control rights specify who makes decisions affecting the tradeoff between cash flow and private benefits. Aghion and Bolton find that the partner that controls the decisions once the project is underway will then divert resources, or make other decisions, in order to serve his or her own interests. Thus, control rights should be assigned for particular events based on which partner will make the least inefficient decision at that point. Although specified as generating a private good, this conclusion corresponds to Besley and Ghatak (2001), with control rights going to the partner with the highest valuation of the output.

8.5   PPRPs AND CONTROL RIGHTS

With PPRPs becoming increasingly prevalent, there is concern that as public funding declines, basic research (public good research) will be neglected and the focus on commercial applications (private good research) increased. There is limited theoretical literature addressing the specifics of research partnerships. Incomplete contracts literature has focused primarily on the optimal allocation of control rights when producing either a private or public good. PPRPs can, however, be structured to accommodate impure goods, as shown in Chapter 9, so that private firms can sponsor research that benefits public good research (Rausser & Stevens, 2009; Rausser et al., 2008).

Other research focuses on the diverging goals held by partners. For example, Aghion and Bolton's (1992) treatment of private benefits could be considered analogous to the nonmonetary benefits sought by public research partners such as the generation of public good research. The firm manager or entrepreneur (interested in both cash flow and the good produced) represents the role of the public research partner while the investor (interested only in cash flow) can represent the private research partner, who is focused on generating applied innovations that may lead to commercialization. If generating innovations that can be commercialized and supporting the local business community are the primary goals, relatively more control rights should be turned over to the private partner because – following Aghion and Bolton (1992) – the private partner is likely to make the least inefficient decision when facing an unexpected turn in the R&D process. If, on the other hand, nonmonetary goals, such as generating basic (public) research, are the primary goals, then the public partner should wield more control.

In further work focusing on the nature of the inputs offered by each partner, Aghion and Tirole (1994) analyze the organization of R&D activity using an incomplete contract framework. They find that the provider of research funding, or "customer" (i.e., investor), will have more control and ownership of resulting innovations relative to the collaborating "research unit" (i.e., manager or entrepreneur) if his or her capital inputs are large relative to intellectual inputs provided by the research unit. They also find that property rights associated with multiple innovations should be split on the basis of "comparative advantage in creating value." This work reflects a general finding from the literature on incomplete contracts: Control of property rights should be allocated to the parties in accordance with the relative potential impacts of their effort. Of course, the relative impact of financial versus intellectual inputs on research is difficult to determine and thus not easily sorted when private and public partners combine assets.

In an analysis of strategic R&D alliances between biotechnology firms and pharmaceutical corporations, Lerner and Merges (1998) consider how the phase of R&D, specifically how close the research is to commercialization, affects the allocation of control rights. The firms provide relatively more intellectual assets and the corporations contribute relatively more financial assets. The analysis suggests that biotechnology firms have more experience with early-stage research and thus these firms should retain more control rights in the earlier stages of a project; that is, the party contributing relatively more intellectual capital to a research collaboration is likely to have a better bargaining position at earlier stages in the research process. Contrary to this hypothesis, Lerner and Merges do not find a consistent association between research phase and the allocation of control rights. They find that when a technology is in its early stages (farther away from commercialization), more control rights are allocated to the partner providing financing. Therefore, the partner supplying intellectual capital may not be taking advantage of the bargaining power implied by their expertise.

8.6 CONCLUSION

Both theoretical and empirical research supports the notion that control rights are a crucial issue in public–private research agreements and that the balance of these rights should be tied to the valuation and, hence, overall goals of the relationship. The implications for PPRPs are clear. Public partners must be savvy in leveraging their intellectual capital to achieve a favorable balance of control over the results of the research collaboration, especially when this research falls on the more fundamental (i.e., early-stage) side of the research spectrum. Public research partners must recognize the full potential value of their contribution to the partnership and negotiate agreements accordingly. And further, public partners should be sure to define control rights over the research process ex ante, rather than as innovations are generated and bargaining power erodes.

Given that PPRPs often require numerous types of inputs from each partner and produce multiple potential products, each falling somewhere on the spectrum from private to public good,[3] partners are negotiating over a set of investments and a set of expected outputs which do not have a one-to-one mapping (i.e., one partnership input is likely to contribute to the production of several outputs). Efficient allocation of control rights in PPRPs will then likely depend on an assessment of the nature of all potential research outputs. In practice, this suggests that control rights should be defined for each output of the partnership. While PPP contracts can accommodate this complexity, accurate ex ante assessment of expected outputs, in order to maximize efficiency, is a challenge. Although the valuation of each partner for each of these outputs may be determined, the relative contribution of each partner's investments to each output is less transparent.

The theoretical research suggests, however, that to the extent that a partnership's outputs can be separated, the nature of each defined, and relative partner contributions identified, different assignments of control rights by partnership output should result (see Table 8.1). For partnership outputs that are primarily a public good, control rights should be assigned to the partner with the highest valuation, while for outputs that are primarily private goods, control rights should be assigned to the partner with the most valuable assets. For those outputs that have attributes of both public and private goods, the partner with the lower valuation should be given control rights given that the high-valuation partner already has sufficient incentives with regard to these outputs. While the theoretical principles for control right assignments for primarily public or private partnership outputs seem feasible in practice, the recommendation to give the low-valuation partner control over outputs that are neither primarily public nor primarily private in nature may be more problematic.

NOTES

1. Cabral and Saussier (2007) base their case studies on earlier empirical studies of prison performance.
2. The database is made up of observations from 1998, 2001, and 2004.
3. For example, Aghion and Bolton (1992) address this issue, separating cash flow from private benefits and control rights on each.

9. Impure goods and the structure of contracts

In the previous chapter we presented the allocation of control rights or authority assignments in partnerships that produce public or private goods. In this chapter we consider the partnerships that produce impure goods. An impure good has attributes of both public and private goods; that is, the good is either non-rival or non-excludable, but not both. In some cases, research discoveries can be classified as impure goods. For example, research discoveries in renewable energy in particular are best classified as impure goods. Though access to advancements in renewable energy can be protected through IP rights, these advancements produce environmental benefits that extend well beyond the commercial appropriation captured by the property right holder. Much of the university research on lignocellulosic ethanol falls squarely into this categorization. Since renewable energy research cannot be classified as a public or private good, the theoretical control right allocations developed in the previous chapter will not be optimal. We present another set of control right allocations that depend on the degree of impurity and the financial investment of each partner.

University research partnerships are not the only partnerships that produce impure goods. PPPs that produce impure goods are especially common in countries attempting to improve management and service provisions of natural resources. Much of the literature on impure goods in PPPs is based on such partnerships in natural and environmental resources. We define natural resources to include both market and non-market goods and services that arise from, inter alia, the use and allocation of water, land, mining, environmental remediation efforts, forestry, fisheries, and energy (whether exhaustible or renewal). Partnerships in natural resources provide unique insights into the optimal PPRP structure because they must address the management and provision of impure public goods. The optimal structure of a PPP depends on the type of good or service produced. The type of good or service is pivotal in the determination of shared authority among partners in the extraction or production and consumptive distribution of natural resources.

Contracts for university research partnerships and PPPs in the natural and environmental resources, and their associated control and property rights, come in many forms, ranging from large, multi-project, multi-year alliances to small-scale projects. We present a framework for analyzing these contracts based on control rights that stem from contingencies in the partnership's production process and are embedded in the contract.

9.1 THEORETICAL FRAMEWORK

Much of the contracting and control right literature focuses on the allocation of control rights within partnerships that generate either private goods or public goods. While providing important insights, this literature does not provide a full framework for evaluating most PPPs which generate impure goods. For example, in the area of natural resources, PPPs produce impure goods such as environmental remediation, water sanitation, infrastructure, or scientific research. As with other PPRPs, PPPs with a R&D focus produce impure goods such as scientific innovation and published analysis.

Francesconi and Muthoo (2011) were the first to develop a framework for evaluating PPPs that generate impure goods. Moreover, in contrast to Grossman and Hart (1986) and Besley and Ghatak (2001), the model allows control rights to be shared between two partners. In the first stage, two agents choose the allocation of control rights. After the initial allocation, the two agents invest in the project. Once the investment decisions are made, the partners can make unilateral or joint decisions through cooperative bargaining, rather than invoking the control rights, and payoffs result. If the partners do not cooperate, the project's value, as determined by the allocated control rights, will be less than if they cooperated, as we discovered in Chapter 7. Any ex post bargaining affects the marginal returns to investment for each partner, which are in turn influenced by the disagreement payoffs coming from the ex ante allocated control rights. The partners bargain over whether the decisions are to be made cooperatively or non-cooperatively and what, if any, transfers are to be made.

Francesconi and Muthoo (2011) find that when the level of impurity is small (i.e., the partnership product is primarily a public good), control rights should go to the partner that values the results of the partnership the highest, following Besley and Ghatak (2001). When the degree of impurity is large (i.e., the partnership product is primarily a private good), control rights should be allocated to the largest investor, as in Grossman and Hart (1986) and Hart and Moore (1990). If the degree of impurity is large and investments are roughly equal, it is optimal for control rights to be shared with a relatively greater share going to the low-valuation partner, a counter-intuitive result. If the degree of impurity is neither small (i.e., public good) nor large (i.e., private good) and the investments are of similar importance, once again the low-valuation partner should be allocated all control rights. Allocating control rights to the low-valuation partner is optimal in these cases because the high-valuation partner already has an incentive to invest and the low-valuation partner will be more willing to invest if they hold a greater share of the control rights.

The major results on the assignment of control rights for all three major types of goods found in the theoretic literature are presented in Table 9.1. The efficient assignment depends on the type of good or value generated (private, public, degree of impurity) and the choices/attributes of the parties entering into the partnership.

In Francesconi and Muthoo's (2011) model for allocating control rights in PPPs, initially two partners, g and n, divide the control rights between themselves. The partner g holds a share $c \varepsilon [0, 1]$ of the control rights and the remaining $(1 - c)$ of the control rights are held by the partner n. After

Table 9.1   Optimal allocation of authority or control rights in a PPP

Type of good	To partner(s) with the most valuable investment	To partner(s) with the highest valuation of output	Shared with greater share to low-valuation partner (output)	All rights to low-valuation partner (output)
Private good (Grossman & Hart, 1986, Hart & Moore, 1990)	X			
Public good (Besley & Ghatak, 2001)		X		
Impure good (Francesconi & Muthoo, 2011)				
• Impurity large (i.e., private good), unequal investment	X			
• Impurity small (i.e., public good)		X		
• Impurity large (i.e., private good), equal investment			X	
• Impurity neither large nor small, equal investment				X

the control rights are allocated, g and n invest a_g, $a_n \geq 0$ respectively in the project. Once the investments are made, the partners can either make decisions unilaterally or jointly through cooperative bargaining. If the partners do not cooperate, the project's value will be $B(c, a_g, a_n)$, and if they do cooperate, the value will be $b(a_g, a_n)$, where $b(a_g, a_n) > B(c, a_g, a_n)$. The non-cooperative project value, $B(c, a_g, a_n)$, is specified to be a linear function of control rights: $B(c, a_g, a_n) = cB^g(a_g, a_n) + (1 - c) B^n(a_g, a_n)$, where $B^i(a_g, a_n)$ is the project's value for partner i when i has sole decision-making authority.

The players bargain over whether the decisions are to be made cooperatively or non-cooperatively and what, if any, transfers there will be from g to n or n to g. If g and n cooperate, their payoffs are $\theta_g b(a_g, a_n) + t$ and $\theta_n b(a_g, a_n) - t$ respectively, where the valuation parameters, θ_n and θ_g, determine each partner's valuation of the project and t is a monetary transfer from n to g which can be positive or negative. But, if the partners choose to make decisions non-cooperatively, the payoffs are $\theta_g[cB^g(a_g, a_n) + (1 - \alpha)(1 - c) B^n(a_g, a_n)]$ and $\theta_n[(1 - \alpha)cB^g(a_g, a_n) + (1 - c) B^n(a_g, a_n)]$ respectively, where the impurity of the good produced by the project is measured by the parameter $\alpha\varepsilon[0, 1]$. The α parameter allows this framework to be extended to PPPs that produce any good on the spectrum between pure private goods and pure public goods.

The broad themes developed from a theoretical perspective yield useful insights when applied to PPRPs in specific industries. PPRPs that conduct research related to natural resources can be structured so that private firms sponsor research that benefits public good research (Spielman et al., 2007; Rausser et al., 2008). Public investment in research can stimulate private investment by creating new technologies that can be profitably exploited by the private sector (Wang, 2007). In forming these relationships, it has been recognized that PPRPs cannot be justified solely as a fund-raising device where public funds are replaced with private funds, because the payout to the private firm can cause greater distortions than a tax levied by the public sector (Sadka, 2006; Engel et al., 2007).[1] Chong et al. (2006) highlight the importance of competition between private partners vying to enter an agreement with a public partner. When private partners and partnership paths are being evaluated, the full range of ex post costs, even those that may arise after the expected conclusion of a relationship, should be accounted for during the partner selection process. Once a partner has been selected, the findings of Francesconi and Muthoo (2011), coupled with those of Cabral and Saussier (2007), support a careful sharing and balancing of control rights between public and private partners in a relationship generating an impure good on a detailed risk-by-risk basis.

9.2 CASE STUDIES: INFRASTRUCTURE INVESTMENT

Infrastructure development projects carry significant risk as they require large capital investments over a long time period to construct, operate, and maintain. Traditionally, infrastructure development was only pursued by the public sector as many of the projects (bridges, roads, telecommunications, railroads, energy, etc.) dealt with natural resources and produced impure public goods. But, as infrastructure development has grown increasingly complex and expensive, governments have looked to improve efficiency by using private sector expertise and financing through PPPs (Engel et al., 1997; Ramamurti, 1997; Estache et al., 2000; Estache et al., 2007). PPPs also allow the government to avoid levying distortionary taxes by tapping private sector funding, which can be repaid by user fees generated by the partnership. PPPs can also reduce the public sector's financial risk in both the cost of the project and the future revenue streams, and some public agencies argue that this risk transfer is the primary benefit flowing from the use of financing by PPPs.

When an infrastructure PPP is formed, the private firms usually manage financing, planning, and constructing the asset base for the services to be generated. Upon completion of the project, the firm is allowed to manage and collect rents from the asset for a length of time, after which the asset reverts to the government. In developing countries, infrastructure financing by PPPs is particularly promising as it allows governments without sufficient funding, risk-bearing capability, or intellectual capital to build their country's infrastructure (World Bank Latin American and Caribbean Studies, 1997; Alonso-Conde et al., 2007).

Infrastructure development projects are typically long-lived, illiquid, capital intensive, and difficult to value, carrying with them significant risks (construction risk, operating risk, revenue risk due to volume shortfall, financial risk, force majeure risk, regulatory risk, and environmental risk). A major challenge in securing private sector involvement in the provision of public infrastructure has been to design contracts that result in appropriate risk sharing. Contracts for infrastructure PPPs can reduce these risks by carefully structuring the renegotiation process so as not to distort each partner's incentives (Gausch, 2004).

A leading example occurred in Australia, where the government has been successful in using PPPs to increase the provision of an impure public good, roads, by forming contracts that directly address the private sector's concerns about risk sharing (Brown, 2005). The government has repeatedly created successful partnerships that have led private firms to invest over $9 billion in the country's roads. Initially, the government learned that the private partners would only enter a contract that included price-setting mechanisms that correctly reflected the risks they assumed by financing and operating these projects. The Australian government addressed this concern by sharing price-setting control rights with the firms in the initial contract. Subsequently the partners would jointly set prices, to reflect the private firms' risks and allow for price flexibility in response to unanticipated shocks. By assigning the firms some control rights for setting prices in the face of unanticipated events and setting prices according to the firms' risks, these contracts aligned the partners' expectations for pricing, which reduced the private firms' risk, and the need for renegotiation. This assignment of control rights has decreased unanticipated shocks (Stage 3) and allowed the Australian government to form successful contracts with the private sector to finance infrastructure.

9.3   CASE STUDIES: RENEWABLE ENERGY[2]

Renewable energy research is best classified as an impure good. IP rights can protect renewable energy discoveries from unauthorized use; these discoveries produce environmental benefits that extend far beyond the commercial profits captured by a property right holder. Much of the university renewable energy research, including research on lignocellulosic ethanol, conversion of heavy hydrocarbons to clean fuel, and carbon sequestration, fall squarely into this categorization. Since this renewable energy research cannot be classified as a public or private good, the theoretical control right allocations for public or private goods (developed in Chapter 8) will not be optimal. The optimal allocation of control rights for such partnerships depends on the degree of impurity and the financial investment of each partner.

The largest renewable energy PPRP is the EBI, a partnership between three public research institutions (UC Berkeley, Lawrence Berkeley National Laboratory, and the University of Illinois at Urbana-Champaign) and BP (see Chapter 6). Formed in 2007, BP committed to provide $500 million in research funding to the EBI over ten years, making this the largest PPRP ever created. The EBI-funded research focuses on energy supply, by developing new biofuels, and energy demand, by reducing the environmental impact of energy consumption. While the scope of the research to be carried out through the EBI is quite broad,[3] much of the research is focused on developing patentable plant material that could be efficiently used as a biofuel.

Both the private and public partners contributed funds to this PPRP. BP was obligated to provide university researchers a total of $350 million in research funding over the course of the partnership, with the remaining $150 million funding research in BP's commercial laboratory space that resides on the campuses of the public partners. The public partners agreed to finance construction of a $159 million research lab complex that would house university researchers and BP research scientists.[4] Since the investment by the public partners amounts to less than one-third of the private partner's research investment, the optimal control right allocation would be skewed toward the private partner, *ceteris paribus*, reflecting the unequal investments and the degree of impurity (see Table 9.1).

Decision-making authority is shared equally by the private and public partners, each having four votes on the eight-member Governance Board (EBI, 2007). Since decisions by the Board require a majority, funding decisions require approval from both partners and each partner has unilateral veto power. The contract also prevents the private partner from terminating the partnership during the first three years, after which BP can reevaluate funding levels.

The EBI agreement grants the private partner more rights over the IP generated by the partnership than the Berkeley–Novartis agreement discussed in Chapter 6. In the EBI agreement, BP is granted the exclusive option to review and license research for 180 days after notification, and the licensing fee cannot exceed $100,000 per year. In addition, if BP licences a research discovery, BP will be granted royalty-free access to other reserch discoveries not funded by BP, but necessary to use their IP ("background inventions"). This gives BP the broad ability to commercialize university research related to the EBI.

Research funded by BP will take place in both traditional academic labs managed by university researchers and corporate labs on the UC Berkeley campus which are managed by BP employees. The IP generated by the coorporate labs is owned by BP, and these labs have strict confidentiality and non-disclosure restrictions, whereas the academic labs have no such restrictions. In essence, the partnership allows BP to operate a commercial research lab on a university campus, giving BP researchers access to university resources without being required to share research discoveries with their counterparts in the academic labs. Commercial laboratories on university campuses are common in PPRPs (Washburn, 2010). Though the benefits to the private partner are clear, it is less obvious that university researchers benefit from these arrangements or whether commercial laboratories conducting confidential research on university campuses is in keeping with the academic charters of these institutions.

In summary, EBI's approach to technology transfer and IP is (President's Council of Advisors on Science and Technology, 2008a):

- Research collaborator inventions will be owned solely by the research collaborator whose employees or contractors are the inventors.
- BP inventions will be owned solely by BP and joint inventions will be jointly owned.
- BP will have a non-exclusive royalty-free license to IP generated from the academic research.
- BP has an option to negotiate for an exclusive license if desired.
- BP gets an initial review period of 30 days for publication delay policies. If there is patentable material, the delay can be extended by an additional 60 days.

In 2002, Stanford University formed the Global Climate and Energy Project (GCEP), a $225 million PPRP with four private firms (Exxon Mobil, GE, Schlumberger, and Toyota) to perform "fundamental research on technologies that will permit the development of global energy systems with significantly lower greenhouse gas emissions" (Global Climate & Energy Project, 2002). This partnership embraced the Kealey non-linear paradigm by directly funding fundamental research in renewable energy. Oversight of the partnership, through the Management Committee, was controlled entirely by the private partners, each of which had a voting representative on the four-person Committee, while the university partner only supplied a non-voting representative in a supervisory role to the Committee. Though the Committee was provided with external peer-reviews to guide decision making, the Committee had final say over the size of the partnership budget, which research projects will be funded, and selecting which discoveries will be licensed, effectively holding all control rights for budgets, research direction, and the licensing.

Though the private partners were given significant control rights in the GCEP, very few restrictions were placed on university researchers' ability to share information provided by the private parties. The private partners provided university researchers with data from the partner's applied research, which helped drive the university's fundamental research. Because there were four private partners, the confidentiality restrictions that are typically included in PPRPs were omitted since they would have hampered communication between researchers. Universities that are concerned about confidentiality restrictions on researchers should consider partnerships with multiple private partners. In these partnerships, each private partner benefits by sharing proprietary data without restrictions because the research teams will have unrestricted access to the other partner's data as well.

Another renewable energy PPRP with multiple private partners is the Center for Biorefining and Biofuels (C2B2), which was founded in 2007.

The C2B2 partnership differs from the GCEP by having multiple university partners as well as multiple private partners. The C2B2 is a partnership between three universities in Colorado (the University of Colorado, Boulder; Colorado State University; and the Colorado School of Mines), one government laboratory (the National Renewable Energy Laboratory), and 27 private partners.[5] The private partners committed $6 million to fund renewable energy research, while the State of Colorado provided $1.75 million in research funding. This partnership is unique in that the PPRP sponsors research in two distinct areas, "shared research" and "sponsored research." Shared research projects are conducted in fundamental fields driven by academic, not private, priorities. The sponsored research projects are focused on applied topics with a commercial orientation and are solicited by the private partners.

Research funding decisions in the shared research areas are made by both the industry and university partners. The Center Executive Board (CEB) manages the research funding process, and the CEB's decisions are controlled by members from each participating university. However, the private partners are given formal channels to evaluate funding proposals and to provide the CEB with recommendations regarding funding decisions. In the sponsored research areas, the private partners issue requests for proposals in specific research areas, evaluate the faculty research proposals, and respond with funding conditions and terms which faculty can choose to accept or not. The private partners are given broad authority over the sponsored research funding process.

Though partnership appears to split authority over funding decisions between the public partners (in shared research) and private partners (in sponsored research), in practice the private partners hold a majority of decision-making power in both the shared and sponsored research areas according to the evaluation presented in Washburn (2010). In both shared and sponsored research the private partners can set the research agenda according to their commerical priorities. Ultimately, the university researchers only have the power to accept or reject the funding terms offered for their individual proposals.

In 2007, Iowa State University began an eight-year, $22.5 million PPRP with ConocoPhillips, "dedicated to developing technologies that produce biorenewable fuels" (Iowa State University, 2007). The partnership was entirely funded by ConocoPhillips and the university did not commit any resources (Washburn, 2010). This PPRP does not have a formal governance structure or collective decision-making process, and all research funding decisions, as well as control rights, are granted to the private partner. ConocoPhillips would initiate the funding process by issuing a request for proposals in research areas of interest to the company, to which Iowa State faculty could respond. ConocoPhillips would evaluate the proposals and set funding levels without a formal mechanism for university comment or feedback. Even though the private partner is the sole funder of the partnership, the theory presented in this chapter shows that it is not efficient for the university to cede all decision-making authority and control rights. At a minimum, this arrangement disadvantages the partnership by removing university faculty and administrators with relevant scientific and management expertise from the decision-making process. A shared governance structure would be in the best interest of both partners.

The licensing concessions in the Iowa State University–ConocoPhillips PPRP appear somewhat less generous. ConocoPhillips is granted a 90 day royalty-free period to use any research discoveries before deciding whether to pursue a license, which would be granted following a non-public pre-negotiated licensing agreement (Washburn, 2010). ConocoPhillips is allowed a maximum of 90 days to review papers prior to publication, and university researchers working with proprietary data provided by ConocoPhillips cannot release the data for 10 years. University researchers are not placed under any other restrictions with respect to the funded research.

The partnership details of the PPRP contracts reviewed above are largely consistent with other major renewable energy partnerships. In a survey of ten major PPRPs between large energy companies and major US universities, Washburn (2010) found that nine out of ten partnerships ceded majority control over partnership governance to the private partner, and four partnerships gave complete control over governance to the private partner. In eight partnerships, the private partner was granted full control over research funding decisions and none of the partnerships required funding proposals to be evaluated via a peer-review process, the typical method for evaluating research proposals. In each case the private partners contributed the majority of partnership's funding and received the majority of control rights. These allocations are not necessarily optimal because the impurity of any impure goods that are generated varied by partnership. In some partnerships where much of the research was basic and openly shared, the impurity was small and the research was more similar to a public good, while in other partnerships where the research was strictly commercial and subject to tight confidentiality restrictions, the impurity was larger and the research was more similar to a private good. It is essential that PPRPs that produce an impure good take into account the degree of impurity along with the financial contributions of each partner when allocating control rights.

9.4   CONCLUSION

Though PPRPs have been efficiently structured to conduct both private and public good research, PPRPs that have been formed for impure good research, particularly in the renewable energy field, have not efficiently allocated decision-making authority or control rights. For example, a survey of PPRPs funded by energy companies found that the private partners were typically granted majority control of governance as well as a majority of the control rights (Washburn, 2010). This allocation of control is suboptimal where the research discoveries resemble public goods more than private goods, as is often the case with renewable energy discoveries.

As PPRPs become more common, it is important to use a conceptual framework that takes into account the type of good the partnership produces to guide contract structure and the governance of PPRPs. The theoretical framework presented in this chapter demonstrates that the assignment of control and property rights can play a major role in determining a PPRP's success. Whether in renewable energy research or infrastructure investment, the assignment of these rights should provide the partners incentives to effectively and efficiently manage the partnership. In particular, using our operational framework to assign control and property rights that align incentives will allow renewable energy PPRPs to achieve more long-run success.

NOTES

1. The authors make the standard assumption that raising $1 in taxes costs society $\lambda > 1$ dollars. An additional dollar invested by a private firm saves society $\lambda - 1 > 0$ dollars in taxes. But the firm must be compensated for their investment with at least an additional $1 in present value. Since this future revenue could have been used by the government to reduce distortions created by taxes, the opportunity cost of losing the future $1 in user fees is the shadow cost of public funds, λ.
2. PPPs in the natural resources typically have long-term project horizons (10–20 years). Since our concern is with PPPs that have completed all three stages of our framework, recently established PPPs are omitted.
3. The EBI Master Agreement (EBI, 2007) lists the following areas of research, "1) feedstock development (growing and harvesting plant material that can be used in biofuels), 2) biomass depolymerization (breaking down plant material for use in biofuels), 3) fossil fuel bioprocessing (converting heavy hydrocarbons to cleaner fuels), 4) carbon sequestration (removing or preventing increases in atmospheric carbon), 5) discovery and development support centers, 6) socio-economic systems (social and economic issues related to these new technologies), and 7) biofuels production."
4. The funding for the Helios complex was detailed in a press release by the UC Berkeley: "The total cost of the Helios building is estimated at $159 million. Of this, $70 million will come from state lease revenue bonds, $74 million from external financing in the form of UC bonds, and $15 million from private support. The bonds will be repaid partly by overhead from the BP grant, which amounts to one-third of all funds coming to UC

Berkeley, and partly by money paid by BP to rent proprietary space in the Helios building" (UC Berkeley News, 2007).
5. The number of private partners in this PPRP is not fixed and new partners have joined and others have left since 2007.

10. The structural setting: The stages of research and development

At the initiation of a research agreement, it is difficult to predict and plan for all events that will occur as the research moves forward. As emphasized in Chapters 8 and 9, by their very nature PPRP agreements are incomplete contracts that cannot account for all contingencies. What can be considered, however, are "control rights" or decision rights. These rights, or "options," determine how decisions will be made when contingencies arise. In other words, control rights represent an option to control a decision or action that will arise at a later date, when more information is available or other contingencies have occurred. In the context of research agreements, control rights specify the degree to which a partner retains control over the research process as it unfolds. These options are embedded within the agreement negotiated by the involved parties, and therefore should be considered ex ante, before committing to a particular contracting party.

In the economics literature, theoretical and empirical research on control rights embedded in contracts is limited. This literature is rooted in the work of Jensen and Meckling (1976) on incentives in corporate finance. They consider the decisions of a firm manager and an investor working on a project. The investor only cares about the value of the project while management cares about both the value of the project and the non-pecuniary benefits. They argue that the value of a firm or project is not fixed; it depends on the actions taken by management and management's consumption of nonpecuniary benefits. Jensen and Meckling use these concepts to analyze different incentive schemes and the tradeoff of various finance choices by management. In essence, they show that if management has control rights over both the value of the project and consumption of nonpecuniary benefits, there is an optimal debt–equity ratio that balances the risk involved with debt and the risk involved with forfeiting equity, or control over the firm, to the investor.

Similarly, Aghion and Bolton (1992) consider a project that yields a cash flow as well as private benefits. As with Jensen and Meckling, each partner in the project cares about different benefits: The investor in the project only cares about cash flow while the entrepreneur receiving the investor's funding is interested in maximizing both cash flow and private benefits, creating a conflict between the partners. In this context, control rights specify who makes decisions affecting the tradeoff between cash flow and private benefits. Aghion and Bolton argue that the partner that controls the decisions once the project is underway will then divert resources, or make other decisions, in order to serve his or her own interests. They argue that control rights should be assigned for particular events based on which partner will make the least inefficient decision at that point.

The structure of the interactions specified in the finance literature can be directly related to PPRPs. Jensen and Meckling's nonpecuniary benefits, and Aghion and Bolton's private benefits, are analogous to the nonmonetary benefits sought by public research partners such as the generation of public good research. It follows that the firm manager or entrepreneur represents the role of the public research partner while the investor, interested only in cash flow, can represent the private research partner who is focused on generating applied innovations that may lead to commercialization. Therefore, both of these works support the notion that control rights are a crucial issue in PPRPs. In fact, Hart (2001) points out that the Aghion–Bolton model, with its emphasis on the independence of control rights from cash flow rights as well as the association of these rights with future contingencies, is supported by empirical work (Kaplan & Stromberg, 2001).

The balance of these rights should be tied to the overall goals of the collective relationship. If generating innovations that can be commercialized along with supporting the local business community are the primary goals, relatively more control rights should be turned over to the private partner because the private partner is likely to make the least inefficient decision when facing unexpected research events (Aghion & Bolton, 1992). If, on the other hand, a nonmonetary goal, such as generating basic, public research is the primary goal, then the public partner should wield more control.

In further work focusing on the nature of the inputs offered by each partner, Aghion and Tirole (1994) analyze the organization of R&D activity using an incomplete contract framework. They find that the provider of research funding, or "customer" (i.e., investor), will have more control and ownership of resulting innovations, relative to the collaborating "research unit" (i.e., manager or entrepreneur), if his or her capital inputs are large relative to the intellectual inputs provided by the research unit. They also find that property rights associated with multiple innovations should be split on the basis of "comparative advantage in creating value." This work reflects a general finding from the literature on incomplete contracts: Control of property rights should be allocated to the parties in accordance with the relative potential impacts of their effort. Of course, the relative impact of financial versus intellectual inputs on research is challenging to determine and therefore difficult to sort out when private and public partners combine assets.

In an analysis of strategic R&D alliances between biotechnology firms and pharmaceutical corporations, Lerner and Merges (1998) consider how the stage of R&D, for example, how close the research is to commercialization, affects the allocation of control rights. They suggest that biotechnology firms have more experience with early-stage research and thus these firms should retain more control rights in the earlier stages of a project; that is, the party contributing relatively more intellectual capital to a research collaboration is likely to have a better bargaining position at earlier stages in the research process. Contrary to this hypothesis, Lerner and Merges do not find a consistent association between the research phase and the allocation of control rights. They find that when a technology is in its early stages (farther away from commercialization), more control rights are allocated to the partner providing financing.

The implications for university–private partnerships are clear. Universities must be savvy in leveraging their intellectual capital to achieve a favorable balance of control over the results of the research collaboration, especially when this research falls on the more fundamental (i.e., early-stage) side of the research spectrum. Public research partners must recognize the full potential value of their contribution to the partnership and negotiate agreements accordingly. Further, universities should be sure to define control rights over the research process ex ante rather than as innovations are generated and their bargaining power may erode.

A critical dimension of any PPRP is the assignment of control rights across the stage of the research. In terms of front-end decisions, or options, the relevant designation is whether the effort will involve more basic research or whether the research will be more applied, focusing on development rather than major discoveries. Of importance are the assets that the respective partners bring to the relationship and how the research agenda is selected under the contract (open call versus directed research). Regardless of whether public, private, or impure goods emerge from the research effort, during the first stage there should be a determination of how the benefits are distributed. The stages of research also come into play when considering whether the relationship is a first-time or renewed collaboration. Renewed relationships are more likely to involve continuing research that is farther from the initial discovery phase and, therefore, universities' bargaining power may be inherently reduced when negotiating a repeated collaboration agreement.

10.1   SETTING THE STRUCTURE

In setting the structural framework for forming and evaluating PPPs for research (or PPRPs), we use the theoretical literature and limited empirical research on PPPs as a guide. PPRPs come in many forms, ranging from large, multi-project, multi-year "strategic alliances" to single, targeted clinical trials. No matter what the exact form of a particular arrangement, these relationships can be characterized by a four-stage operational framework (Rausser & Ameden, 2003; Rausser & Stevens, 2009; Rausser et al. 2000). At the heart of this four-stage operational framework are the control rights that stem from the inherent contingencies in the research process and are embedded in any research agreement. The stages along with many of their key attributes are represented in Table 10.1.

The foundation for negotiating over these control rights is established in Stage 1 when partners engage in "pre-contract" preparations of self-assessment and partner selection. During Stage 2, the private and public partners negotiate an incomplete contract that assigns front-end control rights over decision making and back-end property rights (i.e., control rights) over the partnership assets and the research goods produced by the PPRP. Once these rights are assigned, the partners make investments. In Stage 3, the partners make management decisions through bargaining. This bargaining will lead either to the non-cooperative bargaining solution or to the cooperative bargaining solution that maximizes the joint benefit to both partners (see Chapter 7). In Stage 4, the partners respond to an unanticipated shock by either concluding their partnership or beginning the process again at Stage 2 by renegotiating the allocation of control rights and property rights. If the partners choose to renegotiate, the control rights will generally be redistributed.

Although the four stages are presented separately and successively, in reality they overlap. A public research partner may select an initial set of suitable partners, engage in preliminary negotiations, make a final selection, and then form a final agreement. And once research is underway, evaluation may occur throughout, at predetermined milestones. Moreover, one partner may be selected over another because of the probability of repeat relationships.

The exact order in which the different aspects of the partnership are negotiated is not of much consequence. It is vital, however, for the public partner to be deliberate early in the process when seemingly innocuous decisions ex ante may severely limit its control or flexibility at crucial junctures ex post. At each point in a research relationship, the public institution must consider the long-term consequences of all relationship-related decisions. Private firms often actively seek government contracts and make

Table 10.1   Research partnership structure

Partnership Attributes	Control Rights
Stage 1: Setting the Bargaining Space	
Public partner objectives	What are the binding policies of the
Partner selection process (many vs. single	respective institutions (i.e. what are they
offers)	willing to accept)?
Private partner objectives	What is the intersection?
Type and size of partners	Is there a Pareto frontier?
Type of relationship	
Proximity of private partner(s) to campus	
Primary location of research	
Repeat relationship	
Limitation on funding percentage	
Stage 2: Negotiating the Contract	
Front-End	
Complementary assets	Right to use proprietary data
	Background rights
Governance structure: Oversight committee	Control of governing committee
	Right to expand*
	Right to extend*
	Right to terminate (no cause)*
	Right to terminate projects*
Governance structure: Research focus	Right to define research range
	Right to choose research orientation
Back-End	
Public access to research discovery	Right to control publication delay
	Right to suppress* due to proprietary
	information
	No proprietary information
IP rights: Patents	Filing responsibility
	Ownership*
	Partial ownership*
	Control of patent litigation*
	Right to know-how transfer*
	Ownership of core technology
	Right to blocking patent*
IP rights: Licenses	Initial option (right-to-negotiate vs.
	right-of-first-refusal)
	Right to exclusive/non-exclusive license (right
	to blocking license)
	Percentage (access option)
	Third-party option
	Right to sub-license
Stages 3 and 4: Reviewing and Renewing the Agreement	
Reviewing partnership	Right to transparency
Renewing relationship	Implied right to renew

Note: * Dimensions included in Lerner and Merges (1998) analysis.

restricted partnership offers, leaving public institutions in a passive role. For example, a university's decision to enter negotiations with a single large company for a first round of research may find that the company's competitors are not interested in entering negotiations for the second round due to the perceived "closeness" of the first firm to the university.

The public institution can instead take proactive steps to seek out well-matched partners that complement their strengths. Moreover, by actively evaluating and approaching potential private partners, a public institution can form a consortium with a group of specialized partners rather than responding to offers from single partners. Although self-assessment and actively seeking out partners requires a higher initial investment of effort, it provides the public partner with the greatest degree of control over the selection of partners, and thus implicitly defines the degree of control over the remainder of the partnership process. In other words, a proactive approach can significantly broaden the public institution's choice set. Similarly, a proactive approach by the private firm can significantly increase its control in the negotiating process.

10.1.1   Stage 1: Setting the Bargaining Space

During Stage 1, the potential research collaborators lay the groundwork for the relationship. This process should begin with a self-assessment to identify the institution's primary objectives in seeking out research partnerships, its research strengths and assets, and the individuals or departments within the institution that would be likely to participate. Only with the self-assessment in hand can an institution effectively move forward and consider different partnership options.

The public research institution must decide how to identify and select potential partners. Personal contacts between university personnel and industry researchers as well as networking and viewing new research at professional meetings are important means for making university–industry connections (Thursby & Thursby, 2000). But who should take the lead in initiating a relationship? In the case of public–private relationships, often industry is the one to seek out academic expertise and make specific offers, leaving universities in the passive role of waiting to be approached and weighing each partnership opportunity separately. An alternative approach puts the university in a proactive role.

With a self-assessment in hand, the university can seek out well-matched potential partners that complement their strengths. A university should consider with whom to partner and the best mechanism for doing so given the associated tradeoffs concerning the private partners' objectives and assets, the type and size of the partner, the type of relationship, and the value of previous experience. For example, larger private institutions may have greater financial and scientific resources while smaller institutions may be more flexible. A university may prefer to collaborate with a national company and access its proprietary research tools. Alternatively, it may choose to focus on serving the local business community by partnering with a local startup. The nature and objectives of the partners will dictate certain collaborating mechanisms, perhaps a "strategic alliance" for a larger university and company with all research taking place on campus or alternatively a short-term, targeted research project between a medium-sized university and a small startup with research taking place both off and on campus.

These considerations are in line with the findings from the incomplete contracting theoretical literature (discussed in Chapters 8 and 9) that the partners should focus on the likely nature of any partnership output (i.e., the degree of public versus private output), the likely relative contribution of potential partners' assets, the relative valuation of output likely to be generated by a partnership, and the degree of control that is likely to be demanded or forfeited by a potential partner. Moreover, the pre-contract effort on the part of both partners will lay the foundation not only for developing the formal contract, but also for setting the stage for the relational contract. As discussed by Zheng et al. (2008) and Desrieux et al. (2013), the informal trust and information exchange environment of the relational contract act as a complement to a formal PPP contract. In cases where a PPP is likely to be repeated, the relational contract, and the informal control right allocation within, takes on even greater importance.

10.1.2 Stage 2: Negotiating the Contract

Once a partner has been selected, the public and private partners negotiate a contract that allocates a share of the front-end control rights and back-end property rights to each of the research partners. The front-end control rights specify the resources committed by both partners (i.e., investments) and designate control rights (decision-making power) over the partnership's investments and research processes. The "back-end" specifies the manner in which the results of the research relationship will be handled – how the results will be disseminated and how ownership of the innovations will be designated.

As discussed in the theoretical and empirical literature, the allocation of control and property rights implicitly assigns the risks associated with any partnership. These risks include planning risk, misspecification of output requirements risk, design risk, production (research) and time schedule risk, operation risk, demand risk, risk of changes in public needs, legislative/regulatory risk, financial risk, and residual risk (Iossa et al., 2007).

10.1.3   Negotiating Control of the "Front-end"

When both partners come to the table to negotiate a research agreement, they each bring resources they are willing to dedicate to the relationship. Each partner is interested in minimizing its share of inputs while making sure the combined resources will be sufficient for a successful joint effort. The respective contribution of each partner is an aspect of the agreement that generally receives significant scrutiny from outside observers of the relationship, as well as the potential partners themselves. In fact, each partner implicitly exercises control over the resources dedicated to the relationship through its choice of partnering method and partner. For example, if a public institution is approached by a firm and considers only this single offer, it has a very limited choice set and, in essence, is able to determine only its own commitment of resources. In contrast, if a university considers multiple offers from partners with varied assets, its choice set is obviously broader.

Given the diversity in the nature of partnership investments, it is difficult for partners to balance their respective asset contributions. These asset contributions can be tangible, such as equipment, buildings, or funding, or intangible "knowledge" assets (see Chapter 5). Unlike tangible assets, the value of intangible assets is difficult to determine and relies on many factors such as the nature of the asset and the degree of complementarity. As emphasized in Chapter 5, knowledge assets may be tacit (e.g., know-how) or codifiable. Tacit knowledge draws on skills and techniques and is transferred by demonstration, apprenticeships, personal instruction, and provision of expert services. Codifiable knowledge can be reduced to messages and is easily transferred.

Easily transferred codified knowledge is certainly true of patents, copyrights, and trade secrets. To be sure, exclusive control over a specified set of knowledge assets creates potential rents for its holders. A further, important distinction is between generic and specialized assets (Teece, 1986; Vonortas, 1991). Generic assets are useful for most research, such as basic scientific knowledge concerning biotechnology research. In contrast, specialized assets are suited to a narrow set of specific applications that can be more easily commercialized. In the area of agricultural research, these assets can be further characterized as input-trait (e.g., herbicide-resistant transgenic seed) or output-trait (e.g., high-nutrient content seeds).

All these aspects of research assets come into play when seeking complementarities among the different assets held by the public versus private research partners and when negotiating over the contributions each partner will make to the relationship. Private institutions are likely to hold such assets as funding; specific, state-of-the-art scientific research tools (e.g., expressed sequence tag (EST) sequences, enabling technologies) and associated tacit knowledge about how to work with these technologies; proprietary databases; and commercialization and marketing expertise. In return, public institutions offer scientific expertise, basic science, and leads on new research areas. The ultimate objective is to combine the different attributes of the partners' respective assets in the most productive combinations for the research partnership.

The investment of resources on the front end is fairly transparent while the implications of choosing governance structures for the partnership are not. The governance structure of a partnership assigns control on the front end and ownership at the back end, thus determining how the partners will interact, make decisions, resolve conflicts, and terminate the partnership if necessary.

For research partnerships, the governance structure specifies the composition of any oversight committee, how the research agenda is selected, and the scope of the agreement, which in turn determine the embedded optionality. The composition (i.e., university or industry majority) and operating rules for the oversight group determine the balance of control in the research partnership. The most important consequence of the governance structure is the selection of the research agenda and intellectual leads for the projects. The power to define the research agenda translates into the power to influence the research outcomes. In addition to identifying how the research proposals will be evaluated, the governance structure specifies how the agreement will be administered and if the scope will be changed (i.e., the agreement extended or terminated).

Under strategic alliances, specification of the research agenda usually involves two layers of control. First, the nature of the call for research proposals specified in the agreement defines the set of research options. Under an "open call," any research interest of involved faculty could be considered, giving the selection committee the largest choice set and offering a high level of optionality. In contrast, research proposals may be directed in response to requests for proposals targeted at specific research areas. These research areas could represent the interests of either partner or both. Of course the choice set for the public institution and its researchers becomes more restricted as the research agenda becomes more directed and as the interests of the private partner take priority in defining acceptable research projects. The second layer involves the structure of the body or committee that selects the projects to fund or determines the allocation of funding. This governing body may be a group (or individual) under the control of either the public or private partner, or may be evenly divided. The structure of this body may be specified in the contract along with the criteria that this group is to consider in making their choices.

Depending on the mission of the university and its role in the community, both of these alternative governance structures (public versus private control of the research agenda) have merits. If the research interests of the private partner carry more weight, the partnership may be more likely to generate innovations that result in commercial applications, meeting the objective of serving the community with successful technology transfers. On the other hand, greater control by the private partner may reduce resource commitment by the university. What is important is that the public institution makes conscious decisions about where it is comfortable on this spectrum of control over the research agenda and that they are fully aware of the implicit tradeoffs contained in the related contract language. Several researchers find that the flexibility of governance structures, presence of relational contracts, and even country-specific policy frameworks play a key role in PPRPs (Athias & Saussier, 2007; Zheng et al., 2008; Araujo & Sutherland, 2010; Desrieux et al., 2013).

10.1.4   Negotiating Control of the "Back-end"

If and when the research relationship generates discoveries, the back-end options in the agreement determine how this information is disseminated, the process for establishing ownership (patent rights), and how the innovation will be licensed. Each of these issues is crucial in determining how both the pecuniary and nonpecuniary benefits of the research are shared by the partners and by the general public.

10.1.5   Back-end Control Right: Information Dissemination

The primary interest of universities is to share their research results with colleagues as rapidly as possible, through publications and presentations at conferences, with the hope that scientific knowledge and research will be advanced. This academic mission conflicts with the interest of the private partner to appropriate innovation and technological advancements, thus requiring, for a certain amount of time, that research results are kept from competing interests until the private partner establishes rights to the innovation. As such, the publication delay provisions of research agreements usually come under considerable scrutiny. In fact, guidelines issued by the NIH (1999) recommend a delay of 30 to 60 days. A more relevant question concerns control of the option for terminating the delay period rather than the specified maximum length of this period. For example, the partnership contract could specify that the publication delay ends once the patent is filed. In this case, the partner that controls patent filing controls the publication delay.

10.1.6   Back-end Control Right: IP Rights and Patents

Important issues concerning patenting of innovations that are generated from the partnership include who is responsible for filing for the patents, the right not to file for a patent, control of patent litigation, the right to "know-how" transfer, and ownership of the core technology. Who holds the option to file a patent application is important not only because of control over the publication delay period but because the content of the application defines who is responsible for generating the innovation as well as the nature of the innovation. Both of these parameters can be defined broadly or more conservatively; this will have significant implications for who controls the licensing rights and how strong these rights turn out to be. As far as structuring the research agreement, this issue may be somewhat resolved. It is common practice for the university partner to be responsible for filing the patent applications but the degree to which the private partner provides guidance and is involved in patent litigation is varied.

A more subtle issue is whether a university is obligated to file for a patent if requested to do so by the industry partner or whether it has some discretion. A university partner may wish to avoid expending the effort required to patent innovations if it does not foresee that it will be applied commercially.

10.1.7   Back-end Control Right: Licensing

The nature of the licensing options is a key aspect of PPRPs. It is common for the industry partner to be given a first-to-negotiate licensing option for some subset of the innovations generated under the research agreement. Generally, these options must be exercised within a specified time period, or else the option is extended to third parties. In response to public outcry concerning previous, poorly structured agreements and concerns about blocking patents, right-of-first-refusal options evolved into right-to-negotiate options. In theory, if the industry partner is granted the more limited option of right-to-negotiate, a university has greater control over licensing rights and can prevent blocking licenses (when the private company simply acquires a license and shelves the invention to prevent competitors from accessing the IP) from being awarded.

Other aspects of licensing agreements receive less attention but are also critical. One critical element is the percentage of the total innovations for which the industry partner holds an option to negotiate an exclusive license, or access options. The industry partner may be limited to an "allowable percentage" of patents equal to the percentage of the research funding provided by the private partner. Following the NIH guidelines and many existing agreements, the industry partner holds this option for all patented discoveries generated by the private firm's financial funding. Third-party options are also a critical aspect of license options. These options are the rights that parties outside the agreement have to innovations generated by the agreement.

The economic literature on structuring back-end options has mushroomed over the course of the last decade or so. Modern economics has been used to evaluate moral hazard (Jensen & Thursby, 2001), which recognizes that university faculty may often turn out to prefer basic science research rather than applied research leading to commercial development. This, as the authors note, introduces a realistic moral hazard dimension that may be solved by a contract that includes both a fixed fee (a lump sum payment) and either a royalty rate per unit of output produced or an actual assignment of equity (a share of the licensee's profits) to the faculty inventor. In addition, Dechenaux et al. (2009) argue that the moral hazard problem can also be addressed with the use of milestone payments, where such payments are made when the licensee meets pre-specified milestones in the development process. Such a structure for the back-end options can also prevent possible adverse selection, such as blocking licenses. Adverse selection can also be avoided through up-front fixed fees.

There is also work by Macho-Stadler et al. (2007) that sets the structure for technology transfer offices (TTOs) to provide a service similar to certification. When licensees have incomplete information on the quality of inventions, a TTO can use its capacity to pool the innovations across research units, separating those discoveries that are potentially valuable from those that are not. Quite obviously, to the extent such offices have sufficient intellectual capital, they can also shelve some of the inventions, attempting to establish a credible reputation and thus raising the potential licensee's perceptions of expected quality. Such TTO certification can result in fewer, but more valuable, innovations being licensed. A related concept that arises in structuring the back-end options is the possibility of asymmetric information between the private firm as a licensee and the university as a licensor. As Jensen (2016) notes, "royalties can signal quality when the licensor has private information about the potential profitability of the invention (Gallini & Wright, 1990), when the licensee has private information (Beggs, 1992), or when both do (Macho-Stadler et al., 1996)." In active engagements of collaborative research between university researchers and private firm scientists, asymmetric information complications can be largely avoided through transparent and well-structured PPRPs.

10.1.8   Stage 3: Decision-making through Bargaining

In Stage 3, the partners jointly manage the partnership by making decisions based on a two-person, two-phase bargaining game (see Chapter 7). In the first phase, the partners decide what threats to invoke if no agreement is reached. These threat strategies, chosen to maximize their payoff while minimizing effort based on control right and property right assignments in Stage 2, determine the disagreement payoffs. These strategies may not be carried out and may not be explicit. All that is required is the potential of a threat.

Given the non-cooperative equilibrium determined endogenously, a Pareto move to a cooperative outcome is found given front-end control and back-end property rights that maximize partnership benefits. In this stage, the partners will achieve an efficient outcome in which the partners exercise their rights and share the benefits. The partner holding the relevant control right is aware of the non-controlling partner's influence and selects an action that maximizes the controlling partner's payoff given the non-controlling partner's threats (Rausser et al., 2008).

10.1.9   Stage 4: Responding to Shocks, Reviewing, and Renewing

In Stage 4 of the agreement, the partners respond to unanticipated shocks. Here a shock is an event that affects the partnership once it is underway for which there is no explicit contingency. The partners have two options in response to a shock: (a) they can conclude the partnership and exercise their back-end property rights over the assets and goods produced by the partnership, or (b) they can renegotiate the control rights and property rights designated in Stage 2. If the partners choose renegotiation, the balance of bargaining power may be different than during initial negotiations. A partner may find itself in a more vulnerable position or a stronger position depending on the nature of the shock and the outcome of the partnership to this point.

If terminal conditions of the partnership have been reached, the partners assess outcomes and consider whether to renew the agreement. Public institutions, lacking until recently any formal method for review of partnerships with private institutions, have developed a variety of evaluation policies. These methods rely mainly on anecdotal feedback to evaluate how the partnership proceeded. For example, universities seem to rely mainly on feedback from involved faculty, technology transfer officers, university administrators, and their private-partner counterparts to measure the merits of specific projects and to monitor unintended consequences. The informal review and general impression of both partners are coupled with evaluations of tangible outcomes, such as the number of patents generated by the research and success in meeting project deadlines, to generate an overall assessment of PPRP performance.

10.1.10   Renewing the Agreement

Much of the discussion here and elsewhere on research partnerships focuses on developing proper incentives for behavior covered within the scope of an individual agreement, but little consideration is given to incentives that fall outside a specific agreement. Because many of these agreements are up for renewal once completed, there are incentives for the university to make sure that the private partner is satisfied with the outcome of the research agreement, and given increasing financial pressures, this may affect behavior within a current agreement. In other words, these agreements are not necessarily one-shot games, but instead may be viewed as one round of a repeated game. As such there are incentives for the university to develop a certain reputation so that the private partner will support a renewed relationship.

This speaks to one of the primary concerns with these agreements – that universities will fail to look for funding from other sources, will become dependent on renewing these agreements, and will therefore lose their ability to walk away from negotiations (i.e., they will face diminished bargaining power). If recognized, these issues may be addressed by choosing partners with which there is a strong incentive alignment as well as through extra safeguards in the agreement.

10.2   KEY DIMENSIONS AND PPRP TEMPLATES

Regardless of the type of university–industry partnership, three characteristics or dimensions of these partnerships are key to understanding research partnerships: size, stage, and assignment of control rights. The size of a research partnership is indicated by such factors as the number of partners involved, the amount of financial resources and other assets exchanged and committed to the research relationship, and the length of period of the commitment. Universities may enter agreements with a single private company or, instead, with groups of firms sharing a common interest (industry consortia). Collaborations may cover a single research project or, alternatively, may involve "mega-agreements" that cover a large range of interactions. The amount of resources dedicated to an interaction can range from a one-time gift or small, independently sponsored project to partnerships involving a significant exchange of research funding, research technologies, facility space, equipment, or other assets. Research projects may have short or long time horizons. The stage of research defines a second key dimension: Partnership agreements fall on different segments of the continuum ranging from early-stage, basic research to late-stage, targeted research focused on the commercialization of innovations. A research partnership that involves activities spanning the full continuum from basic to targeted applied research might better capitalize on the complementarities and feedback loops inherent in the chaotic research paradigm (see Chapter 2).

The third dimension may be defined by the consistency between the assignment of control rights with the core values and culture of each research partner. For example, within a specific partnership agreement, the public partner's control rights may locate them somewhere on a continuum representing the tradeoff between academic freedom versus outreach/engaging with the business community to pursue commercial value as defined by the private partner. In fact, this dimension also reflects the tradeoff between basic research representing the long-run culture and core values of most research universities engaged in expanding the frontiers of basic knowledge, and the very focused, applied research traditionally valued by the private partner. This tradeoff has far different implications depending on which of the two paradigms of Chapter 2 is embraced.

Using these first two key dimensions, size and stage of research, five alternative templates exist for characterizing and evaluating PPRPs. The third key dimension of preserving core values in the assignment of any control rights can be used to evaluate partnerships within each particular template. These templates do not capture all types of interactions between industry and universities, but instead focus on characterizing those kinds of relationships that involve collaborative research. Other university–industry interactions, such as technology licensing, IP sharing,[1] and limited exchange of research material, facilitate research though not necessarily collaboration. The PPRP templates are briefly described here.

10.2.1 Template One: Small, Early-stage, Basic Research Partnerships

The basic research focus implies a high level of academic control and a low probability of finding an industry partner. This research is most likely carried out with a university or government lead and little to no private partner involvement.

Under template one, the PPRPs are small and singularly focused on basic research. In practice, industry partners are not likely to be interested in supporting this kind of research unless it is part of a larger, ongoing relationship.

10.2.2 Template Two: Small, Later-stage Research Partnerships as Seen in the Form of Certain Sponsored Research Partnerships and Spinoff and Commercialization Projects

The most common form of these smaller, later-stage partnerships is sponsored research project agreements. The relationship may be initiated by either partner. Research agendas are set at the outset and either the public or private partner may serve as the intellectual lead. Instead of defining a governance structure for selecting research directions, the partners propose a specific research project of certain duration and budget. Under this template, the optionality or control rights for the public partner on both the front-end and back-end can be very limited (especially when the research is overseen by a company researcher). Negotiations concerning these partnerships tend to be passive and policy-determined (e.g., according to university and government policy). Research agenda and scope are generally narrow and directed. Back-end options tend to be severely restricted but are generally still negotiable. Given the certainty involved in these partnerships, sponsored projects may act as testing grounds for interaction between a private partner and a specific industry partner, and therefore may serve as precursors of more far-reaching strategic partnerships.

In the case of startups, universities that have had difficulty finding existing companies interested in undertaking the risk associated with commercializing new research innovations have set up new companies or "spinoffs." The university usually grants the new company licensing rights to a university technology, and in return may take an equity stake in the company. Some universities have aggressively facilitated these arrangements.

Shane (2004) identifies three central problems with university spinoff activity: the lack of broad faculty support, the conflict of the commercial model with traditional university goals, and conflict of interest issues. Many faculty members at most universities do not support the creation of spinoffs. Moreover, Shane indicates that spinoffs exacerbate the conflict between academic departments, in particular between applied, commercially oriented departments like engineering, and less commercially oriented humanities and arts departments.

10.2.3   Template Three: Research Partnerships between a Single Private and Single Public Partner that Involve an Exchange of Significant Resources over Several Years and that Cover a Continuum from Early to Later Stages

This template is also frequently referred to as a strategic alliance. Strategic partnerships are comprehensive, multi-project, multi-year commitments of broad scope between a large company and, in some cases, a single university, or an academic department in a university, and, in other cases, multiple universities. On the front-end, both partners dedicate significant resources to the research agreement. Formal governance structures for determining research agendas and control of back-end assets are specified. Given their size, these agreements tend to come under significant scrutiny and often an ex post evaluation is required. In some instances, once an agreement is concluded, the commitment between the partners is renewed.

Sharp differences between strategic partnerships exist. At one end of the spectrum, a strategic partnership involves a university with academic freedom as its primary objective, selection of private partners on a competitive basis, a private partner that is not necessarily part of the local business community, a first-time relationship between the partners, university-controlled research, and an open call for research proposals. On the back-end, the university controls the termination of the publication delay and the patent application. And finally, the private partner has limited access to licenses; it has a right to first negotiation for only a percentage of the innovations and third parties cannot be excluded once a certain time period has elapsed.

A drastically different strategic partnership involves a repeated partnership between a university focused on serving its local business community and perhaps a local firm. Negotiations with the private partner occur exclusive of offers by other firms. The industry partner holds controlling membership on the oversight committee and a directed call for research proposals adheres to the research interests of the industry partner. On the back end, the industry partner controls the patent application process, is entitled to right-of-first-refusal on licensing options, and is allowed exclusive licenses on technology it does not intend to commercialize. In effect, the private partner or industry controls third-party access to the research (i.e., blocking patents).

This template has a wide spectrum of potential strategic partnerships, negotiations, and therefore control rights. Initially, all aspects of the partnership are on the table, and the university partner retains or relinquishes control of each part of the research process as specified by the contract. The final designation of these rights can be dramatically different.

Negotiating with many partners versus one can vastly widen a university's choice set and bargaining power. In a first-time relationship, a university is likely to have greater flexibility of options because each partner has limited information and the proposed research is likely to involve an earlier stage. On the front end, under an open, versus directed, call for proposals, and with a university-controlled oversight committee, the university holds the options for selecting projects and/or allocating funds. On the back end, if the university controls the patent filing process, it indirectly can set any publication delays, the definition of the patent boundaries, and access of third parties.

For a strategic alliance, the final stages of decision making through bargaining can allow control by both partners. With a single private and single public partner, threat strategies are much less complicated than if more than two partners are involved. Given that the private partner is providing more of the hard assets such as funding and is bound by the contract to do so, while the public partner is often providing more intangible assets like research capabilities with long payoff horizons, the private partner inherently has limited options for threats. How would a private partner call a university to task for not fulfilling research effort commitments? How can this effort be measured? Obviously, it is easier for a public partner to sustain a financial breach of contract by the private partner.

10.2.4   Template Four: Partnerships between Multiple Partners and Significant Resources that Cover a Range of Research from Early to Later Stages

These partnerships come in the form of research centers, open collaboration models, and research consortia. Template four reflects an increase in the number of partners and often an increase in the dedicated assets and length of the relationship over the strategic partnerships than in template three. These larger, more complex arrangements involve establishing research units and centers. The research is not generally conducted within existing academic departments. Instead, research units are set up separately, very often off campus, allowing more distance between the partnership and the academic community at the university. These partnerships can involve funding from a single company to set up a research center or may involve coordinating with multiple partners to establish research parks such as North Carolina State's Centennial Campus and Arizona State University's and Stanford University's Research Parks. The primary motivation of these partnerships is to focus on later-stage research efforts and technology transfer to serve the interests of a local community.

As with strategic partnerships, the bargaining space for this template is active. The industry partners may be small companies with targeted research goals or may involve large, life sciences firms. These interactions may range from tight to loose control rights, open to directed research, and true research collaboration to simple licensing or technology transfer arrangements. Unlike strategic partnerships, the off-campus nature of these agreements means that many aspects of the relationship may not be explicitly defined or revealed; asset flow and entry rights are non-transparent. The length and scope of the relationship is usually indeterminate and uncertain, as are the back-end options. Specific publication delay policies may govern dissemination of research results, or opportunities for the private partner to suppress publications may exist. Public access to the research innovations may also be limited.

A newer model of university–private firm or industry partnerships, open collaborative research, which teams a private partner with several universities to pursue a common interest, also falls under template four by virtue of involving more partners and, potentially, longer time periods. The components of such programs often include university research grants, "lablets" set up adjacent to the universities where, for example, Intel and university researchers work on open and collaborative research side-by-side, and proprietary research projects. These partnerships are governed by an Open Collaborative Research agreement that specifies principles of active collaboration on the front and back end by all parties and non-exclusive IP rights.

10.2.5   Template Five: Interactions between Industry and a University that Come in the Form of Informal Gifts

At almost all universities these interactions do not involve any formal contracting arrangements. The informal agreements under template five are often the initial mode of contact between university and industry partners. Through networking, industry scientists identify valuable counterparts (and vice versa) and set up simple arrangements involving low transaction costs. These agreements can either be transparent, public collaborations or, in most cases, more indirect, non-transparent, informal arrangements such as corporate gifts that are not necessarily tied to any specific research collaboration. These corporate gifts play an important and increasing role in university research, and may involve secrecy agreements along with implicit options to review research results and delay publications as well as ownership of research innovations. No formal contract is negotiated, control rights are uncertain, and opportunities for questionable interactions abound. In many cases, to address some of these issues, universities have gift policies, such as Harvard University's policy on gifts, which "carry no reciprocal obligations between donor and recipient" as distinguished from sponsored research under which "the business interests or mission of the source of external funds is most often related directly to the uses for which the funds are put by the recipient" (Harvard University, 2011). Though these policies are an attempt to address potential pitfalls from informal gifts, the undefined nature of these agreements necessarily makes them difficult to control and thus inherently risky.

10.3   TEMPLATE BARGAINING SPACE

The university contracting perspective for PPRPs and the bargaining space for the five templates are presented in Table 10.2. The bargaining space for templates one and two are passive; active engagement with a private partner is not possible. In the case of template one, a private partner is not likely to engage in a relationship that involves small early-stage research projects. In the case of template two, the private partner has most likely defined both the research agenda and the public access to research products. Only template three and template four offer a specified bargaining space with partners negotiating over a range of options on asset exchange, governance structures, and back-end information and IP access rights. The potential partnerships under these two active templates are the intended focus of the four-stage negotiating structure presented earlier in this chapter. In the next section, we present a case study comparing the bargaining space and contracting terms of two benchmark strategic alliance partnerships, Berkeley–Novartis and WU–Monsanto discussed earlier in Chapter 6.

10.4   CASE STUDY: BERKELEY–NOVARTIS VERSUS WU–MONSANTO

In the late 1990s, two landmark strategic partnerships, each between a major university and a large company, provided benchmarks for how PPRPs could be structured, what benefits could be generated, and what issues should be avoided. As presented in Chapter 6, one partnership, between UC Berkeley (Berkeley) and Novartis Agriculture Discovery Institute (Novartis), began in November 1998 and provided $25 million of research support over five years to voluntary participants from Berkeley's PMB. The other partnership, between Washington University (WU) and Monsanto, has spanned several decades and has involved multiple agreements and over $100 million in research support. One of the agreements

Table 10.2 *University contracting perspective*

Templates	Bargaining Space	Front-End Control Rights		Back-End Control Rights	
		Asset Flow & Entry Rights	Governance Structure/ Research Agenda	Public Access to Research Discovery	Public Access to IP
One: No Agreement	Passive	Transparent	Public Partner Determined	Complete Access	Complete Access
Two: Sponsored Project	Passive	Transparent	Private Partner Determined: Directed	Delay	Restricted to Severely Restricted
Three: Strategic Partnerships	Active	Transparent	Agreement Determined: Open to Directed	Delay	Unrestricted to Severely Restricted
Four: Research Unit	Active	Non-transparent	Uncertain: Open to Directed	Delay	Unrestricted to Severely Restricted
Five: Informal Agreement	Non-transparent	Non-transparent	Uncertain: Open to Informally Directed	Uncertain	Uncertain

under the WU–Monsanto partnership began in 2000 and provided $15 million in support to the Department of Biology over several years.

As explained in Chapter 6, the Berkeley–Novartis partnership was highly controversial from the beginning with widespread negative media attention in such articles as "The kept university" (Press & Washburn, 2000), "Berkeley dispute festers over biotech deal" (Dalton, 1999), and "Is the university–industrial complex out of control?" (Nature Editorial, 2001). The Washington University Medical School (WUMS)–Monsanto agreement was a continuation of a long-standing relationship between the two partners and did not generate any controversy or recorded public discourse. A 2001 report that provided an overview of university–industry collaboration profiled both partnerships (The University–Industry Research Collaborative Initiative, 2001). In a news conference about the release of the report, Hank McKinnell, then CEO of Pfizer and one of the authors, said the report detailed "the best of times and the worst of times" (Abate, 2001). The report gave the then 20-year WUMS–Monsanto partnership as an example of the best collaborations. At a news conference, McKinnell said that the Berkeley–Novartis deal represented the other extreme, presumably because of the media controversy that took place. Another hypothesis, however, could be advanced. In the case of WUMS–Monsanto, the private company, Monsanto, captured the essential control rights while in the case of the Berkeley–Novartis agreement, the critical control rights were held by the university research faculty. Moreover, at least in the case of plant biotechnology research, the Berkeley community has a far different perspective on GMO products than the St. Louis community.

10.4.1   Stage 1: Setting the Bargaining Space

At the initiation of a research partnership, the selection process for partners defines the range of possible outcomes. Either the public or private partner can take the lead in initiating an agreement. That lead partner, having defined its primary research assets and goals as well as the desired attributes of a partner, may then approach a single potential partner or may entertain a range of offers from several partners. For example, when Berkeley's academic unit, CNR, was considering whether to enter a research partnership, it solicited proposals from 16 plant biotechnology companies on a competitive bidding basis. From that group, an offer from Novartis provided the best fit based on the decision criteria set forth by CNR and approved by the university administration. Although deliberately seeking out partners, rather than waiting to be approached with a proposal, required more effort up front, it gave the university the greatest degree of control over the selection of research partners, which in turn implicitly defined the control the university had over all stages of the structuring process.

The WU–Monsanto partnership (with the WU Department of Biology rather than the Medical School) that began in 2000 represented another branch of the long-standing relationship between WU and Monsanto and, as such, represented a limited bargaining space. In contrast to the physical separation between Berkeley and Novartis, the WU–Monsanto agreement was forged between two major institutions in the same community. Monsanto's headquarters are located in St. Louis where WU resides. The major contributor to the establishment of the extraordinary Missouri Botanical Garden was, in fact, Monsanto. The director of the Botanical Garden for many years was Peter Raven, a member of the Department of Biology faculty at WU. Peter Raven was a former president of the American Association for the Advancement of Science and is widely regarded as one of the world's leading botanists. His intellectual leadership is largely responsible for transforming a typical botanical garden into perhaps the greatest botanical garden in the world. It has been reported that the Missouri Botanical Garden, located just a few miles from Monsanto's headquarters, owes "much of its explosive growth to the beneficence of the corporation" (Cockburn, 2015, p. 61). As a result, from the perspective of the community, the WU–Monsanto agreement naturally emerged.

10.4.2 Stage 2: Negotiating the Front- and Back-end

The governance structure, as determined by the composition of the committee administering the research partnership, is key to setting overall tone, process, and focus. Under the Berkeley–Novartis agreement, oversight of the program was conducted by a six-member advisory committee with three Berkeley members and three Novartis members. The Berkeley members did not include faculty from the department that was the focus of the agreement. Throughout the five-year PPRP, this committee was entirely advisory and had no control over the research agenda or the allocation of financial funds. The WU–Monsanto agreement also had a six-member Advisory Committee with three WU members and three Monsanto members. In contrast with Berkeley–Novartis, the WU–Monsanto Advisory Committee was under the direction of the chair of the academic department involved in the research agreement (Department of Biology) and the agreement did not specify how the remaining WU members were selected.

For PPRPs, the control of the research agenda often involves two steps. First, the call for research proposals can range from being open to any and all research proposals by faculty in broad research areas to asking for proposals targeted at specific research areas. As the request for research proposals becomes more limited in scope and perhaps skewed to the interests of the private partner, the choice set for the public institution will become more restricted. The second step is to select research proposals to fund. The structure of the committee given this task will further shape the research agenda.

For example, under the Berkeley–Novartis agreement, Berkeley retained control of an open research agenda and Novartis funds were unrestricted. Initially, an open call was put out to participating faculty[2] for research proposals, and neither Berkeley nor Novartis defined the types of project proposals to be considered. Further, the committee that allocated funding to each project (all proposed projects receive some amount of funding) was made up of three Berkeley faculty members from the participating department. In addition, the criteria used for ranking projects included the quality and intellectual merit of the proposed research, potential advancement of discovery, and the past and present productivity of the researcher. The economic interest of any proposed project to Novartis was not considered.

An alternative structure emerged from the WU–Monsanto agreement. The advisory committee solicited proposals that conformed to research areas specified by the committee. As previously noted, the committee was equally split with three university members and three representatives from Monsanto. Therefore, the interests of Monsanto had more weight, both in defining the choice set of research proposals that were considered by the committee and in selecting which of those proposals were funded. Further, the agreement specifically directed the committee to identify and fund projects that not only had exceptional academic merit, but also served the economic research interests of Monsanto. The WU–Monsanto agreement may have been more likely to generate patentable discoveries and may have had a greater economic effect on the local community. The Berkeley–Novartis agreement would structurally have more adequately protected academic interests.

Under PPRPs, the terms governing publication delay are a critical point of contention. While the university's academic mission is to share research findings rapidly and broadly, the private partner is interested in restricting access to research findings until IP rights are protected by filing for patents. As discussed, research agreements are often guided by specific recommendations concerning publication delay (recall that guidelines issued by the NIH (1999) recommend a delay of 30 to 60 days).

Rather than the specified maximum publication delay period, a more important aspect of information dissemination is the control of the option for terminating the delay period. For example, under the Berkeley–Novartis agreement, Novartis had an initial 30-day delay during which to decide whether an innovation had the potential to be patented. If Novartis decided that the parties should proceed with a patent application, publications could be delayed only up until the time the patent application was filed or 90 days, whichever time period was shorter. Moreover, Berkeley had the right to file the patent application at any time. According to the UC Berkeley Office of Technology Licensing, the filing process could be expedited, with an initial application filed in a day or so. Therefore, under this agreement, although the maximum publication delay was 120 days, Berkeley had complete control to end the delay (past the initial 30-day period). This publication delay provision did not delegate any content control to Novartis but instead allowed Berkeley to protect its IP rights and, if necessary, to remove proprietary information provided in confidence to Berkeley.

The WU–Monsanto agreement also specified an initial 30-day delay period during which Monsanto could determine if innovations were potentially patentable and, if so, invoke its publication delay right. The contract construed this period to be reasonable for patents to be filed and allowed this period to exceed 60 days with the approval of the advisory committee, of which Monsanto held three of six seats. Although implied, the contract did not specifically state that the publication delay period ended when the university filed for a patent. This particular structuring of publication delay rights, subject to the approval of an industry-dominated committee, gives the industry partner greater control rights and may create obstacles if the research partners have differing views as the research progresses.

Both private and public partners have an interest in defining IP rights over research outcomes, including who is responsible for filing for patents, who controls the right not to file for a patent, who controls patent litigation, who controls "know-how" transfer, and who owns the discoveries. The partner that holds the right to file a patent application controls not only the publication delay period, but also the content of the application. In PPRPs, it is common for the university partner to be responsible for filing the patent applications and for the private partner to provide guidance and become involved in patent litigation to varying degrees. Under both the Berkeley–Novartis and WU–Monsanto agreements, the university had the responsibility for filing and prosecuting a patent, but the company was responsible for incurring the associated legal costs.

With respect to blocking patents, an important issue is whether a university must file for a patent at the private partner's request. For example, under the Berkeley–Novartis agreement, Berkeley could elect not to file for a patent that Novartis did not intend to commercialize. In other words, Berkeley could make sure that innovations, or know-how, that would not otherwise be commercialized remained freely available to the public and that limited administrative resources were not diverted to pursue meaningless patents.

Of much importance for PPRPs is the nature of licensing options. Because of concerns about blocking patents, instead of right-of-first-refusal options, it is common for the industry partner to be given a first-to-negotiate licensing option for some subset of the innovations generated under the research partnership. Generally, these options must be exercised within a specified time period or else the option is extended to third parties.

Another key aspect of licensing agreements is the percentage of total innovations for which the industry partner holds an option to negotiate or a right-of-first-refusal for an exclusive license. For example, under the Berkeley–Novartis agreement, Novartis could exercise this option for an "allowable percentage" of patents, equal to the percentage of the total research funding that was sourced with Novartis. Under other agreements, the industry partner holds this option for all patented discoveries generated by the agreement (the percentage of which may exceed the percentage of research funding from the agreement). Novartis's first right of negotiation applied to all research conducted by faculty that had signed on to the agreement, except in the case of research funded privately or by the DOE. While Berkeley would have been expected to negotiate for fair terms, this provision allowed Novartis to cherry pick from the university department's innovations, not just those generated by Novartis funding.

Third-party options are also a critical aspect of license agreements. These options are the rights that parties outside the partnership have to innovations generated by the partnership. Under the Berkeley–Novartis partnership, third parties held open options on patents not included in the allowable percentage and on patented innovations either covered by non-exclusive license or for which Novartis's first-to-negotiate option had expired. Novartis had no recourse once its licensing option expired, and Berkeley was free to enter licensing negotiations with third parties. In contrast, under the WU–Monsanto agreement, third parties held a conditional option. Monsanto had right-of-first-refusal on any licensing arrangement between the university and third parties, even if Monsanto's original licensing option had expired. Thus Monsanto was guaranteed an option of first refusal on any third-party offers made for the WU portfolio. This severely limited the options available to third parties.

10.4.3   Stage 3 and 4: Bargaining, Shocks, Reviewing, and Renewing

Shocks to the partnership may come in different forms such as changes in markets for expected commercialized products, a change in the efficacy of a research input, or changes in primary research staffing. Again, the simplicity of two partners versus multiple partners means navigating negotiations in response to shocks and agreeing whether to conclude the partnership or renegotiate control and property rights is possible. As more partners are added to a research agreement, there is greater risk to successful renegotiation of control rights. At the termination of a strategic alliance, the partners assess outcomes and consider whether to renew. Each partner will use their own evaluation of the agreement to set their bargaining space for the next agreement. If the strategic alliance is one agreement in a long-term relationship between a university and an industry partner, the implicit assumption by both partners will be that the agreement will be renewed and the bargaining space is limited. If the partnership is stand-alone, both partners have a broader choice set (due to a more limited history with the particular partner) in terms of renewing the research agreement. In the case of Berkeley–Novartis, the university or the PMB would have been more than willing to extend the initial agreement beyond five years. However, Novartis had moved on by divesting the NADI research group, combining it with a newly created entity, Syngenta, permanently separating plant biotechnology and agricultural chemicals from its core pharmaceutical commercial operations and thus limiting its life science business largely to humans, not plants and microbials.

10.5 CONCLUSION

Evaluation of the outcomes of a strategic alliance is not straightforward. This type of research relationship, with its broad range of collaborative activities, cannot be captured by quantitative measures alone. The partners necessarily have to consider informal feedback from researchers and from the wider university and industry communities. These qualitative measures of partnership success have to be considered alongside such measures as number of patents, number of students supported, and number of publications.

All types of PPRPs involve either explicit or implicit contracts, or both. The degree to which each partner is able to thoughtfully identify and successfully negotiate the control rights embedded in these contractual relationships will determine the likelihood of partnership success. This chapter presents a practical setting for control right identification and negotiation in the form of a four-stage structure for negotiating PPRPs.

The first stage, setting the bargaining space for the partners, involves conducting a self-assessment and potential partner assessment to establish the broadest choice set for negotiation. The second stage, negotiating the contract, focuses the partners on front-end and back-end options and their implications for research and partnership outcomes. The third stage of decision making through bargaining defines how the partners negotiate once the partnership is underway. During the fourth and final stage, the partners respond to shocks, review partnership outcomes, and choose whether or not they will negotiate to renew the relationship. Throughout all four stages of the structure, the allocation of key control rights is a primary determinate of the success of the research and the relationship between the partners.

Two partnership characteristics, the size of a partnership and the stage of research, are used to allocate the primary types of PPRPs into five templates. Two of the five templates have an active bargaining space for the explicit contracts governing the relationship. Template three, a research partnership between a single private and single public partner that involves an exchange of significant resources over several years and that covers a continuum from early to later stages, is applied to two illustrative benchmark strategic alliances. The two benchmark alliances examined are the Berkeley–Novartis and WU–Monsanto research partnerships. Our case study of these two partnerships focuses on the private partner–university contracting perspective. Primary lessons include the importance of actively engaging potential partners, academic freedom and the allocation of control rights across the structure of the research agenda selection committee, the publication delay and option to end publication delay, and IP and licensing options.

NOTES

1. IP pooling involves consolidating a central portfolio of IP assets to facilitate exchange. Rather than actual IP holdings, IP clearinghouses involve consolidation of information (Graff & Zilberman, 2001). The goal of IP sharing is to reduce transaction costs and address the hold-up problem on the "back-end" of R&D by facilitating access to technologies. Essentially, these approaches are intended to serve as IP market-clearing mechanisms.
2. Each year, each faculty member decides whether he or she wishes to participate or not.

11. Lessons and recommendations

Contractual relationships between universities or other public sector entities and private firms to engage in creative research raise a series of critical questions. Does the profit-driven sponsor shift the university's or public sector's mission away from basic research? Does the industry's desire to exploit IP rights interfere with communication within and between universities to an extent harmful to open science and the pursuit of public good research? Quite naturally, conflicts are an inevitable consequence of the fundamental clash between public systems that encourage openness in science and private sector or industrial systems that focus on financial rewards based on secrecy. In the final analysis, this all boils down to one core question: Can a university or public sector partnership with industry or private firms be socially beneficial or, more precisely, Pareto improving? We demonstrated in Chapter 7 that a collective choice framework for the design and implementation of PPRPs, in the face of conflict between private self-interest versus the public interest, can lead to Pareto optimal cooperative outcomes.

Many lessons have been learned as public criticism and scrutiny of PPRPs has evolved (Press & Washburn, 2000). Issues such as conflict of academic and private firm interest, ownership of and access to IP (e.g., issues of hold-up and blocking patents), academic freedom, and publication delays have fueled the current debate and often present serious obstacles to designing and implementing well-functioning research partnerships (Lach & Schankerman, 2004).

Universities should be wary of ceding control through various terms and conditions of PPRPs. Both theoretical and empirical research has supported the notion that control rights are a crucial negotiation item in the design and implementation of public–private research agreements. Fundamental theoretical research has shown that these decision and/or control rights should be tied to valuation and thus to the overall purposes and goals of the PPRPs. Public partners must be savvy in leveraging their intellectual capital to achieve a favorable balance of control over the results of the research collaboration, especially when this research falls on the more fundamental or basic science end of the research spectrum. Public research partners must recognize the full potential of their contributions to the partnership and negotiate agreements accordingly. Moreover, public partners must define control rights over the research process ex ante rather than ex post, as innovations are generated and bargaining power erodes.

Another crucial lesson, despite the inherent conflicts between public and private interests, is that research partnerships can be structured that serve the mutual benefit of both parties. We have found that, to overcome the obstacles of conflicting objectives, the partners should create contracts that recognize the existence of conflict and clearly lay out a framework for resolving such conflicts. There will always be conflicts in the design and implementation of a research plan, and contracts must directly address such potential disputes.

There are certainly stakeholders who are not direct parties to a PPRP but are convinced that private firms or corporations make inherently unsuitable partners because of their secrecy and profit motives. However, the history of innovation in the United States clearly shows the obvious critical role that the potential for economic rewards and economic growth plays. There is no question that few important innovations could or would have been captured without the financial support of private industry backers. Such motivational incentives are a critical component of the established US patent property rights.

The differing perspectives of outside stakeholders that are not direct parties to the PPRPs must be thoughtfully considered. Every university or public sector research entity must carefully monitor and seek lessons from the results of research partnerships so that best practices can be sharpened for collaborations with the outside world. One lesson, of course, is that the mission of university administrators and faculty should be to foster diverse avenues of investigation, searching for potential points of integration. Along the way, there will inevitably be disagreement, but contention cannot be allowed to block innovation, risk taking, and academic independence, which constitute most universities' culture. If a minority of students and faculty are allowed to control the research agenda for a particular university, fewer outstanding professors will be hired, fewer of the best PhD research students will enroll, and ultimately the university will attract less public support. The public interest is best served when divergent approaches are required to compete on a level playing field of science in lieu of the contentious terrain of politics. Rather than yielding to the fears about PPRPs, research partnerships should ultimately be measured by their results and the lessons learned.

Research is inherently an uncertain process, regardless of whether the focus is on basic or applied investigations. Under such circumstances, PPRPs must be based on contractual commitments that directly address unanticipated events. There is no such thing as a complete contract (see

Chapters 8 and 9). The contract must anticipate a set of implementable actions to be taken when events occur that are unanticipated. Control rights must be clearly articulated, and the stages that any PPRP faces must be formally recognized both ex ante and ex post (see Chapter 10). Well-designed and implementable PPRPs will reflect a bargaining space (see Chapters 1 and 10). The articulation of these stages emerged directly from lessons that have been documented from prior experiences with PPRPs.

The potential benefits from university–industry partnerships have been well articulated. Complementarities between scientific and practical knowledge have the capacity to generate rapid and far-reaching innovation. It follows that each partner is seeking attributes and assets in prospective partners that complement their own abilities and resources. Industry is interested in combining its knowledge of markets with information on new research and innovation in order to identify those developments that are likely to lead to commercial applications (Aghion & Tirole, 1994; Aghion et al., 2005). This motivation may be obvious, but industry is also interested in more subtle assets such as access to academic expertise, networks, and first-hand information about up-and-coming scientists (current graduate students). And while universities are very clearly interested in financial capital, they are also seeking intellectual capital, cutting-edge research technologies, proprietary research tools (e.g., databases), and in many instances enabling IP (Blumenstyk, 2001; Heller & Eisenberg, 1998). Access to these research assets enhances a university's ability to provide first-rate education to its graduate students.

Although the potential benefits of research partnerships are reasonably transparent, the potential risks to both parties are opaque. These risks pose serious obstacles to the successful formation of PPRPs. In addition to the uncertainty inherent in any research process, the differences between university educational objectives and corporate goals are an important source of risk in these relationships (Slaughter & Leslie, 1997; Graff et al., 2002). Recent data show that almost 70 percent of research in universities has been categorized by the NSF as basic, while the proportion is reversed in industry. In 2000, while universities accounted for only 14 percent of total R&D funding in the United States, they performed about 50 percent of the total basic research (Scotchmer, 2004). With private financing comes the concern that the traditional orientation of the academic research agenda toward basic, public good research will be directed toward more applied, appropriable research that serves the objectives of the private partner, and that this, in turn, will result in a loss of academic integrity.

Not only research direction but research results from sponsored studies might be biased toward sponsors' interests. Bekelman et al. (2003), for instance, show that in biomedical research there is a statistically significant association between industry sponsorship and pro-industry conclusions. Industrial sponsors may also impose constraints on communication between grantees and other colleagues which, in turn, may hinder research progress and increase research costs (Scotchmer, 2004). Planning horizons tend to differ; university researchers focus on long-term research while companies often seek quicker payoff projects. In addition, the cultures and values of research partners may simply clash, creating insurmountable blocks to a continuing relationship. Furthermore, the incentives to secure a renewal or extension of an existing contractual agreement may adversely influence university scientist behavior under a current collaboration.

Rights to IP can be contentious (Kenney, 1988; Slaughter, 1988; Brooks, 1993). Hold-up and background rights are of primary concern to an industry partner interested in commercializing the products of a research partnership. Researchers at universities and other public institutions often use proprietary or enabling IP research tools in their research without obtaining rights. They are sometimes blocked, however, from using these tools for commercial purposes. Generally, one researcher in a university institution may freely access another researcher's patented research tool for academic study. This opportunity does not typically extend to private researchers unless a formal agreement is forged. Thus a private company looking to partner with a particular researcher, for example, may experience hold-up at the commercialization stage because the public research partner did not obtain formal rights to all research inputs (i.e., background rights) from some other private company. Note also that if numerous university researchers and graduate students are involved in a research project, industry risks loss of privacy and protection for proprietary information.

11.1 STRATEGIC AND TACTICAL CHOICES

In evaluating PPRPs with private firms, a university must first come to a clear articulation about its culture and comfort zone with respect to such collaborations. If a particular university embraces the first paradigm presented in Chapter 2, the linear decomposition paradigm, there will be less interest on the part of these universities in PPRPs. In fact their natural inclination is to simply respond to RFPs sourced from various governmental agencies, foundations, and research think tanks to pursue pure public good research. In contrast, for those universities that accept paradigm 2, the non-linear, chaotic, feedback paradigm, it is in their interest to pursue private sector involvement in their research activities. In fact, such universities might well embrace both paradigm 1 and paradigm 2, actively engaging in a portfolio that is based on both.

Given a university's selection of either paradigm 2 or a portfolio of both paradigms, the next relevant issue is whether to actively pursue a private partner to support its academic research. Typically, the university and its faculty wait passively until they receive RFPs from governmental agencies or private companies and then prepare responses to the other party's proposed terms and conditions. As a result, they must live with and never dictate the critical terms of the relationships. By contrast, if the public partner or university actively pursues a private partner through competitive interactions, a strategic advantage can be captured that in effect inverts the typical process and changes the entire bargaining process. For this active strategy, universities or public entities generate an RFP, allowing private companies with appropriate R&D interests to compete with one another, but guided and constrained by the university's principle and guidelines that have been established for such partnerships.

Such an active strategy requires an assessment of the faculty researchers' intellectual capital and whether, in a particular area of research inquiry, some subset of the faculty are on the frontiers of knowledge. If there are complementarities that can be identified which are related to access to proprietary data that is controlled by private firms, then such an active strategy may well serve the long-term interest of the university. If such unique intellectual capital on the part of the academic researchers does not exist or there is no complementarity with regard to proprietary data access controlled by private firms, then the natural default position is for the university to pursue a passive strategy. The passive strategy would simply involve responding to any private firm interest. Even a passive strategy may in fact result in significant discoveries that will ultimately benefit both partners to any PPRP. For the active and/or the passive strategy, a key issue that arises for many universities is their position with regard to competing for the very best PhD graduate students. If a university finds itself at a competitive disadvantage in recruiting such students, this too will provide additional incentives for pursuing research agreements with private firms to generate the funding to support the compensation for PhD graduate students.

Regardless of whether a university's culture dictates paradigm 1 or whether it allows for paradigm 2 and possibly some mixture of the two paradigms, negotiating the relevant terms and conditions of any PPRP contract must pay particular attention to all of the issues raised in Chapter 6. These include all of the terms and conditions in what we have characterized as the "front-end options" as well as the "back-end options." This will require a clear specification of the bargaining space (see Chapter 10) as well as the governance structure, including the assignment of control rights across the stages of the research process specified in Chapter 10. Given a partner selection, the collective negotiations and bargaining will be subject to the specific university guidelines (see Chapter 6 and the Appendix to this book). Such guidelines will only set boundaries, but within those boundaries key contract conditions and terms must be negotiated. These terms and conditions include determination of the research agenda, access to proprietary data or research tools provided by the private firm, the nature of any related confidentiality agreements, assurance of academic freedom, publication delays that are only sourced with the time delay on patent filing, and the time limits on the private partner exercising its back-end options to license any codified patents that emerge from the PPRP.

11.2   POTENTIAL INSTITUTIONAL FAILURES AND OBSTACLES

The fundamental issue in forming research partnerships is assessing the value of the suite of options that are defined ex ante, when the partners enter a contractual agreement, before the research takes place. Whether to accept certain contractual provisions is essentially an investment decision that takes place under uncertainty. In the case of research, not only are the probabilities of particular events difficult to determine (i.e., the chance of developing a commercializable innovation), but the stream of financial benefits, given that specific events occur, are uncertain. Although valuing control rights using expected royalty payments seems like an obvious and simple solution, these future payment streams are difficult to predict. Moreover, financial benefits are only one aspect of the full value of control rights. Flexibility options can generate nonfinancial benefits and serve nonpecuniary goals, but currently there is no accepted methodology valuing these flexibility options or control rights. In essence, there is no mechanism for securitization. Put and call options inherent in a research agreement, options to forfeit (sell) or obtain (buy) the benefits of the research, are ill-defined. In essence, there is no system for valuing the key aspects of the partnership, such as time to expiration for licensing options.

The non-existence of a mechanism for determining "real" option values for research means that there is currently no truly practical system for sharing IP. Under the various proposed IP pooling and clearinghouse regimes, it is not clear what control rights are forfeited by IP owners contributing to the pool. Further, how to attribute value when IP in the pool is accessed and utilized is left unspecified.

To solve the primary institutional failure in structuring public–private relationships – no viable securitization mechanism – we must move beyond the current potential solution (e.g., electronic, Internet-based exchanges) and develop a comprehensive system for monetizing the real value of control and flexibility options in R&D. A first step would be to set up an electronic exchange system institutionalized by an academic organization such as the Association of University Technology Managers (AUTM). With academic rather than private oversight, the interests of the academic community can be preserved. The exchanges could focus on facilitating access and alternative arrangements such as materials transfer agreements. For these systems to be effective, call rights for both IP used by university researchers and private use of university discoveries must be designed. And further, methods for quickly assessing the value of options for newly discovered IP must be developed. The most efficient approach, at least initially, is likely to involve constructing specific IP securitization portfolios pertaining to some well-defined area of innovation.

In their pursuit of collaborative research, universities must work with academic organizations, such as the AUTM, to develop and meet uniform standards of practice that successfully incorporate and synthesize relevant policies concerning all aspects of collaborative research agreements. In particular, smaller, inexperienced institutions must be especially mindful. Unfortunately, public scrutiny of public–private interactions tends to focus on larger institutions, leaving smaller universities at risk of entering unbalanced relationships.

References

Abate, T., 2001. Report emphasizes biotech's need for academic-corporate study / Authors discuss how to continue research, avoid ethical lapses. *SFGate.com*, 11 June.

Aghion, P., Bloom, N., Blundell, R., Griffith, R., & Howitt, P., 2005. Competition and innovation: An inverted-U relationship. *Quarterly Journal of Economics*, May, 120(2), 701–728.

Aghion, P., & Bolton, P., 1992. An incomplete contracts approach to financial contracing. *Review of Economic Studies*, 59(3), 473–494.

Aghion, P., Dewatripont, M., & Rey, P., 1994. Renegotiation design with unverifiable information. *Econometrica: Journal of the Econometric Society*, March, 62(2), 257–282.

Aghion, P., & Tirole, J., 1994. The management of innovation. *Quarterly Journal of Economics*, November, 109(4), 1185–1209.

Aghion, P., & Tirole, J., 1997. Formal and real authority in organizations. *Journal of Political Economy*, February, 105(1), 1–29.

Alonso-Conde, A., Brown, C., & Rojo-Suarez, J., 2007. Public private partnerships: Incentives, risk transfer and real options. *Review of Financial Economics*, 16(4), 335–349.

Alston, J. M., Wyatt, T. J., Pardey, P. G., Marra, M. C., & Chan-Kang, C., 2000. *A Meta-Analysis of Rates of Return to Agricultural R&D: Ex Pede Herculem?* Washington, DC: International Food Policy Research Institute.

Araujo, S., & Sutherland, D., 2010. *Public–Private Partnerships and Investment in Infrastructure.* Paris: Organisation for Economic Co-operation and Development (OECD).

Arora, A., Fosfuri, A., & Gambardella, A., 1998. *Licensing in the Chemical Industry.* Stanford, April.

Arora, A., & Gambardella, A., 1990. Complementarity and external linkages: The strategies of the large firms in biotechnology. *Journal of Industrial Economics*, 38, 361–379.

Arora, A., & Gambardella, A., 1994. Evaluating technological information and utilizing it: Scientific knowledge, technological capability, and external linkages in biotechnology. *Journal of Economic Behavior and Organization*, 24, 91–114.

Arrow, K. J., 1962. Economic welfare and the allocation of resources for invention. In: *The Rate and Direction of Inventive Activity: Economic and Social Factors*. Princeton, NJ: Princeton University Press, 609–626.

Arthur, B. W., 1988. Competing technologies: An overview. In: G. Dosi, C. Freeman, R. Nelson, G. Silverberg, & L. Soete, eds. *Technical Change and Economic Theory*. London: Francis Pinter, 590–607.

Arthur, B. W., 1996. Increasing returns and the new world of business. *Harvard Business Review*, July–August, 74, 100–109.

Athias, L., & Saussier, S., 2007. *Contractual Flexibility or Rigidity for Public Private Partnerships? Theory and Evidence from Infrastructure Concession Contracts*. chaire eppp: Discussion Paper Series, May 13.

Association of University Technology Managers, 2012. *The Bayh–Dole Act: It's Working*. [Online] Available at: https://www.autm.net/AUTMMain/media/Advocacy/Documents/BayhDoleTalkingPointsFINAL.pdf.

Association of University Technology Managers, 2014. *AUTM U.S. Licensing Activity Survey: FY2014*. [Online] Available at: https://www.autm.net/resources-surveys/research-reports-databases/licensing-surveys/fy-2014-licensing-survey/.

Association of University Technology Managers, 2015. *Tech Transfer Industry's Iconic Survey Reports Steady Growth*. [Online] Available at: https://www.autm.net/AUTMMain/media/Advocacy/2015-DC-News-Release-FNL.pdf.

Azoulay, P., Ding, W., & Stuart, T., 2006. *The Impact of Academic Patenting on the Rate, Quality, and Direction of (Public) Research*. NBER Working Paper 11917.

Beattie, B., 1991. Some almost ideal remedies for healing land grant universities. *American Journal of Agricultural Economics*, 73, 1307–1321.

Beaudry, C., & Kananian, R., 2013. Follow the (industry) money: The impact of science networks and industry-to-university contracts on academic patenting in nanotechnology and biotechnology. *Industry and Innovation*, 20, 241–260.

Beggs, A. W., 1992. The licensing of patents under asymmetric information. *International Journal of Industrial Organization*, 10, 171–191.

Bekelman, J. E., Li, Y., & Gross, C. P., 2003. Scope and impact of financial conflicts of interest in biomedical research: A systematic review. *Journal of the American Medical Association*, January, 289(4), 454–465.

Bennett, J., & Iossa, E., 2006a. Building and managing facilities for public services. *Journal of Public Economics*, 90(10), 2143–2160.

Bennett, J., & Iossa, E., 2006b. Delegation of contracting in the private provision of public services. *Review of Industrial Organization*, 29(1–2), 75–92.

Berdahl, R., 2004. Berdahl on the Novartis agreement. *The Berkeleyan*, 2 September.

Besley, T. J., & Ghatak, M., 2001. Government versus private ownership of public goods. *Quarterly Journal of Economics*, 116(4), 1343–1372.

Blanc-Brude, F., Goldsmith, H., & Valila, T., 2009. A comparison of construction contract prices for traditionally procured roads and public-private partnerships. *Review of Industrial Organization*, 35(1–2), 19–40.

Blume-Kohout, M., Kumar, K., Lau, C., & Sood, N., 2015. The effect of federal research funding on formation of university–firm biopharmaceutical alliances. *Journal of Technology Transfer*, 40(5), 850–876.

Blumenstyk, G., 2001. A villified corporate partnership produces little change (except better facilities). *Chronicle of Higher Education*, 22 June, 47(41), 024.

Blumenthal, D., Campbell, E. G., Anderson, M. S., Causino, N., & Louis, K. S., 1997. Withholding research results in academic life science: Evidence from a national survey of faculty. *Journal of the American Medical Association*, April, 277(15), 1224–1228.

Blumenthal, D., Campbell, E. G., Causino, N., & Louis, K. S., 1996. Participation of life-science faculty in research relationships with industry. *New England Journal of Medicine*, 335(23), 1734–1739.

Breschi, S., Lissoni, F., & Montobbio, F., 2007. The scientific productivity of academic inventors: New evidence from Italian data. *Economics of Innovation and Technology Management*, 16(2), 101–118.

Brooks, H., 1993. Research universities and the social contract for science. In: L. M. Branscomb, ed. *Empowering Technology: Implementing a U.S. Policy*. Cambridge, MA: MIT Press, 202–234.

Brown, C., 2005. Financing transport infrastructure: For whom the road tolls. *Australian Economic Review*, 38(4), 431–438.

Buchanan, B., & Chapela, D. I., 2002. Novartis revisited. *California Monthly*, February, 112(4).

Bush, V., 1945. *Science, the Endless Frontier: A Report to the President*. Washington, DC: Office of Scientific Research and Development.

Business-Higher Education Forum, 2001. *Working Together, Creating Knowledge: The University-Industry Research Collaboration Initiative*. Washington, DC: Council on Government Relations.

Cabral, S., & Saussier, S., 2007. Organizing prisons through public private partnerships: Evidence from Brazil, France and the United States. *Reflexive Governance in the Public Interest*.

Center on Budget and Policy Priorities, 2014. *States are Still Funding Higher Education below Pre-Recession Levels*. [Online] Available at: http://www.cbpp.org/research/states-are-still-funding-higher-education-below-pre-recession-levels.

Chong, E., Huet, F., Saussier, S., & Steiner, F., 2006. Public-private partnerships and prices: Evidence from water distribution in France. *Review of Industrial Organization*, 29(1–2), 149–169.

Christ, C. F., & Rausser, G. C., 1973. The validity and verification of complex systems models: Discussion. *American Journal of Agricultural Economics*, 55(2), 271–279.

Chung, A., 2015. Schools that sue: Why more universities file patent lawsuits. *Reuters*, 15 September.

Cockburn, A., 2015. Weed whackers: Monsanto, glyphosate, and the war on invasive species. *Harper's Magazine*, September, 331(1984), 57–63.

Cohen, W. M., & Levinthal, D. A., 1989. Innovation and learning: The two faces of R & D. *Economic Journal*, September, 569–596.

Crozie, R., 2013. Meet the man anointed to save Bell Labs. *itnews*, 3 December.

Cyert, R. M., & March, J. G., 1963. *A Behavioral Theory of the Firm*. 2nd ed. Englewood Cliffs, NJ: Wiley-Blackwell.

Dalton, R., 1999. Berkeley dispute festers over biotech deal. *Nature*, 6 May, 399(5).

David, P., 1997. Inside the knowledge factory: A survey of universities. *The Economist*, 345, 1–22. [Online] Available at: http://www.economist.com/node/600142.

David, P. A., Hall, B. H., & Toole, A. A., 2000. Is public R&D a complement or substitute for private R&D? A review of the economic evidence. *Research Policy*, 29(4), 497–529.

Debre, P., 1998. *Louis Pasteur*. Originally published by Flammarion, 1994 ed. Baltimore, MD: Johns Hopkins University Press.

Dechenaux, E., Thursby, M., & Thursby, J., 2009. Shirking, sharing risk and shelving: The role of university license contracts. *International Journal of Industrial Organization*, 27, 80–91.

Department of Agriculture, 2002. *2002 Census of Agriculture, Technical Report, AC-02-A-51, Volume 1, Part 51*. Washington, DC: US Department of Agriculture.

Deresiewicz, W., 2014. *Excellent Sheep: The Miseducation of the American Elite and the Way to a Meaningful Life*. New York: Free Press.

Deresiewicz, W., 2015. The neoliberal arts: How college sold its soul to the market. *Harper's Magazine*, September, 331(1984), 25–32.

Desrieux, C., Chong, E., & Saussier, S., 2013. Putting all one's eggs in one basket: Relational contracts and the management of local public services. *Journal of Economic Behavior and Organization*, 89, 167–186.

Dewatripont, M., & Maskin, E., 1995. Credit and efficiency in centralized and decentrilized economies. *Review of Economic Studies*, 62(4), 541–555.

Diamond, A. M., 1999. Does federal funding 'crowd in' private funding of science? *Contemporary Economic Policy*, 17(4), 423–431.

Energy Biosciences Institute, 2007. *Master Agreement between BP Technology Ventures Inc. and the Regents of the University of California*, November 9. [Online] Available at: http://www.energybiosciencesinsti tute.org/sites/default/files/EBI_Contract.pdf.

Engel, E., Fischer, R., & Galetovic, A., 1997. Highway franchising: Pitfalls and opportunities. *American Economic Review*, May, 87(2), 68–72.

Engel, E., Fischer, R., & Galetovic, A., 2007. *The Basic Public Finance of Public–Private Partnerships*. Center Discussion Paper No. 957. New Haven, CT: Economic Growth Center, Yale University and NBER.

Estache, A., Juan, E., & Trujillo, L., 2007. *Public–Private Partnerships in Transport*. Policy Research Working Paper 4436. World Bank.

Estache, A., Romero, M., & Strong, J., 2000. *The Long and Winding Path to Private Financing and Regulation of Toll Roads*. Policy Research Working Paper 2387. World Bank.

European Commission, 2008. *Communication from the Commission to the European Council, A European Economic Recovery Plan*. Brussels. [Online] Available at: http://ec.europa.eu/economy_finance/publications/ publication13504_en.pdf.

Fabrizio, K. R., & Di Minin, A., 2008. Commercializing the laboratory: Faulty patenting and the open science environment. *Research Policy*, 37(5), 914–931.

Fernald, J., & Wang, B., 2015. The recent rise and fall of rapid productivity growth. In: *Federal Reserve Bank of San Francisco Economic Letter*. February 9. [Online] Available at: http://www.frbsf.org/economic-research/publications/economic-letter/2015/february/economic-growth-information-technology-factor-productivity/.

Francesconi, M., & Muthoo, A., 2011. Control rights in complex partnerships. *Journal of the European Economic Association*, June, 9(3), 551–589.

Fuglie, K. O., Klotz, C., & Gill, M., 1996. Intellectual property rights encourage private investment in plant breeding. *Choices*, 11(1), 22–23.

Gallini, N. T., & Wright, B. D., 1990. Technology transfer under asymmetric information. *Rand Journal of Economics*, 21, 147–160.

Gardner, B. L., 2002. *American Agriculture in the Twentieth Century: How it Flourished and What it Cost*. Cambridge, MA: Harvard University Press.

Gausch, J. L., 2004. Granting and renegotiating infrastructure concessions: Doing it right. In: *WBI Development Studies*. Washington, DC: World Bank.

Geertz, C., 1973. *The Interpretation of Cultures: Selected Essays*. New York: Basic Books.

Gittelman, M., 2005. What makes research socially useful? Complementarities between in-house research and firm–university collaboration in biotechnology. *Revue d'Économie Industrielle*, 2, 57–73.

Glenna, L., Welsh, R., Ervin, D., Lacy, W., & Biscotti, D., 2011. Commercial science, scientists' values, and university biotechnology research agendas. *Research Policy*, 40, 957–968.

Global Climate & Energy Project, 2002. *Stanford University – The Global Climate & Energy Project*. [Online] Available at: http://gcep.stanford.edu/about/index-print.html.

Godin, B., & Gingras, Y., 2000. Impact of collaborative research on academic science. *Science and Public Policy*, 27(1), 65–73.

Goodhue, R. E., & Rausser, G. C., 1999. Value differentiation in agriculture: Driving forces and complementarities. In: G. Galizzi & L. Venturini, eds. *Vertical Relationships and Coordination in the Food System*. Heidelburg: Physica-Verlag, 93–112.

Graff, G. D., Bergman, K., Bennett, A., & Zilberman, D., 2006. Intellectual property clearinghouses as an institutional response to the privatization of innovation in agriculture. *ATDF Journal*, October, 3(3), 11–16.

Graff, G., Heiman, A., & Zilberman, D., 2002. University research and offices of technology transfer. *California Management Review*, 45(1), 88–115.

Graff, G., Rausser, G., & Small, A., 1999. *Agricultural Biotechnology's Complementary Intellectual Assets*. Working Paper. Department of Agricultural and Resource Economics, University of California, Berkeley.

Graff, G., & Zilberman, D., 2001. An intellectual propery clearinghouse for agricultural biotechnology. *Nature Biotechnology*, 1 December, 19(12), 1179–1180.

Green, J. R., & Scotchmer, S., 1995. On the division of profit in sequential innovation. *RAND Journal of Economics*, Spring, 26, 20–33.

Greenberg, D., 2007. *Science for Sale: The Perils, Rewards, and Delusions of Campus Capitalism*. Chicago, IL: University of Chicago Press.

Grossman, S. J., & Hart, O. D., 1986. The costs and benefits of ownership: A theory of vertical and lateral integration. *Journal of Political Economy*, 94(4), 691–719.

Guerzoni, M., Taylor, A., Audretsch, D., & Desai, S., 2014. A new industry creation and originality: Insight from the funding sources of university patents. *Research Policy*, 43, 1697–1706.

Gulbrandsen, M., & Smeby, J. C., 2005. Industry funding and university professors' research performance. *Research Policy*, 34(6), 932–950.

Hamilton, K., 2003. *Subfield and Level Classification of Journals.* CHI Report No. 2012-R. Cherry Hill, NJ: CHI Research Inc.

Hamm, S., 2009. Big blue's global lab. [Online] Available at: http://www.bloomberg.com/bw/magazine/content/09_36/b4145040683083.htm.

Harsanyi, J. C., 1956. Approaches to the bargaining problem before and after the theory of games: A critical discussion of Zeuthen's, Hicks', and Nash's theories. *Econometrica: Journal of the Econometric Society*, 24, 144–157.

Harsanyi, J. C., 1962a. Measurement of social power, opportunity costs, and the theory of two-person bargaining games. *Behavioral Science*, 7(1), 67–80.

Harsanyi, J. C., 1962b. Measurement of social power in n-person reciprocal power situations. *Behavioral Science*, 7(1), 81–91.

Harsanyi, J. C., 1963. A simplified bargaining model for the n-person cooperative game. *International Economic Review*, 4(2), 194–220.

Harsanyi, J. C., 1986. *Rational Behaviour and Bargaining Equilibrium in Games and Social Situations.* Cambridge: Cambridge University Press.

Hart, O., 1995. *Firms, Contracts, and Financial Structure.* Oxford: Oxford University Press.

Hart, O., 2001. Financial contracting. *Journal of Economic Literature*, 4 December, 39, 1070–1100.

Hart, O., 2003. Incomplete contracts and public ownership: Remarks, and an application to public–private partnerships. *Economic Journal*, 113(486), C69–C76.

Hart, O., Drago, R. W., Silanes, F. L., & Moore, J., 1997. A new bankruptcy procedure that uses mulitple auctions. *European Economic Review*, 41(3), 461–473.

Hart, O., & Moore, J., 1988. Incomplete contracts and renegotiation. *Econometrica: Journal of the Econometric Society*, 56, 755–786.

Hart, O., & Moore, J., 1990. Property rights and the nature of the firm. *Journal of Political Economy*, December, 98(6), 1119–1158.

Hart, O., & Moore, J., 1999. Foundations of incomplete contracts. *Review of Economic Studies*, 66(1), 115–138.

Harvard University, 2011. *Gift vs. Sponsored Research Policy.* [Online] Available at: http://osp.finance.harvard.edu/gift-vs-sponsored-research-policy.

Hausman, D. M., & McPherson, M. S., 1993. Taking ethics seriously: Economics and contemporary moral philosophy. *Journal of Economic Literature*, 671–731.

Hayashi, F., 2000. *Econometrics.* Princeton, NJ: Princeton University Press.

Heller, M. A., & Eisenberg, R. S., 1998. Can patents deter innovation? The anticommons in biomedical research. *Science*, May, 280(5364), 698–701.

Hertzfeld, H. R., Link, A. N., & Vonortas, N. S., 2006. Intellectual property protection mechanisms in research partnerships. *Research Policy*, 1 July, 35(6), 825–838.

Huffman, W., & Evenson, R., 1993. *Science for Agriculture*. Ames, IA: Iowa State University Press.

Humphreys, C., 1997. Review of Terence Kealy "The economic laws of scientific research." *European Review*, October, 5(04), 443–445.

Institute for Food and Agricultural Standards, 2004. *External Review of the Collaborative Research Agreement between Novartis Agricultural Discovery Institute, Inc. and The Regents of the University of California.* East Lansing, MI: Michigan State University.

Iossa, E., Spagnolo, G., & Vellez, M., 2007. *Best Practices on Contract Design in Public–Private Partnerships.* Working Paper. World Bank.

Iowa State University, 2007. ConocoPhillips establishes $22.5 million biofuels research program at Iowa State, April 10. News Service: Iowa State University. [Online] Available at: http://www.public.iastate.edu/~nscentral/news/2007/apr/biofuels.shtml.

Isis Innovation, 2003. *Revenue Sharing from Licensing.* [Online] Available at: http://isis-innovation.com/university-members/commercialising-technology/ip-patents-licenses/revenue-sharing-licensing/.

Jensen, M. C., & Meckling, W. H., 1976. Theory of the firm: Managerial behavior, agency costs and ownership structure. *Journal of Financial Economics*, October, 3(4), 305–360.

Jensen, R., 2016. University/industry linkages in the support of biotechnology discoveries. *Annual Revue of Resource Economics*, Forthcoming.

Jensen, R., & Thursby, M., 2001. Proofs and prototypes for sale: The licensing of university inventions. *American Economic Review*, 91(1), 240–259.

Johns Hopkins University, 2011. *Intellectual Property Policy.* [Online] Avaiable at: https://www.jhu.edu/assets/uploads/2014/09/intellectual_property_policy.pdf.

Jong, S., 2008. Academic organizations and new industrial fields: Berkeley and Stanford after the rise of biotechnology. *Resource Policy*, 37, 1267–1282.

Just, R. E., & Huffman, W. E., 2009. The economics of universities in a new age of funding options. *Research Policy*, 38(7), 1102–1116.

Just, R., & Rausser, G., 1993. The governance structure of agricultural science and agricultural economics: A call to arms. *American Journal of Agricultural Economics*, October, 75, 69–83.

Kabir, N., 2013. Tacit knowledge: Its codification and technological advancement. *Electronic Journal of Knowledge Management*, 11(3), 235–243.

Kalt, J. P., & Zupan, M. A., 1984. Capture and ideology in the economic theory of politics. *American Economic Review*, 279–300.

Kaplan, S., & Stromberg, P., 2001. Venture capitalists as principals: Contracting, screening, and monitoring. *American Economic Review*, 91(2), 426–430.

Katz, M. L., & Shapiro, C., 1985. Network externalities, competition, and compatibility. *American Economic Review*, June, 75, 424–440.

Kau, J. B., & Rubin, P. H., 1979. Self-interest, ideology, and logrolling in congressional voting. *Journal of Law and Economics*, October, 22(2), 365–384.

Kealey, T., 1996. *The Economic Laws of Scientific Research*. Basingstoke, UK: Palgrave Macmillan.

Kenney, M., 1988. *Biotechnology: The University–Industrial Complex*. New Haven, CT: Yale University Press.

Kerr, N., 1987. *The Legacy: A Centennial History of the State Agricultural Experiment Stations, 1887–1987*. Columbia: Missouri Agricultural Experiment Station, University of Missouri.

Kim, J., 2009. Where's Bell Labs? Its president responds. *BloombergBusiness*, 10 September.

Kuhn, T. S., 1962. *The Structure of Scientific Revolutions*. 1st ed. Chicago, IL: University of Chicago Press.

Lach, S., & Schankerman, M., 2004. Royalty sharing and technology licensing in universities. *Journal of the European Economic Association*, January, 2(2–3), 252–264.

Larsen, M. T., 2011. The implications of academic enterprise for public science: An overview of the empirical evidence. *Research Policy*, February, 40(1), 6–19.

Lerner, J., & Merges, R. P., 1998. The control of technology alliances: An empirical analysis of the biotechnology industry. *Journal of Industrial Economics*, 46(2), 125–156.

Lexchin, J., Bero, L. A., Djulbegovic, B., & Clard, O., 2003. Pharmaceutical industry sponsorship and research outcome and quality: Systematic review. *British Medical Journal*, 31 May, 326(7400), 1167.

Link, A. N., 2006. *Public/Private Partnerships: Innovation Strategies and Policy Alternatives*. New York: Springer Science and Business Media.

Link, A., & Scott, J., 2005. Opening the ivory tower's door: An analysis of the determinants of the formation of U.S. university spin-off companies. *Research Policy*, 34, 1106–1112.

Macho-Stadler, I., Martínez-Giralt, X., & Pérez-Castrillo, D., 1996. The role of information in licensing contract design. *Research Policy*, 25, 43–57.

Macho-Stadler, I., Pérez-Castrillo, D., & Veugelers, R., 2007. Licensing of university inventions: The role of a technology transfer office. *International Journal of Industrial Organization*, 25, 483–510.

Marco, A. C., & Rausser, G. C., 2008. The role of patent rights in mergers: Consolidation in plant biotechnology. *American Journal of Agricultural Economics*, 90(1), 133–151.

Marco, A. C., & Rausser, G. C., 2011. Complementarities and spillovers in mergers: An empirical investigation using patent data. *Economics of Innovation and New Technology*, 20(3), 207–231.

Milgrom, P., & Roberts, J., 1990. The economics of modern manufacturing: Technology, strategy, and organization. *American Economic Review*, June, 80, 511–528.

Mowery, D., 1983. The relationship between intrafirm and contractual forms of industrial research in American manufacturing, 1900–1940. *Explorations in Economic History*, October, 20, 351–374.

Nagel, J. H., 1968. Some questions about the concept of power. *Behavioral Science*, 13(2), 129–137.

National Defense Research Committee, 1941. *Report of the National Defense Research Committee for the First Year of Operation, June 1940–June 1941*. Washington, DC: National Archives.

National Economic Council, 2009. *A Strategy for American Innovation: Securing our Economic Growth and Prosperity*. [Online] Available at: https://www.whitehouse.gov/innovation/strategy.

National Institutes of Health, 1999. *Principles and Guidelines for Recipients of NIH Research Grants and Contracts on Obtaining and Disseminating Biomedical Research Resources: Final Notice*. [Online] Available at: http://www.gpo.gov/fdsys/pkg/FR-1999-12-23/pdf/99-33292.pdf.

National Science Foundation, 2007. *Survey of Research and Development Expenditures at Universities and Colleges*, Washington DC.

National Science Foundation, 2012. *Science and Engineering Indicators 2012*. [Online] Available at: http://www.nsf.gov/statistics/seind12/c8/c8s2o29.htm.

National Science Foundation, 2013. *National Patterns of R&D Resources: 2011–12 Data Update*. [Online] Available at: http://nsf.gov/statistics/nsf14304/pdf/nsf14304.pdf.

Nature Editorial, 2001. Is the university–industrial complex out of control? *Nature*, 11 January. 409(6817).

Nelson, R. R., 1997. "A science funding contrarian." Review of *The Economic Laws of Scientific Research*, by Terence Kealey. *Issues in Science and Technology*, Fall, 14(1).

Noma, E., 1986. *Subject Classification and Influence Weights for 3,000 Journals*. Cherry Hill, NJ: CHI Research/Computer Horizons Inc.

North, D. C., 1981. *Structure and Change in Economic History*. New York: W. W. Norton.

Olson, M., 1965. *The Logic of Collective Action*. Cambridge, MA: Harvard University Press.

Owen-Smith, J., & Powell, W. W., 2003. The expanding role of university patenting in the life sciences: Assessing the importance of experience and connectivity. *Research Policy*, 32, 1695–1711.

Owen-Smith, J., & Powell, W. W., 2006. Accounting for emergence and novelty in Boston and Bay Area biotechnology. In: P. Braunerhjelm & M. Feldman, eds., *Cluster Genesis: The Emergence of Technology Clusters and Their Implications for Government Policies*. Oxford: Oxford University Press, 61–86.

Polanyi, M., 1958. *Personal Knowledge: Towards a Post-Critical Philosophy*. Chicago, IL: University of Chicago Press.

President's Council of Advisors on Science and Technology, 2008a. *Priorities for Personalized Medicine*. [Online] Available at: https://www.whitehouse.gov/files/documents/ostp/PCAST/pcast_report_v2.pdf.

President's Council of Advisors on Science and Technology, 2008b. *University–Private Sector Research Partnerships in the Innovation Ecosystem*. [Online] Available at: https://www.whitehouse.gov/files/documents/ostp/PCAST/past_research_partnership_report_BOOK.pdf.

President's Council of Advisors on Science and Technology, 2012. *Report to the President on Agricultural Preparedness and the Agriculture Research Enterprise*. [Online] Available at: https://www.whitehouse.gov/sites/default/files/microsites/ostp/pcast_agriculture_20121207.pdf.

Press, E., & Washburn, J., 2000. The kept university. *Atlantic Monthly*, March, 285(3).

Price, R. M., & Goldman, L., 2002. *The Novartis Agreement: An Appraisal, Administrative Review*. [Online] Available at: http://www.berkeley.edu/news/media/releases/2004/07/admin_novartis_review.pdf.

Ramamurti, R., 1997. Testing the limits of privatization: Argentine railroads. *World Development*, November, 25(12), 1983–1993.

Ranga, L. M., Debackere, K., & von Tunzelmann, N., 2003. Entrepreneurial universities and the dynamics of academic knowledge production: A case study of basic vs. applied research in Belgium. *Scientometrics*, 58(2), 301–320.

Rasmussen, W., 1989. *Taking the University to the People: Seventy-five Years of Cooperative Extension*. Ames, IA: Iowa State University Press.

Rausser, G. C., 1974. Technological change, production and investment in natural resource industries. *American Economic Review*, December, 64, 1049–1059.

Rausser, G., & Ameden, H., 2003. *Structuring Public–Private Research Agreements: The Critical Role of Control Premiums*. Draft Working Paper. Berkeley, CA: Center for Studies in Higher Education, UC Berkeley.

Rausser, G. C., & Lapan, H. E., 1979. Natural resources: Goods, bads and alternative institutional frameworks. *Resources and Energy*, December, 2(4), 293–324.

Rausser, G. C., Scotchmer, S., & Simon, L. K., 1999. *Intellectual Property and Market Structure in Agriculture*. Department of Agricultural and Resource Economics, University of California, Berkeley.

Rausser, G., Simon, L., & Ameden, H., 2000. Public-private alliances in biotechnology: Can they narrow the knowledge gaps between rich and poor?. *Food Policy*, 25, 499–513.

Rausser, G., Simon, L., & Stevens, R., 2008. Public vs. private good research at land-grant universities. *Journal of Agricultural and Food Industrial Organization*, 6(2).

Rausser, G. C., & Small, A. A., 2000. Valuing research leads: Bioprospecting and conservation of genetic resources. *Journal of Political Economy*, February, 108(1), 173–206.

Rausser, G. C., & Stevens, R., 2009. Public–private partnerships: Goods and the structure of contracts. *Annual Review of Resource Economics*, 1(1), 75–98.

Rausser, G. C., Swinnen, J., & Zusman, P., 2011. *Political Power and Economic Policy: Theory, Analysis, and Empirical Applications*. Cambridge: Cambridge University Press.

Rausser, G. C., Willis, C., & Frick, P., 1972. Learning, external benefits and subsidies in water desalinization. *Water Resources Research*, December, 8(6), 1385–1400.

Robinson, D., & Medlock, N., 2005. Diamond v. Chakrabarty: A retrospective on 25 years of biotech patents. *Intellectual Property and Technology Law Journal*, 17(10), 12–15.

Rosenberg, N., 1990. Why do firms do basic research (with their own money)? *Research Policy*, April, 19(2), 165–174.

Ruttan, V. W., 1982. *Agricultural Research Policy*. Minneapolis, MN: University of Minnesota Press.

Ruttan, V. W., 2006. *Is War Necessary for Economic Growth?: Military Procurement and Technology Development*. New York: Oxford University Press.

Sadka, E., 2006. *Public–Private Partnerships: A Public Economics Perspective*. IMF Working Paper No. 06/77. International Monetary Fund.

Schacht, W., 2009. *The Bayh–Dole Act: Selected Issues in Patent Policy and the Commercialization of Technology*. Library of Congress, Washington, DC: Congressional Research Service.

Scotchmer, S., 2004. *Innovation and Incentives*. Cambridge, MA: MIT Press.

Shane, S., 2004. *Academic Entrepreneurship: University Spinoffs and Wealth Creation*. Cheltenham, UK and Northampton, MA: Edward Elgar.

Sheridan, C., 2007. Big oil's biomass play. *Nature Biotechnology*, November, 25(11), 1201–1203.

Slaughter, S., 1988. Academic freedom and the state: Reflections on the uses of knowledge. *Journal of Higher Education*, April, 59(3), 241–262.

Slaughter, S., & Leslie, L. L., 1997. *Academic Capitalism: Politics, Policies, and the Entrepreneurial University*. 1st ed. Baltimore, MD: Johns Hopkins University Press.

Spielman, D. J., Hartwich, F., & von Grebmer, K., 2007. *Sharing Science, Building Bridges, and Enhancing Impact*. Discussion Paper No. 00708. Washington, DC: International Food Policy Research Institute, CGIAR.

Stevens, A. J., 2004. The enactment of Bayh–Dole. *Journal of Technology Transfer*, 29, 93–99. [Online] Available at: http://www.bu.edu/otd/files/2011/02/The-Enactment-of-Bayh-Dole.pdf.

Stuart, T., Ozdemir, S., & Ding, W., 2007. Vertical alliance networks: The case of university–biotechnology–pharmaceutical alliance chains. *Research Policy*, 36, 477–498.

Subramanian, A., Lim, K., & Soh, P., 2013. When birds of a feather don't flock together: Different scientists and the roles they play in biotech R&D alliances. *Research Policy*, 42, 595–612.

Sugden, R., 1986. New developments in the theory of choice under uncertainty. *Bulletin of Economic Research*, 38(1), 1–24.

Teece, D. J., 1986. Profiting from technological innovation: Implications for integration, collaboration, licensing and public policy. *Research Policy*, December, 15(6), 285–305.

Thursby, J. G., Jensen, R., & Thursby, M. C., 2001. Objectives, characteristics and outcomes of university licensing: A survey of major US universities. *Journal of Technology Transfer*, 1 January, 26(1–2), 59–72.

Thursby, J. G., & Thursby, M. C., 2000. Interstate cigarette bootlegging: Extent, revenue, losses, and effects of federal intervention. *National Tax Journal*, 53(1), 59–77.

Thursby, J. G., & Thursby, M., 2011a. University–industry linkages in nanotechnology and biotechnology: Evidence on collaborative patterns for new methods of inventing. *Journal of Technology Transfer*, 36(6), 605–623.

Thursby, J. G., & Thursby, M., 2011b. Has the Bayh–Dole Act compromised basic research? *Research Policy*, 40(8), 1077–1083.

Thursby, M., Thursby, J., & Gupta-Mukherjee, S., 2007. Are there real effects of licensing on academic research? A life cycle view. *Journal of Economic Behavior and Organization*, 63(4), 577–598.

Tijssen, R. J. W., 2010. *Discarding the 'Basic Science/Applied Science' Dichotomy: A Knowledge Utilization Triangle Classification System of Research Journals*. CWTS Working Paper No. CWTS-WP-2010-002. Leiden, The Netherlands: Centre for Science and Technology Studies (CWTS), March 2.

Tirole, J., 1999. Incomplete contracts: Where do we stand? *Econometrica: Journal of the Econometric Society*, 67(4), 741–781.

Tsoukas, H., 2003. Do we really understand tacit knowledge? In: M. Easterby-Smith & M. A. Lyles, eds. *The Blackwell Handbook of Organizational Learning and Knowledge Management*. Malden, MA: Blackwell Publishing, 410–426.

University of California, 2014. *Ideas, Inventions, Impact: Technology Commercialization Report*. [Online] Available at: http://oip.ucla.edu/sites/default/files/IAS_Rpt_FY2014.pdf.

University of California, Berkeley, Academic Senate, Committee on Educational Policy, 1998. Available at: http://nature.berkeley.edu/srr/Alliance/past/survey.htm.

University of California, Berkeley News, 2007. *Energy Biosciences Institute: Frequently asked questions*, UC Berkeley News, November 14. [Online] Available at: http://www.berkeley.edu/news/media/releases/2007/11/14_ebi-faq.shtml.

University of Washington, 2015. *APS 59.4, Technology Transfer*. [Online] Available at: http://www.washington.edu/admin/rules/policies/APS/59.04.html.

US Diamond v. Chakrabarty, 1980. 447 U.S. 303.

Van Looy, B., Callaert, J., & Debackere, K., 2006. Publication and patent behavior of academic researchers: Conflicting, reinforcing or merely co-existing? *Research Policy*, 35(4), 596–608.

Van Looy, B., Ranga, M., Callaert, J., Debackere, K., & Zimmerman, E., 2004. Combining entrepreneurial and scientific performance in academica: Towards a compounded and reciprocal Matthew-effect? *Research Policy*, 33(3), 425–441.

Varian, H., 1992. *Microeconomic Analysis*, 3rd ed. New York: W. W. Norton.

Vonortas, N. S., 1991. *Cooperative Research in R&D-Intensive Industries*. Aldershot, UK: Avebury.

Wang, C., 2007. *Public Investment Policy and Industry Incentives in Life Science Research*. PhD Thesis. Oregon State University.

Washburn, J., 2005. *University, Inc: The Corporate Corruption of Higher Education*. Cambridge, MA: Basic Books.

Washburn, J., 2010. *Big Oil Goes to College: An Analysis of 10 research collboration contracts between leading energy companies and major U.S. universities*. Washington: Center for American Progress. [Online] Available at: https://www.americanprogress.org/wp-content/uploads/issues/2010/10/pdf/big_oil_lf.pdf

Washington Post, 2015. Apple is learning an expensive lesson about universities. *SFGate*, 15 October.

Williamson, O. E., 1993. Calculativeness, trust, and economic organization. *Journal of Law and Economics*, April, 36(1) Part 2, 453–486.

World Bank Latin American and Caribbean Studies, 1997. *Dealing with Public Risk in Private Infrastructure*. (T. Irwin, M. Klein, G. E. Perry, & M. Thobani, eds.) Washington, DC: World Bank.

Wuchty, S., Jones, B. F., & Uzzi, B., 2007. The increasing dominance of teams in production of knowledge. *Science*, 316(5827), 1036–1039.

Zheng, J., Roehrich, J. K., & Lewis, M. A., 2008. The dynamics of contractual and relational governance: Evidence from long-term public–private procurement arrangements. *Journal of Purchasing and Supply Management*, 14(1), 43–54.

Zucker, L. G., & Darby, M. R., 1996. Star scientists and institutional transformation: Patterns of invention and innovation in the formation of the biotechnology industry. *Proceedings of the National Academy of Sciences of the United States of America*, 93(23), 12709–12716.

Zucker, L. G., Darby, M. R., & Brewer, M. B., 1998. Intellectual human capital and the birth of U.S. biotechnology enterprises. *American Economic Review*, March, 88(1), 290–306.

Zusman, P., 1993. Participants' ethical attitudes and organizational structure and performance: Application to the cooperative enterprise. In: C. Csaki & Y. Kislev, eds., *Agricultural Cooperatives in Transition*. Boulder, CO: Westview Press, 23–54.

Appendix: University and government guidelines

GUIDELINES: CORNELL UNIVERSITY

APPLIED SPONSORED RESEARCH AGREEMENT
CORNELL UNIVERSITY
OFFICE OF SPONSORED PROGRAMS

THIS AGREEMENT is entered into by and between (_____ a corporation having powers under the laws of the _____ (hereinafter referred to as "Sponsor") and Cornell University, a non-profit, tax-exempt, educational institution having corporate powers under the laws of the State of New York (hereinafter referred to as "University").

WITNESSETH:

WHEREAS, the effort contemplated by this Agreement is applied research, which applies the findings of prior research, towards their development into new products, services, processes, or methods; and

WHEREAS, such applied research is of mutual interest and benefit to University and to Sponsor, each a "Party" and collectively "Parties", and will further instructional and/or research objectives of University in a manner consistent with its status as a non-profit, tax-exempt, educational institution;

NOW THEREFORE, in consideration of the premises and mutual covenants herein contained, the Parties hereto agree to the following:

1. Definitions.

    1.1. "Project" shall mean the work funded under this Agreement as described in Exhibit A, which is made a part of this Agreement hereof.

1.2. "Intellectual Property" shall mean patent rights, copyrights and all other rights resulting from intellectual activity in the industrial, scientific, literary or artistic fields, and shall include the rights relating to (a) literary, artistic and scientific works; (b) inventions in all fields of human endeavor; (c) scientific discoveries; and (d) industrial designs.

1.3. "Sponsor Intellectual Property" shall mean Intellectual Property created, invented or discovered solely by one or more employees of Sponsor without the use of University resources.

1.4. "University Intellectual Property" shall mean Intellectual Property created, invented or discovered solely by one or more employees of University.

1.5. "Project Intellectual Property" shall mean Intellectual Property created during the Period of Performance and within the scope of the Project.

  1.5.1. "Sponsor Project Intellectual Property" shall mean Project Intellectual Property created, invented or discovered solely by one or more employees of Sponsor without the use of University resources.

  1.5.2. "University Project Intellectual Property" shall mean Project Intellectual Property created, invented or discovered solely by one or more employees of University.

  1.5.3. "Jointly Owned Project Intellectual Property" shall mean Project Intellectual Property created, invented or discovered jointly by one or more employees of University and Sponsor or by one or more employees of Sponsor with the use of University resources.

1.6. "Created" shall have the meaning attributed to it under 17 USC § 101, Copyrights. "Invented" and "discovered" shall have the meaning attributed to them under 35 USC Chapter 10 – Patentability of Inventions.

1.7. "Background Intellectual Property" shall mean Intellectual Property documented herein in Exhibit C ("Background Intellectual Property") that is deemed to be relevant to the Project and has 1) been developed by a Party, or 2) is in existence prior to the initiation of the Project, or 3) is developed by a Party during the Period of Performance of the Project but outside of the Project.

1.8. "Confidential Information" means confidential, scientific, business or financial information that is marked or designated in writing as "Confidential", or if disclosed orally, is identified as confidential at the time of disclosure and confirmed in written summary form within (30)

1.9. thirty days of oral disclosure, provided that such information:

(a) is not publicly known or available from other sources who are not under a confidentiality obligation to the source of the information;

(b) has not been made available by its owners to others without a confidentiality obligation;

(c) is not already known by or available to the receiving party without a confidentiality obligation; or

(d) is not independently developed by the receiving party.

2. Work. University agrees to use reasonable efforts to perform the Project.

3. Key Personnel. The following individuals are identified as key personnel for the performance of the Project: _ , Principal Investigator

   If for any reason the Principal Investigator or any other key personnel becomes unable to continue the Project University and Sponsor shall attempt to agree upon a successor. If the Parties are unable to agree upon a successor, this Agreement shall be terminated in accordance with Article 12, Termination for Convenience.

4. Period of Performance. The "Period of Performance" and term of this Agreement will be

   _ through _.

5. Reports

   5.1. During the term of this Agreement, University shall furnish Sponsor with letter reports summarizing the work conducted. A final report setting forth the accomplishments and significant findings shall be submitted by University within ninety (90) days of the expiration of this Agreement

   5.2. Technical reports delivered by University to Sponsor shall include, as appropriate, all non-confidential and unencumbered underlying, relevant data, described in Exhibit A as deliverables. Sponsor agrees to include University's copyright notice in all copies of technical reports reproduced.

6. Costs and Payments.

6.1. It is agreed to and understood by the Parties that University shall be reimbursed for all costs incurred in connection with the Project up to the amount of $ (the "Project Cost") as established by the budget in Exhibit B which is incorporated herein. While it is estimated that the Project Cost is sufficient to support Project expenses, University retains the right to reallocate funding among budget categories for allowable project-related costs in accordance with the budget.

6.2. Sponsor shall not be liable for any payment in excess of the Project Cost unless this Agreement is modified in writing. Within ninety (90) days after the termination of this Agreement University shall submit a final financial report setting forth costs incurred. The report shall be accompanied by a check in the amount, if any, of the excess of funds advanced over costs incurred.

6.3. University shall submit invoices to Sponsor on a monthly basis to the address specified in Article 22, Notices. In order to be eligible for reimbursement, invoices shall be for costs incurred as established by the budget, in accordance with the terms of this Agreement, University policies and OMB Circular A-21, and shall display expenses for reimbursement by budget category. Payment shall be made upon receipt of invoice. All checks shall be made payable to Cornell University and sent to the address specified in Article 22, Notices.

7. Equipment. Title to any equipment purchased or manufactured in the performance of the Project shall vest in University.

8. Use of Name. Neither Party shall use this Agreement or the name of the other Party for endorsement, advertising, news release, or in any other manner (except in publications noted in Article 10 below) without the prior written approval of the other Party. This provision shall not preclude University from publishing Sponsor's name, project title, University's principal investigator, project period and award amount in its publicly-available listing of sponsored projects.

9. Confidential Information.

9.1 Confidential Information shall be used solely for Project-related purposes. The receiving Party retains the right to refuse to accept any Confidential Information that it does not consider to be essential to the completion of the Project.

9.2 Where the receiving Party accepts Confidential Information, it agrees to use the same degree of care to protect the disclosing Party's Confidential Information as it would to safeguard its own information of like nature, but no less than a reasonable degree of care. The receiving Party may disclose Confidential Information to its employees, students, contractors, or agents who need to know such Confidential Information to further the Project, and will ensure that all such persons are informed about the confidentiality obligations associated with such Confidential Information.

9.3 The receiving Party shall be bound to protect the disclosing Party's Confidential Information for a period of two (2) years from the date of disclosure unless such information has already been published or publicly disclosed by the disclosing Party or a third party or is required to be disclosed by law or court order.

9.4 In the event that the Receiving Party (or anyone to whom Confidential Information is furnished by such Party as authorized herein) is required by law to disclose any Confidential Information of the Disclosing Party, the Receiving Party will provide the Disclosing Party with reasonably prompt notice thereof so that the Disclosing Party may seek a protective order or other appropriate remedy. In any event, the Receiving Party will (or will use its reasonable efforts to cause such person to whom Confidential Information was furnished to) furnish only that portion of the Confidential Information which is legally required to be furnished and will use its reasonably best efforts to obtain assurances that confidential treatment will be accorded to that portion of the Confidential Information so furnished.

9.5 Each Party shall deliver to the other Party all documents containing Confidential Information received pursuant hereto and all copies, extracts or other embodiments of such Confidential Information within ten (10) days after being requested to do so by such other Party.

10. Publication.

10.1. The Parties acknowledge that it is the University's mission to discover and disseminate knowledge for the purpose of scholarship, education and research. Consistent with this mission and with University policies on academic freedom, openness of research, classified research, and in accordance with Export Control Laws as defined in Article 17 of this Agreement, University shall have the right, at its discretion, to release information, present or to publish any material resulting from the Project, with the exception of sponsor-provided Confidential Information. University shall provide Sponsor with a thirty (30) day period in which to review each publication. Sponsor may request University to delay release of such proposed publication for a maximum of an additional sixty (60) days in order to protect Intellectual Property or sponsor provided Confidential Information described therein. No such delay shall be imposed on the filing of any student thesis or dissertation.

10.2. Sponsor will be given full credit and acknowledgment for the support provided to University in any publication resulting from the Project.

11. Project Intellectual Property.

11.1. All rights and title to Sponsor Project Intellectual Property shall vest in the Sponsor.

11.2. All rights and title to University Project Intellectual Property shall vest in the University.

11.3. All rights and title to Jointly Owned Project Intellectual Property shall vest jointly in the University and in the Sponsor.

11.4. University will provide Sponsor with a written disclosure of any University Project Intellectual Property promptly after such University Project Intellectual Property is disclosed by a University employee in accordance with University policy to the Center for Technology Licensing at Cornell University ("CTL"). Sponsor will provide CTL with a written disclosure of any Sponsor Project Intellectual Property promptly after such Sponsor Project Intellectual Property is disclosed by a Sponsor employee to Sponsor. Each Party shall treat all Project Intellectual Property disclosures submitted by the other Party as Confidential Information.

11.4.1 After University provides Sponsor a written disclosure of a University Project Intellectual Property, Sponsor shall, within sixty (60) days of the receipt of the written disclosure, inform University in writing of its election of rights provided in 11.7 below. If Sponsor fails to exercise its election rights in writing within said sixty (60) day period, all such rights shall be waived and Sponsor shall have no further rights to University Project Intellectual Property.

11.5 University has the first right to file patent applications for University Project Intellectual Property at its own discretion and expense. At the request of Sponsor, University may file at Sponsor's expense. Patent expenses shall include the cost of patent filing, prosecution, and maintenance in the United States and any foreign country in which the patent is filed. All patent expenses incurred in obtaining and maintaining any patent on Jointly Owned Project Intellectual Property shall be shared equally, except that if one Party declines to share in such expenses the other Party may take over the prosecution and maintenance thereof, provided that title to the patent remains in the names of both Parties.

11.6 Each Party will grant to the other a non-exclusive, fee-free and royalty-free, irrevocable, non-transferrable, world-wide license without the right to sublicense, to each Party's Project Intellectual Property created pursuant to and during the course of the Project solely for research and education purposes.

11.7 If Sponsor pays for patenting and/or other costs associated with the protection of University Project Intellectual Property and agrees to demonstrate reasonable efforts to commercialize University Project Intellectual Property in the public interest, Sponsor may, subject to any third party rights, elect from the legal rights described below in 11.7.1.1 and 11.7.1.2.

11.7.1.1 A non-exclusive and royalty-free license (a "NERF License") that is non-transferrable and without the right to grant sublicenses to third parties to University Project Intellectual Property in the jurisdiction in which Sponsor is paying for the patenting and/or other costs associated with protection; or

11.7.1.2   For a reasonable licensing fee to be negotiated with CTL, an exclusive, royalty-free license (an "ERF License") that is non-transferrable and without the right to grant sublicenses to third parties to University Project Intellectual Property and/or University's Interest in Jointly Owned Project Intellectual Property in the jurisdiction in which Sponsor is paying for the patenting and/or other costs associated with protection in an appropriate field-of-use to make, have made, use, have used, import and sell and have sold products that are: 1) protected by University Project Intellectual Property and 2) are uniquely and directly related to Sponsor's Background Intellectual Property. A University Project Intellectual Property is uniquely and directly related to Sponsor's Background Intellectual Property when: a) Sponsor's Confidential Information is either disclosed in a claim or as part the patent prosecution process of the University Project Intellectual Property; b) the University Project Intellectual Property incorporates Sponsor's Confidential Information and/or Sponsor's Background Intellectual Property; or c) the use of Sponsor's Confidential Information is required to practice the invention.

11.7.2   If University and Sponsor do not enter into a license agreement within three (3) months after Sponsor's election to proceed under Sections 11.7.1.1 or 11.7.1.2, then Sponsor's rights under Sections 11.7.1.1 and 11.7.1.2 shall expire.

11.7.3   Within the 30 days of University's written disclosure under Section 11.4, Sponsor additionally may:

(1)   elect to negotiate with CTL (with payment of a one-time fee), during the Option Period described below, an option to include in the NERF License secured in Section 11.7.1.1 or in the ERF License secured in Section 11.7.1.2 the additional right to grant sublicenses to third parties under certain sublicense revenue-sharing arrangements between Sponsor and University.

The Option Period shall begin on the date Sponsor secures the NERF License or the ERF License as provided for in Sections 11.7.1.1 and 11.7.1.2, respectively, above and shall expire three (3) months thereafter; or

(2) elect a free, six (6) month option to negotiate with CTL an exclusive, fee- and royalty-bearing license for any University Project Intellectual Property, University's interest in Jointly Owned Project Intellectual Property, and related, necessary Background Intellectual Property not otherwise encumbered. The exclusive license may include the right to grant sublicenses in the negotiated field-of-use and territory and other customary contractual terms.

12. Termination for Convenience. This Agreement may be terminated at any time by either Party giving the other Party at least sixty (60) days written notice of termination. In the event of termination, University will be reimbursed for all expenses and non-cancellable commitments incurred in accordance with the terms of this Agreement prior to the date of termination. In no event shall the liability of Sponsor exceed the Project Cost.

13. Independent Contractor.

   13.1. In the performance of the Project University shall be deemed to be and shall be an independent contractor and, as such, University shall not be entitled to any benefits applicable to employees of Sponsor.

   13.2. Neither Party is authorized or empowered to act as an agent for the other for any purpose and shall not on behalf of the other enter into any contract, warranty, or representation as to any matter. Neither shall be bound by the acts or conduct of the other.

14. Insurance.

   14.1. University warrants and represents that University has adequate liability insurance, such protection being applicable to officers, employees, and agents while acting within the scope of their employment by University. University has no liability protection for any other person.

14.2.   Each Party hereby assumes any and all risks of personal injury and property damage attributable to the negligent acts of that Party and the officers, employees, and agents thereof.

15.   Warranties. Sponsor acknowledges and agrees that the Project results are delivered "as is". University makes no warranties, express or implied, as to those results or any inventions created, invented or discovered under this Agreement or as to the merchantability or fitness for a particular purpose of the Project results or any such inventions. University shall not knowingly infringe the legally protected intellectual property rights of third parties. Sponsor expressly understands that University will not complete a comprehensive patent, trade secret, or copyright search of the results presented and that Sponsor should complete its own search.

16.   Limitation on Liability/Assumption of Risk. University expressly disclaims and Sponsor expressly assumes all liability and shall defend and indemnify University against any third party claims, including under any theory of strict liability, for any direct, consequential or other damages that result from the use of or reliance upon the Project results or any such inventions by Sponsor, licensee, or any third party.

17.   Export Control. Each Party acknowledges that certain information or materials provided by the other under this Agreement may be subject to U.S. export control laws and regulations (collectively, "Export Control Laws"), which include (without limitation) the International Traffic in Arms Regulations (ITAR, 22 CFR Chapter 1, Subchapter M, Parts 120-130), Export Administration Regulations (EAR, 15 CFR Chapter VII, Subchapter C, Parts 730-774), and regulations and orders administered by the Treasury Department's Office of Foreign Assets Control ("OFAC Regulations"). Each Party agrees to comply with all Export Control Laws. Neither Party shall disclose any information subject to Export Control Laws unless and until a plan for the transfer, use, dissemination and control of the information has been approved by both Parties. Sponsor expressly acknowledges and agrees that University shall conduct the Project as "fundamental research" for purposes of Export Control Laws compliance, such that the Project results qualify as "public domain" under ITAR Parts 120.10(a)(5) and 120.11 or as "publicly available" under EAR Parts 734.3(b)(3) and 734.8(a) and (b).

18.   Force Majeure. University shall not be liable for any failure to perform as required by this Agreement to the extent such failure to

perform is reasonably beyond University's control, or by reason of any of the following: labor disturbances or labor disputes of any kind, accidents, failure of any governmental approval required for full performance, civil disorders or commotions, acts of aggression, floods, earthquakes, acts of God, energy or other conservation measures, explosion, failure of utilities, mechanical breakdowns, material shortages, disease or other such occurrences.

19. Governing Law. This Agreement shall be governed and construed in accordance with the laws of the State of New York.

20. Assignment. This Agreement shall not be assigned by either Party without the prior written consent of the other Party.

21. Agreement Modification. Any modification to the terms of this Agreement shall be valid only if the change is made in writing and approved by mutual agreement of **authorized representatives** of the Parties hereto.

22. Notices. Notices, invoices, communications, and payments hereunder shall be deemed made if given by registered or certified envelope, postage prepaid and addressed to the party to receive such notice, invoice, or communication at the address given below or such other address as may hereafter be designated by notice in writing.

If to Sponsor:

    Contractual:

    Technical:

    Invoices:

If to University:

    Contractual: Office of Sponsored Programs
    373 Pine Tree Road
    Cornell University
    Ithaca, New York 14853-2820 USA
    Phone:
    Fax: 607-255-5058
    Email:

    Technical:

Payments: Cornell University
Sponsored Financial Services
P.O. Box 22
Ithaca, NY 14851-0022 USA

Intellectual Property:

Center for Technology Licensing at
Cornell University
395 Pine Tree Road, Suite 310
Ithaca NY 14850
Phone: 607-254-4698
Fax: 607-254-5454

23.   Survivability. The obligations set forth in Articles 5.2, 8, 9, 11 and 15 shall survive the expiration or termination of this Agreement.

This Agreement is the complete agreement of Sponsor and University and supersedes all prior understandings regarding the Project.

IN WITNESS WHEREOF, the Parties have caused these presents to be executed in duplicate on the dates indicated below.

SPONSOR   CORNELL UNIVERSITY
OFFICE OF SPONSORED
PROGRAMS

_____   _____

_____   _____

Date   Date

Source: Cornell University, Office of Sponsored Programs, 2015. *Applied Sponsored Research Agreement*, June. https://www.osp.cornell.edu/Policies/Spons-Res-Agrmt-Applied-Res-June_2015.pdf.

GUIDELINES: MASSACHUSETTS INSTITUTE OF TECHNOLOGY

MASSACHUSETTS INSTITUTE OF TECHNOLOGY OFFICE OF SPONSORED PROGRAMS

EXPLANATION OF MIT'S STANDARD SPONSORED RESEARCH AGREEMENT

THE HYPERLINKED ANNOTATIONS IN THIS DOCUMENT ARE INTENDED SOLELY TO HELP THE READER UNDERSTAND THE BASIS IN LAW OR MIT POLICY FOR TERMS IN MIT'S STANDARD SPONSORED RESEARCH AGREEMENT. THESE ANNOTATIONS IN NO WAY ALTER OR MODIFY THIS CONTRACT. IN THE EVENT THERE IS ANY DISPUTE AS TO THE INTENT OR MEANING OF THE POP-UP ANNOTATIONS VERSUS THE ACTUAL CONTRACT, ONLY THE TEXT OF THE CONTRACT ITSELF SHALL BE INTERPRETED.

This Research Agreement ("Agreement") is made effective as of ———————(the "Effective Date"), by and between **Massachusetts Institute of Technology**, located at 77 Massachusetts Avenue, Cambridge, Massachusetts 02139 (hereinafter referred to as "MIT"), and ——————— ———, located at ——————— (hereinafter referred to as the "Sponsor"). Party shall mean the Sponsor or MIT as the context dictates, and when used in the plural, shall mean the Sponsor and MIT.

WHEREAS, the research program contemplated by this Agreement is of <u>mutual interest and benefit to MIT and to the Sponsor</u>, and will further the instructional and research objectives of MIT in a manner consistent with its status as a non-profit, tax-exempt, educational institution.

NOW, THEREFORE, the Parties hereto agree as follows:

1. **STATEMENT OF WORK.** MIT agrees to use <u>reasonable efforts</u> to perform the research program as described in **Attachment A** (the "Research") to this Agreement.

2. **PRINCIPAL INVESTIGATOR.** The Research will be supervised by ———————the "Principal Investigator". If, for any reason, ——————— is unable to continue to serve as Principal Investigator and a successor reasonably acceptable to both MIT and the Sponsor is not available, this Agreement shall be terminated as provided in Article 6.

3. **PERIOD OF PERFORMANCE.** The Research shall be conducted during the period commencing _____(the "Start Date") and, unless earlier terminated in accordance with this Agreement, ending ——————— (the "Completion Date"). The Completion Date may be modified or extended only by mutual written agreement of the Parties.

4. **REIMBURSEMENT OF COSTS.** In consideration of the foregoing, the Sponsor shall reimburse MIT for all <u>direct</u> and <u>F&A (Facilities & Administrative or indirect)</u> costs incurred in the performance of the Research, including business class fares for international travel of faculty and staff. Total reimbursements shall not exceed the total estimated project cost of $ ———————without written authorization from the Sponsor.

5. **PAYMENT.** Payment(s) shall be made to MIT by the Sponsor <u>in advance</u> in U.S. dollars, <u>excluding taxes or impost</u> of any kind, as follows:

   $ due

   Information for payment(s) by wire transfer appears in **Attachment B** to this Agreement.

   A final financial accounting of all costs incurred and all funds received by MIT hereunder, together with a check for the amount of the unexpended balance, if any, shall be submitted to the Sponsor within ninety (90) days following the Completion Date or termination of this Agreement.

6. **TERMINATION.** This Agreement may be terminated by either Party upon sixty (60) days' prior written notice to the other Party. Upon termination by either Party, MIT will be reimbursed as specified in Article 4 for all <u>costs and non-cancelable commitments</u> incurred in connection with the Research up to and including the effective date of termination, such reimbursement not to exceed the total estimated cost specified in Article 4.

7. **CONFIDENTIAL INFORMATION.** If, in the performance of the Research, the Principal Investigator and members of the MIT research team require and accept access to the Sponsor's "Confidential Information" (as defined in **Attachment C** to this Agreement), the rights and obligations of the Parties with respect to such information shall be governed by the terms and conditions set forth in **Attachment C** to this Agreement.

8. **PUBLICATIONS.** MIT will be free to publish the results of the Research after providing the Sponsor with a <u>thirty (30) day period in which to review each publication</u> to identify patentable subject matter and to identify any inadvertent disclosure of Confidential Information. If necessary to permit the preparation and filing of U.S. patent applications, the Principal Investigator may agree to an additional review period not to exceed sixty (60) days. Any further extension will require subsequent agreement between the Sponsor and MIT.

9. **SPONSOR <u>INTELLECTUAL PROPERTY</u>.** Title to any invention conceived or first reduced to practice in performance of the Research solely by the Sponsor's personnel without significant use of MIT administered funds or facilities ("Sponsor Invention") shall remain with the Sponsor. Title to and the copyright in any copyright-able material first produced or composed in the performance of the Research solely by the Sponsor's personnel without significant use of MIT administered funds or facilities ("Sponsor Copyright") shall remain with the Sponsor. Neither Sponsor Inventions nor Sponsor Copyrights shall be subject to the terms and conditions of this Agreement.

10. **JOINT INTELLECTUAL PROPERTY.**

    A. JOINT INVENTIONS. The Parties shall have joint title to (i) any invention conceived or first reduced to practice jointly by employees and/or students of MIT and the Sponsor's personnel in the performance of the Research and (ii) any invention conceived or first reduced to practice by the Sponsor's personnel in the performance of the Research with significant use of funds or facilities administered by MIT (each, a "Joint Invention"). The Sponsor shall be notified of any Joint Invention promptly after an invention disclosure is received by MIT's Technology Licensing Office. MIT shall have the first right to file a patent application on a Joint Invention in the names of both Parties. All expenses incurred in obtaining and maintaining any patent on such Joint Invention shall be equally shared except that, if one Party declines to share in such expenses, the other Party may take over the prosecution and maintenance thereof, at its own expense, provided that title to the patent remains in the names of both Parties.

    B. LICENSES. Each Party shall have the independent, unrestricted right to license to third parties any such Joint Invention without accounting to the other Party, except that the Sponsor shall be entitled to request an exclusive license to MIT's interest in a Joint Invention as provided under paragraph 11.B.2. below.

C. JOINTLY DEVELOPED COPYRIGHTABLE MATERIALS. Copyrightable materials, including computer software, developed in the performance of the Research (i) jointly by employees and/or students of MIT and the Sponsor's personnel, or (ii) by the Sponsor's personnel with significant use of funds or facilities administered by MIT, shall be jointly owned by both Parties, who shall each have the independent, unrestricted right to dispose of such copyrightable materials and their share of the copyrights therein as they deem appropriate, without any obligation of accounting to the other Party.

11. **MIT INTELLECTUAL PROPERTY.**

A. MIT INVENTIONS. MIT shall have sole title to (i) any invention conceived or first reduced to practice solely by employees and/ or students of MIT in the performance of the Research (each an "MIT Invention") and (ii) any invention conceived or first reduced to practice by the Sponsor's personnel with significant use of funds or facilities administered by MIT, if the invention is conceived or reduced to practice other than in the performance of the Research. The Sponsor shall be notified of any MIT Invention promptly after a disclosure is received by MIT's Technology Licensing Office. MIT may (a) file a patent application at its own discretion or (b) shall do so at the request of the Sponsor and at the Sponsor's expense.

B. LICENSING OPTIONS. For each MIT Invention on which a patent application is filed by MIT, MIT hereby grants the Sponsor a non-exclusive, non-transferable, royalty-free license for internal research purposes. The Sponsor shall further be entitled to elect one of the following alternatives by notice in writing to MIT within six (6) months after MIT's notification to the Sponsor that a patent application has been filed:

1. a non-exclusive, non-transferable, world-wide, royalty-free license (in a designated field of use, where appropriate) to the Sponsor, without the right to sublicense, in the United States and/or any foreign country elected by the Sponsor pursuant to Section 11.C. below, to make, have made, use, lease, sell and import products embodying or produced

through the use of such invention, provided that the Sponsor agrees to demonstrate reasonable efforts to commercialize the technology in the public interest and reimburse MIT for the costs of patent prosecution and maintenance in the United States and any elected foreign country; or

2. a royalty-bearing, limited-term, exclusive license (subject to third party rights, if any, and in a designated field of use, where appropriate) to the Sponsor, including the right to sublicense, in the United States and/or any foreign country elected by the Sponsor pursuant to Section 11.C. below, to make, have made, use, lease, sell and import products embodying or produced through the use of such invention. This option to elect an exclusive license is subject to MIT's concurrence and the negotiation of commercially reasonable license terms and conditions and conditioned upon Sponsor's agreement to reimburse MIT for the costs of patent prosecution and maintenance in the United States and any elected foreign country and <u>to cause any products produced pursuant to this license that will be used or sold in the United States to be substantially manufactured in the United States.</u>

If the Sponsor and MIT do not enter into a license agreement within three (3) months after the Sponsor's election to proceed under paragraph 11.B.1. or 11.B.2. above, the Sponsor's rights under paragraphs 11.B.1. and 11.B.2. will expire.

C. FOREIGN FILING ELECTION. If the Sponsor elects a license under 11.B.1 or 11.B.2., the Sponsor shall notify MIT of those foreign countries in which it desires a license in sufficient time for MIT to satisfy the patent law requirements of those countries. The Sponsor will reimburse MIT for the out-of-pocket costs, including patent filing, prosecution and maintenance fees, related to those foreign filings.

D. CONFIDENTIALITY OF INVENTION DISCLOSURES. The Sponsor shall retain all invention disclosures submitted to the Sponsor by MIT in confidence and use its best efforts to prevent their disclosure to third parties. The Sponsor shall be relieved of this obligation only when this information becomes publicly available through no fault of the Sponsor.

E. COPYRIGHT OWNERSHIP AND LICENSES. Title to and the copyright in any copyrightable material first produced or composed in the performance of the Research solely by employees and/or students of MIT shall remain with MIT.

1. For any copyrights or copyrightable material other than computer software and its documentation and/or informational databases required to be delivered in accordance with Attachment A, the Sponsor is hereby granted an irrevocable, royalty-free, non-transferable, non-exclusive right and license to use, reproduce, make derivative works, display, distribute and perform all such copyrightable materials for the Sponsor's internal purposes.

2. The Sponsor shall be entitled to elect, by notice to MIT within six (6) months following MIT's notification or delivery to the Sponsor of computer software and its documentation and/or informational databases required to be delivered to the Sponsor in accordance with Attachment A, a royalty-free, non-transferable, non-exclusive right and license to use, reproduce, make derivative works based upon, display, and distribute to end users, such computer software and its documentation and/or databases for internal and/or commercial purposes. If the use of the software would infringe claims of a patent application filed pursuant to paragraph 11.A. above, then the Sponsor will need to elect license rights in such patent as set forth in 11.B. above in order to elect the license contemplated by this paragraph. If such computer software is a derivative of MIT software existing prior to the start of the Research, then such license may not be royalty-free.

F.   RIGHTS IN TRP. In the event that MIT elects to establish property rights other than patents to any tangible research property (TRP), including but not limited to biological materials, developed during the course of the Research, MIT and the Sponsor will determine the disposition of rights to such property by separate agreement. MIT will, at a minimum, reserve the right to use and distribute TRP for non-commercial research purposes.

G.   LICENSE EFFECTIVE DATE. All licenses elected by the Sponsor pursuant to Sections B., E. and F. of this Article 11 become effective as of the date the Parties sign a separate license agreement.

12. **USE OF NAMES**. The Sponsor and its affiliates shall not use the name "Massachusetts Institute of Technology" or any variation,

adaptation, or abbreviation thereof, or the name of any of MIT's trustees, officers, faculty members, students, employees, or agents, or any trademark owned by MIT, in any promotional material or other public announcement or disclosure without the prior written consent of MIT's Technology Licensing Office, which consent MIT may withhold in its sole discretion.

13. **REPRESENTATIONS AND WARRANTIES**. MIT MAKES NO REPRESENTATIONS OR WARRANTIES OF ANY KIND CONCERNING THE RESEARCH OR ANY INTELLECTUAL PROPERTY RIGHTS AND HEREBY DISCLAIMS ALL REPRESENTATIONS AND WARRANTIES, EXPRESS OR IMPLIED, INCLUDING, WITHOUT LIMITATION, WARRANTIES OF MERCHANTABILITY, FITNESS FOR A PARTICULAR PURPOSE, NONINFRINGEMENT OF INTELLECTUAL PROPERTY RIGHTS OF MIT OR THIRD PARTIES, CREATION, VALIDITY, ENFORCEABILITY AND SCOPE OF ANY INTELLECTUAL PROPERTY RIGHTS OR CLAIMS, WHETHER ISSUED OR PENDING, AND THE ABSENCE OF LATENT OR OTHER DEFECTS, WHETHER OR NOT DISCOVERABLE.

IN NO EVENT SHALL EITHER PARTY, ITS TRUSTEES, DIRECTORS, OFFICERS, EMPLOYEES, STUDENTS AND AFFILIATES, BE LIABLE FOR INCIDENTAL OR CONSEQUENTIAL DAMAGES OF ANY KIND, INCLUDING ECONOMIC DAMAGES OR LOST PROFITS, REGARDLESS OF WHETHER THE PARTY WAS ADVISED, HAD OTHER REASON TO KNOW OR IN FACT KNEW OF THE POSSIBILITY OF THE FOREGOING. THIS ARTICLE 13 SHALL SURVIVE THE EXPIRATION OR ANY EARLIER TERMINATION OF THIS AGREEMENT.

14. **NOTICES**. Any notices required to be given or which shall be given under this Agreement shall be in writing and be addressed to the Parties as shown below. Notices shall be delivered by certified or registered first class mail (air mail if not domestic) or by commercial courier service and shall be deemed to have been made as of the date received.

MIT	SPONSOR
Contractual Matters	**Contractual Matters**
MIT Office of Sponsored Programs 77 Massachusetts Avenue, E19-750 Cambridge, MA 02139-4307 USA Attention: [CA name] Phone: + 1-617- Fax: + 1-617-253-4734 Email: @mit.edu	
Invoice and Payment Matters	**Invoice and Payment Matters**
MIT Office of Sponsored Programs 77 Massachusetts Avenue, E19-750 Cambridge, MA 02139-4307 USA Attention: [CA name] Phone: + 1-617- Fax: + 1-617-253-4734 Email: @mit.edu	
Technical Matters	**Technical Matters**
MIT [Dept/Lab/Center] 77 Massachusetts Avenue, [Rm #] Cambridge, MA 02139-4307 USA Attention: [PI name] Phone: +1-617- Fax: +1-617- E-mail: @mit.edu	
Intellectual Property Matters	**Intellectual Property Matters**
MIT Technology Licensing Office One Cambridge Center, Kendall Square Room NE18-501 Cambridge, MA 02142-1601 Attention: Director Phone: 617-253-6966 Fax: 617-258-6790 Email: tlo@mit.edu	

15. **ASSIGNMENT.** This Agreement shall be binding upon and inure to the benefit of the Parties hereto and their respective successors and permitted assigns. Neither Party may assign this Agreement without the prior written consent of the other Party, except to a successor to all or substantially all of its business and assets. Any attempted assignment in violation of this Article 15 is void.

16. **GOVERNING LAW.** The validity and interpretation of this Agreement and the legal relationship of the Parties to it shall be governed by the laws of the Commonwealth of Massachusetts and the applicable U.S. Federal law.

17. **MEDIATION.** If a dispute arises between the Parties, either Party may notify the other of its desire to mediate the dispute and the dispute shall be mediated.

    A. MEDIATOR. The mediation shall be conducted by a single mediator. The Party requesting mediation shall designate two (2) or more nominees for mediator in its notice. The other Party may accept one of the nominees or may designate its own nominees by notice addressed to the American Arbitration Association (AAA) and copied to the requesting Party. If within thirty (30) days following the request for mediation, the Parties have not selected a mutually acceptable mediator, a mediator shall be appointed by the AAA according to the Commercial Mediation Rules.

    B. NON-BINDING; EXPENSES. The mediator shall attempt to facilitate a negotiated settlement of the dispute, but shall have no authority to impose any settlement terms on the Parties. The expenses of the mediation shall be borne equally by the Parties, but each Party shall be responsible for its own counsel fees and expenses.

    C. FAILED MEDIATION. If the dispute is not resolved by mediation within forty-five (45) days after commencement of mediation, each Party shall be entitled to pursue any right or other legal remedy the Party may otherwise have.

    D. RIGHT TO SEEK EQUITABLE RELIEF. Notwithstanding the provisions of this Section, a Party may bring suit in a court of competent jurisdiction for equitable relief from the other Party's alleged breach of its confidentiality obligations without first mediating the issue.

18. **FORCE MAJEURE.** Neither Party shall be liable to the other for failure to perform any of its respective obligations imposed by this

Agreement provided such failure shall be occasioned by fire, flood, explosion, lightning, windstorm, earthquake, subsidence of soil, governmental interference, civil commotion, riot, war, terrorism, strikes, labor disturbance, or any other cause beyond its reasonable control.

19. **EXPORT CONTROLS.** Each Party acknowledges that any information or materials provided by the other under this Agreement may be subject to U.S. export laws and regulations, including the International Traffic in Arms Regulations (ITAR, 22 CFR Chapter 1, Subchapter M, Parts 120-130), Export Administration Regulations (EAR, 15 CFR Chapter VII, Subchapter C, Parts 730-774)), and Assistance to Foreign Atomic Energy Activities (10 CFR Part 810); each Party agrees to comply with all such laws.

    Because MIT is an institution of higher education and has many students, faculty, staff, and visitors who are foreign persons, MIT intends to conduct the Research as fundamental research under the export regulations, such that the results generated by MIT qualify as "public domain" under ITAR Parts 120.10(a)(5) and 120.11 or "publicly available under EAR Parts 734.3(b)(3) and 734.8(a, b)

    Sponsor will not knowingly disclose, and will use commercially reasonable efforts to prevent disclosure to MIT of any information subject to ITAR controls or in the Commerce Control List (EAR Part 774 and Supplements) or 10 CFR Part 810 Restricted Data or Sensitive Nuclear Technology. If for purposes of the Research, Sponsor intends to disclose export-controlled information to MIT, Sponsor will not disclose such information to MIT unless and until a plan for transfer, use, dissemination and control of the information has been approved by MIT's Export Control Officer. In the event Sponsor inadvertently (i) discloses export-controlled information or (ii) breaches this Section, any deadlines contemplated by the Statement of Work will be adjusted based on the time it takes to address the disclosure.

20. **COUNTERPARTS.** This Agreement and any amendment hereto may be executed in counterparts and all such counterparts taken together shall be deemed to constitute one and the same instrument. If this Agreement is executed in counterparts, no signatory hereto will be bound until all the Parties named below have duly executed a counterpart of this Agreement.

21. **ENTIRE AGREEMENT.** Unless otherwise specified, this Agreement and its Attachments embody the entire understanding between MIT

and the Sponsor with respect to the Research, and any prior or contemporaneous representations, either oral or written, are hereby superseded. No amendments or changes to this Agreement, including, without limitation, changes in the statement of work, period of performance or total estimated cost, shall be effective unless made in writing and signed by authorized representatives of the Parties.

IN WITNESS WHEREOF, the Sponsor and MIT, intending to be legally bound, have executed this Agreement as of the Effective Date by their respective duly authorized representatives.

MASSACHUSETTS INSTITUTE
OF TECHNOLOGY   **SPONSOR**

By_____   By_____

Name_____   Name_____

Title_____   Title_____

Date_____   Date_____

ATTACHMENT A

MIT <u>STATEMENT OF WORK</u>

ATTACHMENT B

INSTRUCTIONS FOR MAKING WIRE TRANSFERS IN USD ONLY TO MIT

Name of bank to which funds are to be wired:	Bank of America, NA
Bank address:	100 Federal Street Boston, MA 02110
WIRE PAYMENT ABA Routing Number:	026 009 593
SWIFT CODE:	BOFAUS3N
DDA Account Number:	# 004632424694 (MIT Incoming Wire)
ACH ABA ROUTING Number:	011 000 138
Wire Details: Please include Name of MIT Program, MIT Principal Investigator, MIT account number or MIT invoice number to credit:	

Sponsor, please provide as much information as possible to identify the objective of the wire transfer, such as MIT Principal Investigator' s name, MIT department, MIT account number, project title or descriptor, to facilitate identification of the incoming wire transfer. If there is limited space, the MIT Principal Investigator and Research Program (Title) are probably the minimum information needed to identify the objective for the wire transfer.

Sponsor, please notify wire-transfers@mit.edu or Patricia Crosby in MIT Accounts Receivable at 1.617.253.2751, pcrosby@mit.edu, that you are making a wire transfer. Provide your company name, the name of the bank or party wiring the money, the amount of the wire, the MIT Principal Investigator, Research Program (Title) and/or account number to which this money should be transferred, and the date when the wire is expected to be made. Please include a contact at the Principal Investigator's MIT department in case of questions and the date when the wire is expected to be made.

ATTACHMENT C

SPONSOR CONFIDENTIAL INFORMATION

If, in the performance of the Research, the Principal Investigator and members of the MIT research team designated by him/her require and accept access offered by the Sponsor to certain information that the Sponsor considers confidential, the rights and obligations of the Parties with respect to such information are as follows:

1. CONFIDENTIAL INFORMATION. When used in this Agreement, "Confidential Information" means confidential and proprietary information of any kind which is disclosed by the Sponsor to MIT that (i) prior to disclosure, is marked with a legend indicating its confidential status or (ii) is disclosed orally or visually, if the Sponsor identifies such information as confidential at the time of disclosure and, within 30 days of such disclosure, delivers to the Principal Investigator a notice summarizing the confidential information disclosed. Notwithstanding the foregoing, in no event is information Confidential Information if it (a) was in MIT's possession before receipt from the Sponsor; (b) is or becomes a matter of public knowledge through no fault of MIT; (c) is received by MIT from a third party having an apparent bona fide right to disclose the information without a duty of confidentiality to the Sponsor; or (d) is independently developed by MIT without use of the Confidential Information.

2. LIMITATIONS ON USE. MIT shall use the Confidential Information solely for the purposes of the Research. Disclosure by the Sponsor of the Confidential Information does not constitute a grant to MIT of any right or license to the Confidential Information except as set forth herein or in a duly executed license agreement.

3. CARE OF CONFIDENTIAL INFORMATION. MIT shall exert reasonable efforts to maintain the Confidential Information in confidence, except that MIT may disclose or permit disclosure of any of the Confidential Information to its directors (members of the MIT Corporation), officers, employees, consultants, advisors, students, subcontractors and agents, who need to know such Confidential Information in the performance of the Research and who have been advised of and have agreed to maintain the confidential nature of the Confidential Information.

MIT shall be deemed to have discharged its obligations hereunder provided MIT has exercised the foregoing degree of care and provided further that MIT shall immediately, upon discovery of any disclosure not authorized hereunder, notify the Sponsor and take reasonable steps to prevent any further unauthorized disclosure or unauthorized use.

MIT's obligations of confidentiality with respect to use and non-disclosure of Confidential Information provided under this Agreement shall survive for a period of three (3) years following receipt of the information.

4. REQUIRED DISCLOSURES. Nothing in this Agreement shall be construed to prevent MIT from disclosing Confidential Information as required by law or legal process, as long as MIT, if permitted by applicable law, promptly notifies the Sponsor of its obligation to disclose and provides reasonable cooperation to the Sponsor in any efforts to contest or limit the scope of the disclosure.

5. RETURN OR DESTRUCTION OF CONFIDENTIAL INFORMATION. When the Confidential Information is no longer required for the purposes of this Agreement, MIT shall, at the direction of the Sponsor, either destroy or return to the Sponsor all Confidential Information and shall destroy any electronic or digital manifestations of the Confidential Information, except that MIT may retain one copy of the Confidential Information solely for the pur-poses of monitoring its obligations under this Agreement.

Annotations

Mutual interest: Research projects undertaken by MIT in collaboration with industry provide opportunities for mutual learning and resources to advance MIT research and education, and may lead to discoveries that significantly benefit the public, thereby supporting MIT's mission.

1. **Reasonable efforts**: Since fundamental research is by nature unpredictable and without guarantee of success, MIT research is conducted on a reasonable efforts basis. MIT cannot accept contract provisions which establish firm performance deadlines, impose penalties for failure to complete the statement of work within the estimated cost, or provide for withholding of payment if the sponsor is not satisfied with the results.

4. **Direct costs** are labor, materials, travel, student tuition, purchased equipment, consultant fees, and subcontracts.

4. **F&A** (financial and administrative, also known as indirect) **costs** cover occupancy, facilities and general research support functions.

5. **Payment in advance**: As a non-profit institution, MIT cannot spend funds needed to support its educational programs to support sponsored research projects. Thus MIT must receive funds in advance of sponsored research activities to enable these activities to proceed. Furthermore, due to the unpredictable nature of fundamental research, results are uncertain and therefore MIT cannot agree to payment arrangements that are based upon attaining specific milestones or delivering specified research results.

5. **Excluding taxes**: Because MIT is a non-profit 501(c)(3) institution, taxes should not be assessed upon sponsored research payments. However, if taxes *are* assessed by a taxing authority in the US or a foreign country, the Sponsor must pay these taxes so the funds committed to supporting the research are not reduced.

6. **Non-cancelable commitments** typically include non-reversible contractual obligations already incurred plus support of students through the end of the academic calendar unit in which termination occurs.

8. **Publications**: Research at MIT is considered fundamental research, the results of which are shared broadly within the scientific and academic communities. Furthermore, timely publication of research results in the most respected academic, peer-reviewed journals and conferences is essential to the career advancement of MIT's faculty, research associates and graduate students. Nevertheless, MIT recognizes a Sponsor's interests in preventing its confidential information from inadvertent public disclosure,

and in protecting patentable results, and provides Sponsor with a 30-day pre-publication review for this purpose.

11. **INTELLECTUAL PROPERTY**: Title to inventions or copyrightable materials arising during a sponsored research program is assigned to the employer of the inventor/author:

- to MIT if created by an MIT employee or student
- to the Sponsor if created by an employee of the Sponsor
- or jointly to MIT and the Sponsor if created jointly by inventors/authors from both parties.

Licensing options provide the routes that enable the Sponsor to practice MIT-developed project Intellectual Property in the Sponsor's research and commercial activities.

11. **other than in the performance of the Research**. If an employee of the Sponsor develops an invention or a copyrightable work using MIT-administered funds or facilities, the Sponsor and MIT will jointly own those inventions and works *as long as they result from the research described in the agreement*. However, if an employee of the Sponsor makes an invention using MIT-administered funds or facilities *for research not covered under the Agreement*, MIT will solely own that invention. (This latter situation should not occur.) This condition is required to comply with US tax regulations that forbid the use of MIT's tax-exempt facilities for the sole benefit of a private user.

11. **entitled to elect (licenses)**: US tax regulations (IRS Revenue Procedure 2007–47) prohibiting private business use of MIT's tax-exempt facilities prohibit MIT from granting commercial licenses to intellectual property *before the specific technology to be licensed is actually developed*. MIT cannot grant commercial licenses in the Sponsored Research Agreement because no inventions have yet been made as a result of the Agreement. Therefore, in the Agreement, MIT can only provide Sponsors with *options to elect* commercial licenses to practice IP that may arise from the proposed research.

11.B.2. **substantially manufactured in the United States.** This US federal government requirement must be acknowledged in the Agreement because US government funding supports about 80% of the research at MIT. Even when no federal funds directly support a research project, there may be background research relevant to the research project that was developed with US federal funds. *When manufacture in the US is required by law, and a licensee requests a waiver of this requirement, MIT will assist the licensee in applying to the US government for this waiver but cannot guarantee it will be granted.*

11.F. **TRP**: Tangible Research Property (TRP) is tangible (or corporeal) items produced by MIT in the course of research projects. TRP may include but is not limited to such items as biological materials, engineering drawings, integrated circuit chips, prototype devices, circuit diagrams, and fabricated equipment.

13. **Representations and Warranties**: Fundamental research is by nature risky and novel, and may be used by sponsors or their agents for applications not expected or intended by MIT, including commercial product development. Use of research deliverables should be at the sponsor's risk only. MIT will not make any representations regarding the application of research deliverables. In addition, while MIT maintains reasonable policies to address the potential for IP infringement, we cannot ensure that such allegations will not arise, regardless of whether they are without merit. MIT will not warrant that exploitation of the research will not infringe any third-party IP rights.

Liable: It is appropriate to exclude such damages from recovery under a research agreement involving a non-profit organization like MIT; otherwise the non-profit organization's ability to engage in research would be severely restricted due to the risk of this potential financial exposure, which may be difficult to evaluate until a claim arises.

Attachment A: The statement of work for the research project is inserted here and thus becomes a part of the Agreement.

Attachment C: The rules governing the disclosure of Sponsor's confidential information to the MIT research project team, and MIT's obligations to protect the confidential information, are set forth here and are consistent with the terms of MIT's standard non-disclosure agreements.

Source: Massachusetts Institute of Technology, Office of Sponsored Programs, 2011. *Explanation of MIT's Standard Sponsored Research Agreement*, May 11. http://osp.mit.edu/sites/osp/files/uploads/mit_research_agreement_050111_annotated. pdf.

GUIDELINES: STANFORD UNIVERSITY

SPONSORED RESEARCH AGREEMENT

This Agreement is between _____ ("Sponsor") and The Board of Trustees of The Leland Stanford Junior University ("Stanford"), an institution of higher education having powers under the laws of the State of California.

Agreement Number:
Research Program Title:
Principal Investigator:
Effective Date:
End Date:
Cost:
Payment Schedule:

The following authorized party representatives have executed this Agreement, including all its terms and conditions.

Sponsor	The Board of Trustees of the Leland Stanford Junior University
Signature _____	Signature _____
Name _____	Name _____
Title _____	Title _____
Date _____	Date _____

I, _____, named as Principal Investigator, acknowledge that I have read this Agreement in its entirety and will use reasonable efforts to uphold my obligations and responsibilities set forth herein:

Signature:_____

Date:_____

1. DEFINITIONS

1.1 "Research Program" means the research to be performed as set forth in Exhibit A.

1.2 "Confidential Information" means Sponsor-owned, confidential, scientific, business or financial information that is provided in written form and clearly marked as Confidential provided that such information:

(a) is not publicly known or available from other sources who are not under a confidentiality obligation to the source of the information;

(b) has not been made available by its owners to others without a confidentiality obligation;

(c) is not already known by or available to the receiving party without a confidentiality obligation;

(d) is not independently developed by the receiving party; or

(e) does not relate to potential hazards or cautionary warnings associated with the performance of the Research Program, or is not required to be disclosed under operation of law.

1.3 "Cost" means all direct and indirect costs incurred by Stanford in conducting the Research Program up to the amount indicated on Page 1.

1.4 "Technology" means all tangible materials, inventions, works of authorship, software, information, and data conceived or developed in the performance of the Research Program and funded under this Agreement.

2. BACKGROUND

2.1 **Performance of the Research Program.** Stanford will use reasonable efforts to perform the research described in Exhibit A, Research Program, which is incorporated and made part of this Agreement.

2.2 **Objectives.** The performance of the Research Program is of mutual interest to Sponsor and Stanford, and is consistent with the instructional, scholarship, and research objectives of Stanford as a non-profit, tax-exempt, educational institution.

3. PRINCIPAL INVESTIGATOR

3.1 **Identity.** The Principal Investigator for the performance and supervision of the Research Program is the person identified on Page 1.

3.2 **Change.** If for any reason the Principal Investigator cannot conduct or complete the Research Program, Stanford will appoint a successor, subject to the approval of Sponsor. If the parties cannot agree on a successor, either party may terminate this Agreement in accord with the terms of Section 12. EARLY TERMINATION.

4. PERIOD OF PERFORMANCE

The Agreement is effective as of the Effective Date and terminates as of the End Date.

5. COSTS

5.1 **Designation.** This Agreement is designated as:

_____

5.2 **Cost-Reimbursable Agreement.** If this Agreement is designated as "Cost-Reimbursable," Sponsor will reimburse Stanford for the Cost of conducting the Research Program. The parties estimate that the Cost is sufficient to support the Research Program, but Stanford may submit to Sponsor a revised budget requesting additional funds if costs are reasonably projected to exceed the Cost. Sponsor is not liable for any payment in excess of the Cost except on Sponsor's written agreement. Stanford has the authority to rebudget Costs from time to time, at the discretion of the Principal Investigator, as long as the rebudgeting is consistent with the goals of the Research Program. At the end of the Research Program, if there is a balance owed to Sponsor of $100 or less, Stanford may keep the balance. Any amounts over $100 will be returned to Sponsor unless the parties agree otherwise. Stanford will provide its customary final financial report upon Sponsor's written request.

5.3 **Fixed-Price Agreement.** If this Agreement is designated as "Fixed Price," Sponsor will pay Stanford the Cost indicated on Page 1. The parties estimate that the Cost is sufficient to support the Research Program. Stanford may submit to Sponsor a revised budget requesting additional funds if Sponsor requests a change in the Research Program scope of work. Sponsor will not be liable for any payment in excess of the Cost except on Sponsor's written agreement. Stanford has the authority to rebudget costs at the discretion of the Principal Investigator, as long as the rebudgeting is consistent with the goals of the Research Program. Sponsor is not entitled to any refund of funds not spent if all Research Program commitments have been met. Stanford will provide its customary final financial report upon Sponsor's written request.

6. PAYMENT

6.1 **Schedule.** Sponsor will pay Stanford in accord with the Payment Schedule on Page 1.

6.2 **Payment Information.** Sponsor will pay by wire transfer to:

Wells Fargo Bank
420 Montgomery Street
San Francisco, CA 94163
(Account numbers to be provided by Stanford contract officer)
or by checks made payable to Stanford University and sent to:
Stanford University
P.O. Box 44253
San Francisco, CA 94144-4253

6.3 **Payment Identification.** For purposes of identification each wire or check payment must refer to the Research Program title, the Agreement number, and the name of the Principal Investigator.

6.4 **Stanford Payment Contact.**

Chris Nodohara, Accountant
Office of Sponsored Research
Stanford University
Encina Hall
616 Serra St., Room 3
Stanford, CA 94305

6.5 **Sponsor Payment Contact.** Invoices to Sponsor will be sent to:

[Name]

[Address]

[Telephone Number]
[Fax Number]

6.6 **Purchase Orders.** To the extent any conflict arises between the terms of this Agreement and the terms of any purchase order subsequently issued by the Sponsor, the terms of this Agreement shall govern.

7.   TAXES

Stanford is a nonprofit 501(c) (3) corporation. Sponsor agrees that if this Agreement is subject to taxation by any governmental authority, Sponsor will pay these taxes in full. Stanford will have no liability for the payment of these taxes.

8.   EXPENDABLES AND EQUIPMENT

Stanford owns all expendables and equipment purchased or fabricated to perform the Research Program.

9.   INTELLECTUAL AND OTHER PROPERTY

9.1   **Ownership of Technology.** Stanford owns the entire right, title, and interest, including all patents, copyrights, and other intellectual property rights, in and to all Technology developed using Stanford facilities and by Stanford personnel ("Stanford Technology") under this Agreement. Sponsor owns all interests, including all patents, copyrights, and other intellectual property rights, in and to all Technology developed using Sponsor facilities and by Sponsor personnel under this Agreement ("Sponsor Technology"). Technology that is jointly developed by Stanford and Sponsor personnel will be jointly owned ("Joint Technology").

9.2   **Disclosure.** Stanford will provide Sponsor with a complete, written, confidential disclosure of any Stanford Technology after the disclosure is received by the Stanford Office of Technology Licensing.

9.3   **Patent Filing and Expenses.** Stanford may file patent applications at its own discretion and expense, or at the request of Sponsor at Sponsor's expense. If Sponsor elects to license Stanford Technology, Sponsor will pay for the costs of patent filing, prosecution and maintenance in the United States and any foreign country.

9.4   **License Election.** By giving written notice to Stanford within 3 months after notice of patentable Stanford Technology, Sponsor may elect one of the following alternatives:

(a)   **Non Exclusive License.** Subject to third party rights, if any, a nonexclusive, nontransferable (without the right to sublicense), worldwide license in a designated field of use to make, have made, use, and sell products covered by the patent application on terms to be negotiated. Stanford may at its option discontinue patent prosecution or maintenance of any invention licensed to Sponsor under this alternative for which Stanford is paying patent-related costs; or

b) **Exclusive License.** Subject to third party rights, if any, a royalty-bearing, limited-term, exclusive, field-of-use license (subject to third-party rights, if any), including the right to sublicense, in the United States or any other country elected by Sponsor (subject to Paragraph 9.7 below) to make, have made, use, and sell products covered by the patent application, in exchange for Sponsor's agreement to diligently commercialize the invention.

9.5 **License Terms and Conditions.** All licenses of this Section 9 elected by Sponsor are effective as of the date the parties negotiate and sign a separate license agreement, which will contain indemnity, insurance, and no-warranty provisions, in addition to other customary terms and conditions. Sponsor agrees all licenses will be subject to any applicable laws and regulations.

9.6 **License to Joint Technology.** Sponsor may, at its option under 9.4(b), exclusively license Stanford's rights in Joint Technology.

9.7 **Foreign-Filing Election.** Sponsor will notify Stanford of those countries outside the United States in which it desires a license in sufficient time for Stanford to satisfy the patent-law requirements of those countries. Sponsor will reimburse Stanford for out-of-pocket costs for those filings, including patent filing, prosecution, and maintenance fees.

9.8 **Copyright Licenses.** Sponsor may elect to negotiate a nonexclusive or exclusive (subject to third party rights, if any) royalty-bearing license to use, reproduce, display, distribute and perform computer software and its documentation for commercial purposes in a designated field of use. Sponsor must elect within 3 months of notice of Stanford's disclosure of copyrightable material available for license. Computer software for which a patent application is filed is subject to Paragraph 9.4.

9.9 **Non-Election.** If Sponsor does not provide written notice of election to Stanford within 3 months of a written disclosure under Paragraphs 9.4, 9.6 or 9.8, Stanford has no further obligations to the Sponsor and may license the Stanford Technology to third parties. If Stanford and Sponsor fail to complete license negotiations within 6 months after written election, Stanford has no further obligations to the Sponsor and may license the Stanford Technology to third parties.

9.10 **Assignment.** Stanford represents that all of its employees, students, and consultants who participate in the Research Program will be obligated to assign to Stanford all their rights in patentable or copyrightable Technology.

9.11 **Other Intellectual Property.** For the avoidance of doubt, all intellectual property developed outside of this Agreement shall remain the property of its owner. Except as explicitly provided in this Agreement, neither party receives any right to the other's intellectual property developed outside of this Agreement.

10. REPORTS

The Principal Investigator will submit a final report to Sponsor within 90 days of the End Date. The report will summarize the Research Program accomplishments and significant research findings.

11. PUBLICATION

11.1 **Objective.** The basic objective of research activities at Stanford is the generation of new knowledge and its expeditious dissemination for the public's benefit. Sponsor will provide all reasonable cooperation with Stanford in meeting this objective.

11.2 **Review.** As a matter of basic academic policy, Stanford retains the right at its discretion to publish freely any results of the Research Program. Stanford will provide Sponsor with a copy of any manuscript or other publication at the time it is submitted for publication. Sponsor may review the manuscript or publication:

   (a)   To ascertain whether Sponsor's Confidential Information would be disclosed by the publication;

   (b)   To identify potentially patentable Technology so that appropriate steps may be taken to protect the Technology; and

   (c)   To confirm that the privacy rights of individuals are adequately protected.

11.3 **Comments.** Sponsor will provide comments, if any, within 30 days of receiving the manuscript or publication. If patentable Technology is disclosed in the manuscript or publication, Sponsor will promptly advise Stanford whether it requests Stanford to file and prosecute a patent application.

11.4 **Acknowledgment.** Stanford will acknowledge the Sponsor in resulting publications for its sponsorship of the Research Project.

12. EARLY TERMINATION

12.1 Either party may terminate this Agreement upon 60 days' written notice. If this Agreement is terminated before the End Date, Sponsor will pay the reasonable cost incurred by Stanford in winding down and terminating the Research Program, including the Cost of the Research Program during the wind-down period and all costs and non-cancelable commitments made before termination. If any Stanford student is supported under this Agreement, Sponsor will remain responsible for the full cost of the student support through the end of the academic quarter in which this Agreement is terminated. After termination, Stanford will submit a final report of all Costs incurred and all funds received under this Agreement. The report will be accompanied by a check for funds remaining after allowable Costs and non-cancelable commitments have been paid.

12.2 Stanford reserves the right to cease performance and terminate this Agreement immediately if Sponsor fails to pay any invoice within 60 days of receipt.

13. NOTICE

Any notices given under this Agreement will be in writing and delivered by mail, by hand, or by facsimile, addressed to the parties as follows:

Stanford

Industrial Contracts Officer
Stanford University
1705 El Camino Real
Palo Alto, CA 94306-1106
Telephone: (650) 723-0651
Facsimile: (650) 725-7295

Sponsor

[Sponsor Cognizant Official]
[Sponsor Name]
[Sponsor Address]

[Sponsor Telephone Number]
[Sponsor Fax Number]

14. PUBLICITY

14.1 **Stanford Name.** Sponsor will not identify Stanford in any promotional statement, or otherwise use the name of any Stanford faculty member, employee, or student, or any trademark, service mark, trade name, or symbol of Stanford or Stanford Hospitals and Clinics, including the Stanford name, unless Sponsor has received Stanford's prior written consent. Permission may be withheld at Stanford's sole discretion.

14.2 **Sponsor Name.** Stanford will not identify Sponsor in any promotional statement, or otherwise use the name of any Sponsor employee, or any trademark, service mark, trade name, or symbol of Sponsor, including Sponsor's name, unless Stanford has received Sponsor's prior written consent. Permission may be withheld at Sponsor's sole discretion.

15., 16. MATERIAL PROVIDED BY SPONSOR

If Sponsor: a) provides any materials, equipment, or other property to Stanford for use in the Research Program; or b) is granted a commercial license in this Agreement to any Research Program results, Sections 15 and 16 of Appendix 1 are incorporated into this Agreement.

17. HUMAN SUBJECTS RESEARCH AND PROTECTION

If the Research Program involves human subjects, Sections 15 and 16 of Appendix 1 and Appendix 2 are incorporated into this Agreement.

18. NO WARRANTIES

Stanford provides Sponsor the rights granted in this Agreement AS IS and WITH ALL FAULTS. Stanford makes no representations and extends no warranties of any kind, either express or implied. Among other things, Stanford disclaims any express or implied warranty:

(a)   of merchantability, of fitness for a particular purpose,

(b)   of non-infringement or

(c)   arising out of any course of dealing.

19. FORCE MAJEURE

Stanford is not liable for any failure to perform as required by this Agreement if the failure to perform is caused by circumstances reasonably beyond Stanford's control, such as labor disturbances or labor disputes of any kind, accidents, failure of any governmental approval required for full performance, civil disorders or commotions, acts of aggression, acts of God, energy or other conservation measures, explosions, failure of utilities, mechanical breakdowns, material shortages, disease, theft, pandemic, or other occurrences.

20. SCIENTIFIC RESEARCH

20.1 **No Guarantee.** Sponsor acknowledges that the Research Program is a scientific undertaking and, consequently, Stanford will not guarantee any particular outcome or specific yield.

20.2 **Freedom of Research.** This Agreement does not limit the freedom of individuals participating in this Research Program to engage in any other research.

21. GENERAL PROVISIONS

21.1 **Laws and Regulations.** Each party is subject to all local, state and federal laws and regulations applicable to its obligations under this Agreement.

21.2 **Export Control.** Both parties agree to adhere to applicable export laws and regulations, subject to all available exclusions and exceptions thereto.

21.3 **Animal Studies.** Stanford does not conduct animal studies that are intended to support applications for research or marketing permits for FDA-regulated products (as described in Title 21, Code of Federal Regulations (CFR) Part 58-Good Laboratory Practice (GLP) for Nonclinical Laboratory Studies).

21.4 **Dispute Resolution.** If any dispute arises between the parties in connection with payments due under this Agreement and it cannot be resolved by mutual agreement after meetings between the parties, it will be finally settled under the JAMS Comprehensive Arbitration Rules and Procedures, by one or more arbitrators appointed in accordance with the Rules. Arbitration will be held in Palo Alto, California, or at some other mutually agreeable location.

21.5 **Assignment.** Neither party may assign this Agreement without the prior written consent of the other party.

21.6 **Severability.** If any provision of this Agreement becomes or is declared illegal, invalid, or unenforceable, the provision will be divisible from this Agreement and deemed to be deleted from this Agreement. If the deletion substantially alters the basis of this Agreement, the parties will negotiate in good faith to amend the provisions of this Agreement to give effect to the original intent of the parties.

21.7 **Independent Contractors.** Stanford and Sponsor are independent contractors and neither is an agent, joint venturer, or partner of the other.

21.8 **Governing Law.** This Agreement is governed by the laws of the State of California, without regard to its conflict of laws doctrine. Any legal action involving this Agreement or the Research Program will be adjudicated in the State of California.

21.9 **Non Discrimination.** Stanford shall follow its normal employment policies, which prohibit discrimination against any employee or applicant for employment on the basis of race, color, creed, religion, national origin, sexual preference, marital status, age, sex, or handicap (except where bona fide occupational qualification so requires), with respect to this Agreement. Qualified individuals will not be denied the opportunity to contribute to the work to be conducted at Stanford under this Agreement on those bases or on the basis of citizenship.

21.10 **Prevailing Terms.** In the event of any inconsistency between the terms of this Agreement and the documents referenced or incorporated into this Agreement, the terms of this Agreement prevail.

21.11 **Entire Agreement.** This Agreement represents the entire agreement and understanding between the parties with respect to its subject matter. It supersedes all prior or contemporaneous discussions, representations, or agreements, whether written or oral, of the parties regarding this subject matter.

21.12 **Amendments or Changes.** Amendments or changes to this Agreement must be in writing and signed by the parties' authorized representatives.

21.13 **Electronic Signatures.** The parties to this Agreement agree that a copy of the original signature (including an electronic copy) may be used for any and all purposes for which the original signature may have been used. The parties further waive any right to challenge the admissibility or authenticity of this Agreement in a court of law based solely on the absence of an original signature.

21.14 **Counterparts.** This Agreement and any amendment to it may be executed in counterparts and all of these counterparts together shall be deemed to constitute one and the same agreement.

[Signatures on front page]

Appendix 1

15. INDEMNIFICATION

15.1 **Duties of the parties.** Sponsor will indemnify, defend, and hold harmless The Board of Trustees of the Leland Stanford Junior University, their respective trustees, directors, employees, agents, volunteers, subcontractors, and students ("Indemnitees") from any liability, damage, loss, or expense (including reasonable attorneys' fees and expenses of litigation) incurred by or imposed upon the Indemnitees or any one of them in connection with any claims, suits, actions, demands, or judgments arising out of or connected with this Agreement or the research done under this Agreement, except to the extent that the liability is due to the gross negligence and willful misconduct of Stanford. Stanford will promptly notify Sponsor of any claim and will cooperate with Sponsor in the defense of the claim. Sponsor will, at its own expense, provide attorneys reasonably acceptable to Stanford to defend against any claim with respect to which Sponsor has agreed to indemnify Stanford. This indemnity will not be deemed excess coverage to any insurance or self-insurance Stanford may have covering a claim. Sponsor's indemnity will not be limited by the amount of Sponsor's insurance.

15.2 **Survival.** The provisions of this clause will survive termination of this Agreement.

16. INSURANCE

16.1 **Stanford Coverage.** Stanford will maintain Worker's Compensation insurance or other coverage on its employees as required by California law, and will self-insure or maintain insurance covering its liability under this Agreement.

16.2 **Sponsor Coverage.** Sponsor will procure and maintain during the term of this Agreement comprehensive liability and product liability insurance to the full amount of Sponsor insurance limits, but in no event less than $5,000,000 per occurrence, with a reputable and financially secure insurance carrier. The insurance will include The Board of Trustees of the Leland Stanford Junior University, their respective trustees, directors, employees, agents, subcontractors, and students as additional insureds with respect to this Agreement. This insurance will be written to cover claims incurred, discovered, manifested, or made during or after the expiration of this Agreement.

16.3 **Certificate.** Before executing the Agreement, Sponsor will provide Stanford with a Certificate of Insurance evidencing primary coverage and requiring 30 days prior written notice of cancellation or material change to Stanford. Sponsor will advise Stanford in writing that it maintains excess liability coverage (following form) over primary insurance for at least the minimum limits set forth above. Conditions of the Certificate of Insurance will be subject to approval in advance by Stanford's Office of Risk Management.

16.4 **Primary Coverage.** Sponsor's insurance will be primary coverage. Stanford's insurance or self-insurance will be excess and noncontributory.

16.5 **Continued Coverage.** If Sponsor's insurance is written on a claims-made basis, as opposed to an occurrence basis, Sponsor will purchase the coverage necessary to ensure continued and uninterrupted coverage of all claims, including those made after the policy expires or is terminated.

Appendix 2

17. HUMAN SUBJECTS RESEARCH AND PROTECTION

Sponsor agrees to provide Stanford with any data and safety monitoring reports related to the Research Program, and Stanford agrees they will be submitted to the IRB as required. During the Research Program and for at least two (2) years following the completion of the Research Program at all sites, Sponsor shall promptly provide Stanford and Principal Investigator with the written report of any routine monitoring findings in site monitoring reports and data safety monitoring committee reports including, but not limited to, data and safety analyses, and any Research Program information that may (i) affect the safety and welfare of current or former Research Program subjects, or (ii) influence the conduct of the Research Program. Stanford and/or Principal Investigator will communicate findings to the IRB and Research Program Subjects, as appropriate.

Exhibit A

Research Program

Source: Stanford University, 2012. *Sponsored Research Agreement (template)*, May 14. http://web.stanford.edu/group/ICO/industry/documents/SRA%20template%20 5-14-12.doc.

GUIDELINES: UNIVERSITY OF CALIFORNIA

University of California
Office of the President
May 1989

GUIDELINES ON UNIVERSITY-INDUSTRY RELATIONS

INTRODUCTION

These Guidelines, which supersede the Interim Guidelines on University-Industry Relations, dated November 3, 1982, are issued in response to a growing recognition of the importance and complexity of relations between the University of California and private industry. University-industry collaborations can result in benefits to both parties, if there is a clear understanding of fundamental University policies and procedures and of the complementary but differing goals of the University and private industry.

The Guidelines are designed primarily to assist faculty in their relations with industry. They summarize relevant University policies and seek to clarify relationships and obligations between the University of California and private industry. They address issues that arise for faculty and academic researchers in particular. Some of the policies, however, such as the University Copyright and Patent Policies and Regulation 4, also apply to staff and non-faculty academic employees. For these employees, further policies bearing on University-industry relationships can be found in the Executive Program Personnel Policies, the Management and Professional Program Personnel Policies, and in Business and Finance Bulletins. (See also Compendium of Specialized University Policies Guidelines and Regulations Related to Conflict of Interest.)

In general, faculty members are encouraged to engage in appropriate outside professional relationships with private industry. Such outside activities can provide the individual faculty member with experience and knowledge valuable to teaching and research and also help students gain valuable educational opportunities and experiences. Such activities also facilitate the transfer of technology to improve the well-being and productivity of society and offer research opportunities through which the faculty member can make a contribution to knowledge.

They also can constitute suitable public service. Individual faculty members have the responsibility for assuring that such outside professional relationships do not interfere with their obligations to the University in teaching, research, and public service.

The premise that underlies these Guidelines is that first consideration must be given to the University's mission of teaching, research, and public service. In pursuing relationships with industry, the University must keep the public trust and maintain institutional independence and integrity to permit faculty and students to pursue learning and research freely.

The University's long history of cooperation with industry in the support of research, instruction, and public service reflects the University's land-grant origins. University-industry relations consist of a variety of activities, including:

- Direct funding of research costs through contracts and grants.
- Formal licensing to industry of University-owned patents and technology.
- Gifts and endowments (including endowed chairs) designated for colleges, schools, departments, or individuals.
- University-industry exchange programs and student internships.
- Specialized programs designed by the University for continuing education and training of professionals, primarily through University Extension.
- Participation of industry representatives on campus and Universitywide advisory groups.
- Cooperative research projects, some of which include government participation and the use of specialized facilities.
- Use of unique University facilities on a fee-for-service basis.
- Research and development facilities of industries housed on University property (industrial parks).
- Activities of Cooperative Extension.
- Faculty consulting.
- Research activities of the Agricultural Experiment Station and its affiliated field stations.

In recent years there has been heightened interest and activity in University-industry relationships. Federal patent and tax laws have changed to facilitate and encourage University-industry collaboration and technology transfer. The Department of Energy National Laboratories are under a Federal mandate to facilitate technology transfer. Moreover, legislators increasingly see such cooperation as a way of enhancing national research and development efforts and of helping to make the State and the nation more competitive.

For those individuals and groups of faculty and the private sector who want to embark on cooperative efforts, the means for doing so are readily available. The University is exploring innovative organizational approaches to assure support of worthy research and education that provide significant contributions to the body of scholarship and knowledge, that are responsive to industry interests, and that advance the public's interest in these productive relationships.

GUIDELINES

1. *Open Academic Environment*

   All University research, including research sponsored by industry, is governed by the tradition of the free exchange of ideas and timely dissemination of research results. The University is committed to an open teaching and research environment in which ideas can be exchanged freely among faculty and students in the classroom, in the laboratory, at informal meetings, and elsewhere in the University. Such an environment contributes to the progress of teaching and research in all disciplines.

   Reasonable steps should be taken to insure that commercial pressures do not impede faculty communication with their colleagues or their students about the progress of their research or their findings. Indicators of possible problems include the disruption of the informal exchange of research findings and products, the lessening of collegiality, and the rise of competitive and adversarial relations among faculty.

   Guideline: The Administration and the Academic Senate are responsible for assuring that an open environment exists throughout the University. It is the responsibility of the campus administration, departmental faculty, and the Academic Senate to establish appropriate norms and to assure the existence of an open environment.

2. *Freedom to Publish*

   Freedom to publish and disseminate results is a major criterion of the appropriateness of any research project. University policy precludes assigning to·extramural sources the right to keep or make final decisions about what may be published. A sponsor may seek a short delay, however, in order to comment upon and to review publications for disclosure of its proprietary data or for potentially patentable inventions. Such a delay in publication should normally be no more than 60 to 90 days. Chancellors, and Vice Presidents, in their areas of responsibility, may make exceptions to this policy under a few limited conditions. This is outlined in full in the Contract and Grant Manual. If any doubt remains concerning an exception, the Chancellor may resolve it by further referring the matter to the Office of the President.

The freedom to publish is not an obligation to publish. Under the Faculty Code of Conduct, a faculty member "... accepts the obligation to exercise critical self-discipline and judgment in using, extending, and transmitting knowledge ..." The exercise of this self-discipline and Judgment, not external factors, should determine the content and timing of publication.

Guideline: Freedom to publish is fundamental to the University and is a major criterion of the appropriateness of a research project.

3. *Outside Professional Activities*

    Faculty are encouraged to engage in appropriate outside professional activities. Each year faculty must submit an annual report on outside professional activities to the department chair. This information is included in the faculty member's record and evaluated in the academic review process.

    It is the responsibility of each faculty member to assure that such outside activities do not interfere with obligations to the University in teaching, research, and public service; and that no portion of time due the University is devoted to private purposes. Provisions of outside consulting agreements must not limit a faculty member's ability to carry out ongoing obligations under University policies such as the Patent Policy.

    Guideline: Faculty are encouraged to engage in appropriate outside professional activities. Responsibility rests with each faculty member to assure that such activities do not interfere with the performance of University duties.

4. *The Obligation to Avoid Conflict of Interest*

    University employees must avoid conflict of interest. A conflict of interest is a situation in which an employee has the opportunity to influence a University decision that could lead to financial or other personal advantage, or that involves other conflicting official obligations. The California Political Reform Act of 1974 prohibits any University employee from making or participating in the making of a University decision from which personal financial gain is foreseeable. Exempted from the Act are decisions on the selection of teaching and other program materials and some decisions about research. The Universitywide Statement on Conflicts of Interest gives some examples of conflict-of-interest situations. It goes on to say, however:

"It has long been recognized that the only truly effective safeguard against conflicts of interest situations is the integrity of the faculty and staff. A codification of the complex ethical questions involved, even if possible, would be unduly restrictive. At the same time, even the most alert and conscientious person may at times be in doubt concerning the propriety of certain actions or relationships. Whenever such doubt arises, the University expects the individual involved to consult with the Office of the Chancellor, or the Chancellor's designated representative, before making a decision."

Guideline: Faculty may not engage in any activity that places them in a conflict of interest between their official University activities and any other interests or obligations.

5. *Disclosure Responsibilities*

Principal Investigators who have a financial interest in any non-governmental sponsor proposing to fund their research must disclose that interest. The written statement of disclosure must be reviewed and approved independently and substantively by local campus committees on the basis of specific criteria in the University's disclosure policy and guidelines before funding for the research can be approved. This report is required by both University policy and State law. A project completion statement is also filed. Such statements of disclosure are open to public inspection. As noted in Guideline 3, faculty must also submit to the department chair after-the-fact annual reports on outside professional activities.

Guideline: Principal Investigators who have a financial interest (such as equity, directorship, or consultant relationship) in any non-governmental sponsor proposing to fund their research must disclose this interest prior to acceptance of funding.

6. *Responsibility to Students*

University regulations protect the academic freedom of students, and responsibility for adherence to these principles rests with the faculty. Students who have reasons to believe they are in situations which violate those principles are advised to seek the advice of the

Department Chair or campus ombudsperson. The Academic Senate's Divisional Graduate Councils and the Universitywide Coordinating Committee on Graduate Affairs are also responsible for making sure that closer University-industry relations do not create strains in the professor-student relationship.

Students must be able to choose research topics for educational reasons without being overly influenced by the need to advance investigations of direct interest to a particular firm; they must be protected against the premature transmittal of research results; and they must be advised objectively on career choices.

The Faculty Code of Conduct states:

"As teachers, professors encourage the free pursuit of learning in their students. They hold before them the best scholarly and ethical standards of their discipline. Professors demonstrate respect for students as individuals, and adhere to their proper roles as intellectual guides and counselors. Professors make every reasonable effort to foster honest academic conduct and to assure that their evaluations of students reflect each student's true merit. They respect the confidential nature of the relationship between professor and student. They avoid any exploitation, harassment, or discriminatory treatment of students. They acknowledge significant academic or scholarly assistance from them. They protect their academic freedom." (AAUP Statement, 1966; Revised, 1987)

Guideline: Faculty members must not allow any outside professional activities or interests to adversely affect their responsibilities to students as teachers, mentors, or supervisors of research.

7. *Patent Policy*

All University employees must disclose all potentially patentable inventions conceived or developed while employed by the University and must assign all those inventions that occur in the course and scope of their employment to the University. Whether inventions are or are not patentable is a matter of Federal patent law. Whether the University will prosecute any specific patent is a determination to be made by the UC Patent, Trademark, and Copyright Office.

While all patentable inventions must be disclosed, inventions resulting from permissible consulting activities without use of University funds or facilities need not be assigned to the University. Consulting agreements should be reviewed carefully, however, to make sure they do not conflict with obligations under University patent and other relevant policies.

The University of California Patent Policy seeks to assure balance among several objectives: 1) facilitating prompt and effective development of useful inventions; 2) preventing the inappropriate use of public funds for private gain; 3) maintaining good relations with industry to make the best use of opportunities for education and research funding; and 4) obtaining appropriate revenues for the University from the licensing of patents. For these purposes, the University Patent Policy provides for: 1) mandatory disclosure to the University of potentially patentable inventions by employees or those who otherwise use facilities or research funds of the University; 2) assignment of patent rights to inventions developed in the course of University employment, or with use of University research facilities, or University funds; 3) sharing of royalties with inventors; and 4) transferring of technology to industry for the public benefit.

Although the primary purpose of University research is not commercially applicable discoveries or inventions, the University recognizes the need to encourage the practical application of the results of research for the public benefit. Thus, the University maintains an active program for identifying and patenting potentially useful inventions and for licensing them to firms which have the capability of developing, manufacturing, and marketing them.

Guideline: All University employees and others who use University funds or facilities must sign patent agreements and must adhere to the University of California Patent Policy.

8. *University Practice on Licensing the Use of Technology Resulting from Research*

The major purposes of licensing to industry the use of technology resulting from University research are: 1) to provide a mechanism for transferring, disclosing, and disseminating the results of University research to the public for the public benefit; and 2) to meet obligations to research sponsors. Licensing also provides a financial return to support further research and education.

Terms and conditions for licensing agreements should consider the nature of the technology, the stage of development of the invention, the effect on the research endeavor in question, the public benefit, and the marketplace. Agreements are negotiated on a case by case basis. If a company needs time to evaluate a research result, an option agreement may be negotiated to allow a limited time for a review for licensing purposes. The University will grant the right of first refusal to the sponsor for an exclusive or nonexclusive license, based on the level of sponsor support. Any license of a patentable invention must at least provide for diligent development by the licenses and, in most cases, for the payment of royalties. Reproduction of copyrightable expressions may be separately licensed. Agreements, options, non-exclusive licenses, and exclusive licenses must not interfere with the principle of open dissemination of research results.

Guideline: University practice permits the licensing of technology resulting from its research as long as the university retains the right to disseminate the results publicly. The principle of the right of open dissemination of research results must not be compromised.

9. *Copyright Policy*

In keeping with academic tradition, University Copyright Policy provides that ownership of copyrights to scholarly or aesthetic works that are prepared through independent academic effort and not as part of a directed University assignment generally reside with the author (unless the work in question was commissioned by the University, or the work was created under extramural support). Such scholarly or aesthetic works include, but are not limited to, books, articles, lectures, and computer software resulting from independent academic study; or artistic works such as novels, videotapes, and musical compositions. Otherwise, all rights in copyright arising from University employment or the use of University resources belong to the University. Title to the copyrightable material that is developed under a contract or grant from a commercial sponsor normally belongs to the University. In limited cases, where the purpose of the agreement is to develop a copyrightable work for the sponsor's publication, the copyright may be assigned to the sponsor, but only if there is a provision surrendering this right to the University after a reasonable interval of time, in the event the extramural fund source has not published within that time. Each campus has a designated official who is able to answer questions about applicability of the Copyright Policy.

Guideline: All University employees and others who use University funds or facilities must adhere to the University Copyright Policy.

10. *Tangible Research Products*

Tangible research products include a wide range of tangible property resulting from the conduct of research, as distinct from copyrightable expressions and patentable inventions. Tangible research products may confer a public benefit through commercial licensing and may include biological materials, such as cell lines and plasmids; chemical compounds; electrical schematic diagrams; mechanical design drawings; and more abstract products such as detailed descriptions or compilations of laboratory procedures, analytical methods, or other such "know-how." The University's Intellectual Property Advisory Council is developing a written policy on tangible research products.

In the event that research results are to be licensed, the University prefers that they be patented or copyrighted when possible. When this is not practical, licensing of tangible research products consistent with these Guidelines is permissible. When the University licenses tangible research products, it is willing to restrict commercial availability of such materials, but such agreements must permit the University to retain the discretion to publish any results of research at any time and to disseminate the tangible materials for educational and research purposes. Such publication and dissemination rights are essential to an academic institution of education and research.

Licensing of tangible research products must have the written concurrence of the involved researchers and the approval of the appropriate Chancellor, Laboratory Director, or Vice President. All such licenses must follow standard University policy and procedures for contracts. Chancellors are further responsible for monitoring the effects of such arrangements on the openness of academic exchange.

Guideline: The University will permit the licensing of tangible research products as long as no inappropriate restrictions are placed on publication or dissemination of research results and materials.

11. *Use of University Facilities*

University facilities are to be used for activities appropriate to the University's mission. Regulation 4, Special Services to Individuals and Organizations, which governs the use of research facilities, establishes guidelines limiting research to activities which are appropriate to the University. In a limited number of instances within the scope of Regulation 4, the University does permit the use of unique or very specialized University facilities by outside parties, both industry and government agencies, on a fee-for-use basis.

Regulation 4 states:

"University participation in tests and investigations shall be limited to activities which lead to the extension of knowledge or to increased effectiveness in teaching. Routine tasks of a commonplace type will not be undertaken.

University laboratories, bureaus and facilities are not to be used for tests, studies, or investigations of purely commercial character, such as mineral assays, determination of properties of materials, the performance efficiencies of machines, analyses of soils, water, insecticides, fertilizers, feeds, fuels, and other materials, statistical calculations, etc., except when it is shown conclusively that satisfactory facilities for such services do not exist elsewhere. Those requiring such tests or services should apply to business firms or to . . .public agencies . . ."

Guideline: University facilities and resources should be devoted to activities that support teaching and research and that lead to the advancement of knowledge. They should not be used for routine tasks of a commercial character. Unique or special facilities may be made available to outside users on a fee-for-use basis.

12.   *Recovering Costs from Research Sponsors: Gift/Grant Distinctions*

In accepting contracts and grants from extramural sources, the University expects to recover full direct and indirect costs of the activity. This is a protection against the use of public funds for private gain. In the case of nonprofit and Federally sponsored research, the University may agree to share some costs, usually in the form of contributed effort. In the case of grants from independent philanthropic foundations, the University does occasionally waive indirect costs as a form of cost sharing. The University views cost recovery in the case of gifts differently. With a gift, the donor does not impose contractual obligations and funds are awarded irrevocably. The criteria that distinguish gifts from grants are provided in the University Policy on Review of Gifts/Grants for Research. Contracts with commercial entities should provide for full direct and indirect cost recovery.

Guideline: The proper distinction between gifts and grants, with the different obligations in each case, is important to the integrity of the University's sponsored research program.

13. *Organizational Arrangements*

Innovative organizational approaches for promoting University-industry relations and funding University research, if compatible with University policy, should be considered. Campuses are entering into various combinations of arrangements including those with government funding, with multiple corporate sponsors, with a single company, and with other campuses and universities.

Primarily because of its need to be even handed in its support of faculty members and in its openness to competing commercial enterprises, the University has not arranged for investment in firms whose products derive from University research, when the principal purpose is to promote faculty inventions. If the University were to be an equity participant in the work of one or more faculty members, it could be seen as favoring those faculty members, and could be in conflict with the University's role to support scholarship and allocate institutional resources in an even-handed manner. Moreover, this kind of relationship with certain companies could preclude or inhibit research sponsorship by other competing companies.

Guideline: In general, it is not appropriate for the University to invest directly in enterprises when such investment is tied to the commercial development of new ideas created or advanced through University research.

FOOTNOTES

Policies and Documents Pertaining to University Relations with Industry

1. Compendium of Specialized University Policies, Guidelines and Regulations Related to Conflict of Interest, Business and Finance Bulletin G-39 (April 15, 1986).

2. Publication Policy and Guidelines on Rights to Results of Extramural Projects or Programs, Contract and Grant Manual, Chapter 1 (1989).

3. University Policy on Faculty Conduct and Administration of Discipline (June 14, 1974), including the Faculty Code of conduct (Revised by The Regents on May 15, 1987; issued by the President on January 19, 1988; and issued with technical changes by Senior Vice President Frazer on August 26, 1988).

4. Policy on Outside Professional Activities of Faculty Members (April 13, 1979) and Guidelines for Reporting Outside Professional

Activities (August 6, 1979), Academic Personnel Manual, Section 025.

5. Standing Order of The Regents of the University of California 103.l(b), Special Provisions Concerning Officers, Faculty Members, and Employees of the University, Service Obligations.

6. Compendium of Specialized University Policies, Guidelines and Regulations Related to Conflict of Interest, Business and Finance Bulletin G-39 (April 15, 1986).

7. Statement of Conflicts of Interest, Office of the President (September 19, 1967; issued on October 5, 1967 and October 12, 1967).

8. Policy on Disclosure of Financial Interest in Private Sponsors of Research, Office of the President (April 26, 1984).

9. Guidelines for Disclosure and Review of Principal Investigators' Financial Interest in Private Sponsors of Research, Office of the President (April 27, 1984).

10. Policy on Outside Professional Activities of Faculty Members (April 13, 1979) and Guidelines for Reporting Outside Professional Activities (August 6, 1979), Academic Personnel Manual, Section 025.

11. University Policy on Faculty Conduct and Administration of Discipline (June 14, 1974), including the Faculty Code of Conduct (Revised by The Regents on May 15, 1987; issued by the President on January 19, 1988; and issued with technical changes by Senior Vice President Frazer on August 26, 1988).

12. University of California Patent Policy (November 18, 1985).

13. University Copyright Policy (August 1, 1975).

14. Publication Policy and Guidelines on Rights to Results of Extramural Projects or Programs, Contract and Grant Manual, Chapter 1 (1989).

15. Regulation 4, Special Services to Individuals and Organizations, Academic Personnel Manual, Section 020 (June 23, 1958).

16. Review of Gifts/Grants for Research, Office of the President (July 8, 1980).

Source: University of California, 1989. *Guidelines on University-Industry Relations*, June 6. http://www.ucop.edu/raohome/cgmemos/89-20.html.

GUIDELINES: US DEPARTMENT OF AGRICULTURE

ARTICLES

Article 1. Definitions

1.1 ARS means the United States Department of Agriculture, Agricultural Research Service.

1.2 COOPERATOR means [XYZ].

1.3 Agreement means this Cooperative Research and Development Agreement.

1.4 Confidential Information means trade secrets or commercial or financial information that is privileged or confidential under the meaning of 5 USC 552(b)(4).

1.5 Subject Invention means any invention or other intellectual property conceived or first reduced to practice under this Agreement which is patentable or otherwise protectable under Title 35 of the United States Code, under 7 USC 2321, et seq., or under the patent laws of a foreign country. *Specifically not included in the definition of Subject Inventions are inventions made outside the Scope of Agreement or prior to the execution of this Agreement.* [**NOTE: You may want to list inventions that may be used in this CRADA but are not Subject Inventions.**]

1.6 Scope of Agreement means those activities set forth in Schedule 2, entitled "Statement of Work."

1.7 Period of Agreement means that period set forth under the Period of Agreement on the ARS Office of Technology Transfer cover form for the Agreement.

Article 2. Publications

2.1 Subject to the requirements of confidentiality and preservation of rights in Subject Inventions, either party may publish the results of this Agreement, PROVIDED:

    a. The other party is allowed to review the manuscript at least sixty (60) days prior to submission for publication by submission to the Authorized Agent.

    b. The publication shall acknowledge this Agreement and the contributions of each party's personnel.

    c. The final decision as to the publication content rests with the party that writes the publication.

2.2 Publication and/or other disclosure of the results of this Agreement shall be delayed as necessary to preserve both United States of America and foreign patent rights in a Subject Invention.

    a. Such a delay will only be granted if requested in writing; and

    b. The requesting party demonstrates promptness and diligence in seeking patent protection on the Subject Invention.

Article 3. Confidentiality

3.1 Confidential Information, which is owned by one party to this Agreement and disclosed to the other, shall be labeled "CONFIDENTIAL" by the submitter and shall not be disclosed by the recipient without permission of the owner, EXCEPT in accordance with Article 2.

3.2 To the extent either party orally submits its Confidential Information to the other party, the submitting party will prepare a document marked "CONFIDENTIAL" embodying or identifying in reasonable detail such orally submitted Confidential Information and provide the document to the other party within thirty (30) days of disclosure.

3.3 Neither party shall be bound by confidentiality if the Confidential Information received from the other party:

    a. Already is available to the public or known to the recipient;

    b. Becomes available to the public through no fault of the recipient; or

    c. Is nonconfidentially received from another party legally entitled to it.

Article 4. Meetings, Reports and Records

4.1 Frequent and effective communication is essential to the successful accomplishment of the objectives of this Agreement. To this end, the scientific representatives of ARS and COOPERATOR shall meet (meetings need not be in person if agreed upon) at least once every six (6) months to exchange results, perform critiques, and make plans and recommendations. Written progress reports shall be supplied by each party to the other at least fifteen (15) calendar days prior to each semi-annual meeting.

4.2 Any such plan or recommendation that is outside the Scope of Agreement shall be reduced to writing and referred to the Authorized

Agent of each party for appropriate action. Any such plan or recommendation so referred shall not be binding upon either party unless incorporated into this Agreement by written amendment.

4.3 Each party shall keep complete records relating to this research. All such records shall be available for inspection by either party at reasonable times. The records, or true copies of them, shall be delivered to either party upon request.

4.4 The results of this Agreement and research data that are collected, compiled, and evaluated under this Agreement shall be shared and mutually interchanged by COOPERATOR and ARS.

4.5 A final report summarizing all data shall be submitted by each party, separately or jointly, to both party's Authorized Agents within sixty (60) days of the completion of this Agreement.

Article 5. Research Exclusion

5.1 The results of this Agreement owned or co-owned by the U.S. Government may be made available to others by ARS for bona fide research purposes if:

a. Confidentiality is not breached; or

b. Patent or Plant Variety Protection Certificate rights are not compromised.

5.2 Plants and animals, their genetic material or information relating thereto, or parts thereof, covered by Plant Variety Protection Certificates, Plant Patents, or Utility Patents, owned or co-owned by ARS, may be made available by ARS to third parties for bona fide research purposes including the development of new animals or plants.

Article 6. Ownership of Inventions

6.1 All rights, title, and interest in any Subject Invention made solely by employee(s) of ARS shall be owned by ARS.

6.2 All rights, title, and interest in any Subject Invention made jointly by at least one (1) employee of ARS and at least one (1) employee of COOPERATOR shall be jointly owned by ARS and COOPERATOR.

6.3 All rights, title, and interest in any Subject Invention made solely by employees of COOPERATOR shall be owned by COOPERATOR.

Article 7. Subject Invention Licenses

7.1   COOPERATOR is granted an option to negotiate an exclusive license in each Subject Invention owned or co-owned by ARS for one or more field(s) of use encompassed by the Scope of Agreement. This license shall be consistent with the requirements of 35 USC 209(a), 209(b) (manufactured substantially in the U.S.), and 209(f) and other such terms and conditions as may be reasonable under the circumstances, as agreed upon through good faith negotiations between COOPERATOR and ARS.

7.2   This option shall terminate whenever COOPERATOR fails to:

a.   Submit a complete application for an exclusive license within sixty (60) days of being notified by ARS of an Invention's availability for licensing; or

b.   Submit a good faith written response to a written proposal of licensing terms within sixty (60) days of such proposal.

7.3   COOPERATOR grants ARS, on behalf of the U.S. Government, a royalty free, nonexclusive, worldwide, irrevocable, nontransferable license for any COOPERATOR solely owned Subject Invention. The purpose of this license shall be to practice the Subject Invention or have it practiced, by or on behalf of the U.S. Government, for research or other U.S. Government purposes. 15 USC 3710a(b)(2).

Article 8. Subject Invention Information

8.1   The Authorized Agents or designees of each party shall promptly make written disclosure to each other of each Subject Invention.

8.2   This information shall be treated in confidence by the receiving party, EXCEPT: it may be shared with those having a need to know.

8.3   Each party shall provide, when requested by the other, all information in its possession, or true copies thereof, pertaining to a Subject Invention which may be necessary or useful in the preparation, filing, and prosecution of patent or Plant Variety Protection Certificate applications covering the Subject Invention.

Article 9. Intellectual Property Protection Applications

9.1   ARS and COOPERATOR agree to cooperate with the other in the preparation, filing, and prosecution of Patent or Plant Variety Protection Certificate applications on Subject Inventions in the United States of America and any other country.

9.2 ARS shall provide COOPERATOR'S Authorized Agent or their designee with a copy of any such application on a Subject Invention within fourteen (14) calendar days of filing.

9.3 ARS shall have the first option to prepare and prosecute patent or Plant Variety Protection Certificate applications on Subject Inventions that are owned or co-owned by the U.S. Government, which option may be waived in whole or in part.

Article 10. Use of Name or Endorsements

COOPERATOR shall not in any way state or imply that this Agreement or the results of this Agreement are an endorsement of its organizational units, employees, products, or services except to the extent permission is specifically granted by ARS.

Article 11. Regulatory Compliance with Government Rules & Regulations

11.1 COOPERATOR is responsible for obtaining appropriate opinions, permits, or licenses from Federal or State agencies, which regulate research materials, or commercial products that may arise from the research work performed within the Scope of Agreement.

11.2 In carrying out its responsibilities under this Article, COOPERATOR shall:

    a. Consult and coordinate regulatory approval actions with ARS; and

    b. Give ARS' Authorized Agent or designee a copy of any applications and opinions, permits, or licenses issued.

11.3 Both parties acknowledge and agree to comply with all applicable laws and regulations of the Animal and Plant Health Inspection Service, the Center for Disease Control, and /or Export Control Administration pertaining to possession or transference of technical information, biological materials, pathogens, toxins, genetic elements, genetically engineered microorganisms, vaccines, and the like.

Article 12. Liability

It is understood and agreed that neither party to this Agreement shall be responsible for any damages or injuries arising out of the conduct of activities governed by this Agreement, except to the extent that such damages and/or injuries were caused by the negligent or wrongful acts or omissions of its employees, agents or officers. ARS' liability shall be limited by the Federal Tort Claims Act, 28 USC 2671, et seq.

Article 13. Termination

13.1   Either party may unilaterally terminate this entire Agreement at any time by giving the other party written notice not less then sixty (60) calendar days prior to the desired termination date.

13.2   Articles 2. "Publications", 3. "Confidentiality", 6. "Ownership", 7. "Subject Invention Licenses", 10. "Use of Name or Endorsements", and 12. "Liability" shall survive the expiration or termination of this Agreement.

13.3   If either party unilaterally terminates this Agreement pursuant to Article 13.1, each party shall return to the other or destroy, as shall be then agreed, any and all data and materials originated or provided by one party to the other that is still in the receiving party's possession within 30 days of termination.

Article 14. Availability of Appropriations

The continuance of this Agreement is subject to the passage by the Congress of the United States of an appropriation of funds from which expenditures may legally be made to cover ARS' contributions.

Article 15. Disputes

15.1   Any dispute arising under this Agreement, which cannot be readily resolved, shall be submitted jointly to the Authorized Agents, identified in Article 16.

15.2   Each party agrees to seek in good faith to resolve the issue through negotiation or other forms of nonbinding dispute resolution processes mutually acceptable to the parties.

15.3   Pending the resolution of any dispute or claim pursuant to Article 15, the parties agree that performance of all obligations shall be pursued diligently.

Article 16. Notices and Authorized Agents

Notices between the parties and copies of correspondence among the scientific and/or technical representatives of each party that interpret or may have a bearing on the legal effect of this Agreement's terms and conditions shall be sent to the Authorized Agents. Referencing Agreement Number 58-3K95-X-XXX thereon, send copies to:

ARS' Authorized Agent   Cooperator's Authorized Agent
Robert J. Griesbach   Name
USDA-ARS-OTT   Organization
5601 Sunnyside Ave.   Mailing Address
Beltsville, Maryland 20705-5131   City, State, Zip
Tel.: 301-504-6905   Tel.:
Fax: 301-504-5060   Fax:
E-mail: crada.ott@nps.ars.usda.gov E-mail:

Article 17. Limitation on ARS' Scientific Representative's Authority

ARS' Scientific Representative, also known as the Authorized Departmental Officer's Designated Representative ("ADODR"), is authorized to perform the research and development falling within the Scope of Agreement. This individual is not authorized to change or interpret with authority the terms and conditions of this Agreement.

Article 18. Assignments

18.1   Neither this Agreement nor any rights or obligations of the parties hereto shall be assigned or otherwise transferred by either party without the prior written consent of the other party, which consent shall not be unreasonably withheld.

18.2   In no case shall COOPERATOR assign or transfer this Agreement to a party not a citizen or legal resident of the United States.

18.3   ARS is an agency of the U.S. Government and any rights or obligations created under this Agreement are freely transferable within the U.S. Government and shall not be deemed an "assignment" as contemplated by this Article 18.

Article 19. Relationship of Parties

19.1   ARS and COOPERATOR act in their independent capacities in the performance of their respective functions under this Agreement and neither party is to be considered the officer, agent, or employee of the other.

19.2   Each party shall allow, consistent with policies and procedures of ARS and the COOPERATOR, access to their facilities, as needed.

19.3   Each party shall separately assign personnel, equipment, supplies, transportation, and facilities, as needed and available to meet respective responsibilities hereunder, such resources to remain the property of the assignor.

Article 20. Force Majeure

20.1 Neither party shall be liable for any unforeseeable event beyond its reasonable control not caused by the fault or negligence of such party:

    a. Which causes the party to be unable to perform its obligations under this Agreement; and

    b. Which it has been unable to overcome by the exercise of due diligence.

    c. This includes, but is not limited to, flood, drought, earthquake, storm, fire, pestilence, lightning and other natural catastrophes, epidemic, war, riot, civil disturbance or disobedience, strikes, labor dispute, failure, or sabotage of either party's facilities or any order or injunction made by a court or public agency.

20.2 In the event of the occurrence of such force majeure event, the party unable to perform shall promptly notify the other party. It shall also:

    a. Use its best efforts to resume performance as quickly as possible;

    b. Suspend performance only for such period of time as is necessary as a result of the force majeure event.

Article 21. Amendment

21.1 If either party desires a modification in this Agreement, the parties shall confer in good faith to determine the desirability of such modification.

21.2 Such modification shall not be effective until a written amendment is signed by the Authorized Agents of both parties.

Article 22. Severability

The illegality or invalidity of any provision of this Agreement shall not impair, affect, or invalidate the other provisions of this Agreement.

Article 23. Ambiguities

ARS and COOPERATOR agree that each party has reviewed this Agreement and that any rule of construction to the effect that ambiguities are to be resolved against the drafting party shall not apply to the interpretation of this Agreement.

Article 24. Officials Not To Benefit

24.1 No Delegate to or Member of the Congress of the United States of America shall have a part of or benefit from this Agreement.

24.2 This requirement does not include corporations if this Agreement is entered into for the corporation's general benefit.

Article 25. Subcontracting Approval

25.1 A party hereto desiring to obtain and use the services of a third party via contract or otherwise shall give prior notice to the other party, including details of the contract or other arrangement.

25.2 This requirement is to assure that confidentiality is not breached and rights in Subject Inventions are not compromised.

Article 26. Governing Law

The construction, validity, performance, and effect of this entire Agreement shall be governed by the laws applicable to the Government of the United States of America as practiced in the Federal Courts located in the District of Columbia.

Article 27. Entire Agreement

27.1 This Agreement constitutes the entire agreement between COOPERATOR and ARS and supersedes all prior agreements and understandings between them with respect to its subject matter.

27.2 Any representations, promise, or condition in connection with such subject matter, which is not incorporated in this Agreement, shall not be binding upon either party.

27.3 No modification, renewal, extension, waiver, or termination of this Agreement or any of its provisions shall be binding upon the party against whom enforcement of such modification, renewal, extension, waiver, or termination is sought, unless made in writing and signed on behalf of such party by that party's Authorized Agent.

27.4 As used herein, the word "termination" includes any and all means of bringing to an end prior to its expiration by its own terms of this Agreement, or any provision thereof, whether by release, discharge, abandonment, or otherwise.

ARTICLES 1, 2, 3, 6, 7 AND 8 OF SCHEDULE 1 ARE NOT USED IN AGREEMENTS WITH A FOREIGN ORGANIZATIONS

SCHEDULE 1

CERTIFICATIONS

COOPERATOR certifies that it:

1. __ is, __ is not, a small business.

2. __ is, __ is not, a minority business.

3. Operates as:

   __ an individual
   __ a partnership
   __ a corporation
   __ limited liability corporation
   __ public institution
   __ private institution
   __ educational institution;

   (if applicable) and is incorporated in the State of (INSERT).

4. _____Tax ID # **ONLY IF MONEY CRADA**

5. Has not paid or agreed to pay any company or person (other than a bona fide employee working solely for COOPERATOR) any fee, commission, percentage, or brokerage fee, contingent upon the award of this Agreement, and if so, agrees to furnish information relating thereto, as requested, by the Authorized Departmental Officer.

6. Has not employed or retained any company or person (other than a fulltime bona fide employee working solely for COOPERATOR) to solicit or secure this Agreement.

7. Its Principal Officers are not listed on the U.S. Government's list of debarred and suspended organizations and individuals; shall notify the Authorized Departmental Officer if so listed; and shall not subcontract or otherwise award to any organization or individual so listed.

8. Agrees to comply with the provisions of the Civil Rights Act of 1964, as amended, and Executive Order 11246, addressing equal opportunity and affirmative action.

9. Agrees to comply with the provisions of Title IX of the Education Amendment of 1972, 20USC1681, *et seq.*; Section 504 of the Rehabilitation Act of 1973, as amended, 29 USC 794; Age Discrimination Act of 1975, 42 USC 61016107; Clean Air Act, 42 USC 7401, *et seq.*; and DrugFree Workplace Act of 1988, 41 USC 701, *et seq.*

10. Is in a position to undertake, perform, and complete this Agreement and will diligently perform work in accordance with its provisions.

SCHEDULE 2

STATEMENT OF WORK

A. *Introduction/Background*

State the problem, why ARS and COOPERATOR are interested in collaborating, what each brings to the collaboration, and what results each expects. Beware of unintentionally expanding the Scope of Agreement through verbosity.

B. *Objective*

State the objective of this Agreement.

C. *Approach and Methodology*

(Be sure to cover the activities of both ARS and COOPERATOR.)

D. *ARS' Responsibilities*

1. Conduct these portions of the research project or perform the following tasks:

    a. (LIST)

    b. . . . .

    c. . . . .

    d. . . . .

2. **(USE D.2.a. and D.2.b. only if applicable)**

    a. Provide xxx square feet of (describe) space in Building —, Room—, at the ARS location for those Cooperator personnel assigned to this project.

    b. Provide utilities, services, and general support to COOPERATOR'S personnel, as needed and available.

E. *COOPERATOR'S Responsibilities*

1. Perform these portions of the research effort:

    a. (LIST)

    b. . . . .

    c. . . . .

d. Describe any personnel and/or equipment the Cooperator will furnish ARS.

2. Pay $ to ARS.

   a. The payment schedule is:

      (1) $ by .;

      (2) $ on before _____; etc.

   b. Make checks or money orders out to the "Agricultural Research Service, " cite Agreement No. 58-3K95-X-XXX thereon, and send to:

      USDA, ARS, BA, Budget and Fiscal Office

      [address]

3. (OPTIONAL) COOPERATOR may pay the travel and per diem of ARS scientific representatives traveling pursuant to this Agreement if such payment receives the prior approval of the appropriate ARS Area Director.

F. *ARS & COOPERATOR'S Joint or Mutual Responsibilities*

1. Perform these portions of the effort jointly:

   a. (LIST)

   b. . . .

   c. . . .

ESTIMATED BUDGET INSTRUCTIONS
[REMOVE THIS PAGE BEFORE FINALIZING]

1. Purpose: To gather data on the total value of resources dedicated to a Cooperative Research and Development Agreement.

The U.S. Department of Agriculture is required to report the total value of the resources dedicated to an Agreement and to submit the reports to the U.S. Congress, the General Accounting Office, the Office of Management and Budget, and the Department of Commerce.

Not only are the dollar contributions to ARS to be reported but also the value of our in-house contributions and the in-house contributions of COOPERATOR.

2. How: Prepare a budget for each Program Year the Agreement is anticipated to be in effect and a summary budget. Add additional years, as needed, to this template.

What: For each line item, enter the value of our and COOPERATOR'S in-house contributions and, if there is a payment from COOPERATOR to ARS, what will we pay for using that payment.

Examples: A senior scientist will use 10% of his or her time on the Agreement and the salary is contributed by ARS, enter the dollar value of that person's salary and fringe benefits.

A Cooperator is paying ARS for a postdoctoral scientist, enter the amount paid.

A Cooperator is paying us for materials and supplies, enter the dollar value of that payment.

A Cooperator is contributing its facilities to evaluate the commercial potential of a product, enter the dollar value of those facilities so used.

ARS is using laboratory and greenhouse space, enter the space charges assessed the management unit for that space.

Indirect
Costs: Indirect costs are gathered from all payment to ARS. ARS= Indirect Cost rate is 20% of Item I or the amount of Item G x .25.

IPSC: ARS does not have an Indirect Cost rate to apply against in-house contributions. ARS does have a IPSC assessed against all in-house CRIS projects. Estimate IPSC for ARS in-house costs by using 20% of Item G, entering the product in Item F, then re-tallying the total.

SCHEDULE 3

ESTIMATED BUDGET

TOTAL YEARS

	ARS Receive Funds for	ARS In-House	Cooperator In-House
A. Salaries and Wages			
B. Equipment			
C. Materials and Supplies			

D. Travel
   1. Domestic
   2. Foreign			

E. Facilities			
F. Other Direct Costs			
G. TOTAL DIRECT COSTS			
H. Indirect Costs			
I. TOTAL COSTS. . . ..$			

YEAR 1

	ARS Receive Funds for	ARS In-House	Cooperator In-House
A. Salaries and Wages			
B. Equipment			
C. Materials and Supplies			

E. Travel
   3. Domestic
   4. Foreign			

E. Facilities			
F. Other Direct Costs			
G. TOTAL DIRECT COSTS			
H. Indirect Costs			
I. TOTAL COSTS. . . ..$			

Instructions: Prepare an Estimated Budget for each year the Agreement is to be in effect and a Summary Budget for the entire planned period of the Agreement.

Source: United States Department of Agriculture, 2013. *Articles of Agreement – Agricultural Research Service – USDA* http://www.ars.usda.gov/sp2UserFiles/ Place/12000000/Partnering/articles.doc April 18.

GUIDELINES: US DEPARTMENT OF ENERGY

> **DOE M 483.1-1**

Approved: 1-12-01
Sunset Review: 1-12-03
Expiration: 1-12-05

DOE COOPERATIVE RESEARCH AND DEVELOPMENT AGREEMENTS MANUAL

U.S. DEPARTMENT OF ENERGY

Office of Science and Technology Policy Analysis

DISTRIBUTION:	**INITIATED BY:**
All Departmental Elements	**Office of Science and Technology Policy Analysis**

DOE M 483.1-1   i(and ii)
1-12-01

DOE COOPERATIVE RESEARCH AND DEVELOPMENT
AGREEMENTS MANUAL

1. <u>PURPOSE</u>. This Manual provides detailed requirements to supplement DOE O 483.1, DOE COOPERATIVE RESEARCH AND DEVELOPMENT AGREEMENTS, dated 1-12-01, which establishes requirements for the performance of technology transfer through the use of Cooperative Research and Development Agreements (CRADAs).

2. <u>REFERENCE</u>. DOE O 483.1, DOE COOPERATIVE RESEARCH AND DEVELOPMENT AGREEMENTS, dated 1-12-01.

3. <u>CONTACT</u>. Questions concerning this Manual should be addressed to the Office of Science and Technology Policy Analysis at 202-586-3900.

BY ORDER OF THE SECRETARY OF ENERGY:

T.J. GLAUTHIER
Deputy Secretary

DOE COOPERATIVE RESEARCH AND DEVELOPMENT
AGREEMENTS MANUAL

1. <u>INTRODUCTION</u>. The purpose of this Manual is to provide practical guidelines that will expedite the Cooperative Research and Development Agreement (CRADA) process. The Manual provides detailed information on Department of Energy (DOE) approval requirements and processing guidelines. This information has been developed to promote consistency among sites entering into CRADAs.

2. <u>DEFINITIONS</u>.

   a. <u>Amendment</u>. A change to a DOE-approved Joint Work Statement (JWS)/CRADA document.

   b. <u>Funds-In</u>. Monies provided by a participant(s) to a DOE contractor for a CRADA project.

   c. <u>In-Kind Contributions</u>. Noncash contributions provided by the participant or contractor. In-kind contributions must include collaboration in the research and development efforts of the CRADA and may also include personal property (equipment and supplies), capital equipment, work to be performed at either party's facilities, real property, or services that are directly beneficial, specifically identifiable, and necessary for performance of the project. In-kind contributions generally do not include work performed prior to execution of the CRADA.

   d. <u>Joint Work Statement</u>. A proposal prepared for a Federal agency by the director of a Government-Owned, Contractor-Operated facility (or his/her delegate) describing the purpose, scope, schedule, and estimated cost of a proposed CRADA; assigning responsibilities among the agency, contractor, and any other party or parties to the proposed agreement; and, to the extent known, assigning rights among the various parties.

3. <u>JWS/CRADA PROCESS</u>. The JWS is intended to be the primary tool for ensuring that the contractor and DOE have a common understanding of the purpose, scope, schedule, and cost of work for a CRADA. DOE's approval of a JWS sets the parameters within which

the contractor may negotiate the CRADA. A JWS must be approved before a CRADA can be approved by DOE.

The DOE field program manager will review the JWS for compliance with Federal and agency regulations and guidelines. All issues and problems will be identified and resolved prior to approval. Appendix A, Joint Work Statement Format, presents the DOE JWS format to be used for all CRADAs. This format is also to be used by contractors when developing multi-laboratory CRADAs. The Statement of Work approved in the JWS will be made an attachment to the CRADA. This JWS format may be supplemented by local field offices.

The Modular CRADA (Appendix B, DOE Modular Cooperative Research and Development Agreement) contains the approved language to be used in a CRADA. Once a CRADA has been approved, any amendment to the CRADA, other than a no-cost extension, requires DOE approval. The mechanics for the approval of such an amendment shall be developed by the cognizant field office and should be consistent with this Manual. It is recognized that there are other models that have been developed through appropriate entities in DOE. These include the Short Form CRADA and the USIC CRADA models. If there is any question as to the validity of other models, consult with the Assistant General Counsel for Technology Transfer and Intellectual Property.

4. <u>TECHNOLOGY TRANSFER NOTIFICATIONS FOR UNUSUAL CIRCUMSTANCES</u>.

    a. <u>Background</u>. DOE and its laboratory system are involved in large numbers of technology transfer activities. Most proceed smoothly and significantly benefit the Department, the private sector, and the nation as a whole. Some activities result in exceptional success, which DOE may want to promote. Other activities involve unusual circumstances (real or perceived issues that can attract significant attention), which need to be communicated to higher levels in DOE management.

    b. <u>Notification Process</u>. When concern arises about unusual circumstances in an existing or proposed CRADA activity, the operations/field office will notify the appropriate Secretarial Officers. These include, if different, the Lead Program Secretarial Officer, Cognizant Secretarial Officer, and Program Secretarial Officer. Members of the technology transfer working group can provide advice or guidance as to whether a particular concern should be reported to a Secretarial Officer.

c.   Notification Criteria. Some notification criteria are specifically addressed in this Manual or imposed by other Orders.

(1)   The following criteria are examples of situations that each have a well-defined notification or approval process in place which identifies when higher management must be notified.

(a)   Modular CRADA. Deviation from the double-underlined language in the Modular CRADA standard terms, conditions, and options, and the related Modular CRADA guidance.

(b)   Multi-laboratory CRADAs. These require notification of the relevant field offices, which are responsible for ensuring coordination and resolution of any conflicting or varying terms or arrangements.

(c)   Sensitive technologies. Projects related to sensitive technologies (as outlined in the Sensitive Subjects List available from the Nuclear Transfer and Supplier Policy Division, NN-43), nuclear applied technologies, or work involving export controlled information require the relevant approvals.

(d)   Human or animal subject involvement.

1   Human subject involvement. If the laboratory holds an assurance of compliance with human subject regulations, it may approve such activities; however, the field office must be notified. If the laboratory does not hold an assurance of compliance (either Department of Health and Human Services or DOE), the Office of Science must approve the activities.

2   Animal subject involvement. If the laboratory has an institutional animal care and use committee, it may approve such activities; however, the field office must be notified. If the laboratory does not have an institutional animal care and use committee, it is not authorized to conduct research activities involving animals.

(e)   Environment, Safety and Health and National Environmental Policy Act. Normal considerations are handled within the standard process.

(2)   For all other circumstances the judgment and experience of field office personnel is the primary determiner of when notification should occur. DOE encourages early discussion among laboratories, field offices, and program offices to make this determination. The following are examples of circumstances under which Headquarters notification might be appropriate based on field office judgment:

(a)   foreign participation and issues;

(b)   alternative benefits to U.S. manufacturing requirements having a potential for significant impact on the U.S. economy;

(c)   size of activity and impact on the laboratory;

(d)   large Funds-in from the partner;

(e)   activities that may involve unique or unusual health, safety, or environmental issues or a significant real or perceived potential environmental impact;

(f)   potential for major economic impact to the relevant industrial or commercial sector or for the appearance of inappropriate competition with the private sector; and

(g)   potential for significant political or media interest or significant public or private sector controversy.

Source: United States Department of Energy, 2001. *DOE Cooperative Research and Development Agreements Manual*, January 12. file:///C:/Users/sbianchimcelwee/Downloads/DOE013CLB2_DOE_CRADA_Form_and_Guidebook_.pdf.

Index